Paul Messaris

VISUAL PERSUASION

The Role
of
Images
in
Advertising

SAGE Publications
International Educational and Professional Publisher
Thousand Oaks London New Delhi

To my mother and the memory of my father

For information address:

SAGE Publications, Inc.
2455 Teller Road
Thousand Oaks, California 91320
E-mail: order@sagepub.com

SAGE Publications Ltd.
6 Bonhill Street
London EC2A 4PU
United Kingdom

SAGE Publications India Pvt. Ltd.
M-32 Market
Greater Kailash I
New Delhi 110 048 India

Printed in the United States of America

Library of Congress Cataloging-in-Publication Data

Messaris, Paul.
  Visual persuasion : the role of images in advertising / Paul
Messaris.
    p. cm.
  Includes bibliographical references and index.
  ISBN 0-8039-7245-8 (alk. paper). — ISBN 0-8039-7246-6 (pbk. :
alk. paper)
    1. Advertising—Psychological aspects. 2. Visual communication.
  3. Commercial art. I. Title.
  HF5822.M415 1996
  659.1′042—dc20   96-25184
              02 03 10 9 8

Acquiring Editor:	Margaret Seawell
Editorial Assistant:	Renée Piernot
Production Editor:	Michèle Lingre
Production Assistant:	Sherrise M. Purdum
Typesetter/Designer:	Danielle Dillahunt
Cover Designer:	Lesa Valdez
Print Buyer:	Anna Chin

CONTENTS

ACKNOWLEDGMENTS

◄O► The research that led to this book was supported extensively by the resources of the Annenberg School for Communication at the University of Pennsylvania. I am deeply grateful to the school's Dean, Kathleen Hall Jamieson; to my research assistants, Alison Andrews and Jennifer Khoury; to Kimberly Maxwell, Ellen Reynolds, and Deb Porter for their help with the book's illustrations; and to my colleague Larry Gross for his role in ensuring the continuing vitality of visual scholarship at Annenberg.

My wife, Carla Sarett, gave me valuable advice on much of what I have written in these pages. I have also profited from the comments, assistance, and support of many colleagues and friends, including: Derek Bouse, Henrik Dahl, Kirsten Drotner, Geri Gay, Klaus Jensen, Yolanda Lazo, Louise Mares, Kim Schroeder, Sari Thomas, Joe Turow, as well as three anonymous reviewers provided by Sage Publications. To all of these, my heartfelt thanks.

This book was originally commissioned for Sage Publications by Sophy Craze, and it was completed under her successor, Margaret Seawell. Many thanks to both of them for their encouragement and advice. It is also a pleasure to express my gratitude to Editorial Assistant Renée Piernot and the other people I worked with at Sage Publications —Production Editor Michèle Lingre and Production Assistant Sherrise Perdum, Copy Editor Liann Lech, and Design Director Ravi Balasuriya— for their courtesy and efficiency. Finally, special thanks to Permissions Editor Jennifer Morgan for her help on matters of copyright.

iv

INTRODUCTION
A Theory of Images in Advertising

◄o► I was leafing through the pages of a newspaper while my 11-year-old niece and her girlfriend watched television. A change in noise level signaled the onset of a commercial. Suddenly, both girls began to make loud, theatrically exaggerated swooning sounds. I looked up. On the screen was the face of TV star Luke Perry, appearing in an ad for Mars Bars®. The girls' display of melodramatic emotion continued, until finally my niece went up to the TV set and pretended to kiss Luke Perry's image. Later that afternoon, we drove into town to do some shopping. As soon as we entered the supermarket, first one girl and then the other went running off to buy Mars Bars®.

This little incident, which happened several years ago, has stayed in my mind as an emblematic illustration of the way in which successful visual advertising is supposed to affect its viewers. Despite their theatricality, the girls' responses should not be dismissed as simply childish behavior. I do not know how common it is for viewers of whatever age to pretend to kiss a screen image. I suspect it is exceedingly rare, although I would not be surprised to be told that I am ignorant of a widespread phenomenon in the world of preadolescents. However, not only among preadolescents but also among fully mature adults, the underlying reaction that motivated the kiss—seeing an image as an embodiment of the physical attractions of the real world—is certainly no rarity. On the contrary, it is a central ingredient of the response that visual ads typically aim for in all of us, old and young alike. A major reason for using images in ads is to elicit this response.

But the image in this particular ad was produced by a camera, and that fact adds a further dimension to its appeal. Unlike handmade images, such as drawings or paintings (which are uncommon in TV commercials but do appear occasionally in print ads), photographs and images on video are typically seen as direct copies of reality. This quality strengthens the viewer's illusion of interacting with real-world people and places, and it also does something else. In many ads, the use of photographs or video serves as evidence that what is being shown in the ad really did happen—for example, that Luke Perry really did pose with a Mars Bar. Of course, that kind of evidence itself may be quite illusory, especially in an age in which photographs can be manipulated so easily by computer. But here I am getting ahead of my story, because my aim at this point is only to outline the intended functions of advertising images, not to question the basis of those functions.

I suppose that, if I were an advertiser, I would probably be happy to hear about my niece and her friend's strong reactions to Luke Perry's screen image. But I am sure that I would be absolutely delighted by their subsequent behavior in the supermarket. Their behavior encapsulates, in a nutshell, a process that many scholars see as the basic selling mechanism of commercial advertising, and an important component of other types of visual persuasion as well (e.g., political propaganda). On the TV screen, the girls saw a juxtaposition of two images: on one hand, an attractive TV star; on the other, a product. In their everyday lives, the enthusiasm that they originally had expressed for the TV star was directed later toward the product.

Clearly, the visual connection established on the screen elicited some form of mental connection in the girls' minds (because I do not, for a moment, believe that their purchase of the Mars Bars was a coincidence). But I think we need to be very cautious about interpreting the nature of that mental connection. Although the girls' behavior may seem, at first blush, to be a straightforward example of an artificially induced, displaced desire—something for which advertising is often blamed, especially when it involves sex, and even more so when it involves young people—I think that what actually happened here was more complicated. For one thing, as I have tried to suggest, the girls' reactions to the TV image of Luke Perry appeared to contain a considerable amount of self-conscious parody. Moreover, each girl's response to the commercial clearly was due in part to the presence of her friend; consequently, the commercial's role in bringing about those responses cannot be accounted for by any simple model of direct causality. However, once again, my goal at the moment is not to address this issue in detail but just to raise it.

I have outlined three major roles that visual images can play in an ad. They can elicit emotions by simulating the appearance of a real person or object; they can serve as photographic proof that something really did happen; and they can establish an implicit link between the thing that is being sold and some other image(s). I will argue below that these three functions of advertising images stem from underlying, fundamental characteristics of visual communication—characteristics that define the essential nature of images and distinguish them from language and from the other modes of human communication. In turn, these three functions of advertising images give rise to a wide variety of specific advertising practices, ranging from celebrity endorsements to hidden-camera interviews to shots of politicians standing in front of flags.

To gain a systematic understanding of the connections between the basic properties of images, on one hand, and the multiplicity of visual advertising techniques, on the other, we need a comprehensive theory of the persuasive uses of visual images. Although the study of persuasive communication has a history of more than two millennia, the focus of this scholarly tradition has tended overwhelmingly to be on verbal strategies. With a few notable exceptions (for example, Lester, 1995; Moriarty, 1987; see also Jowett & O'Donnell, 1992, passim), the systematic investigation of visual persuasion is still in its infancy. The aim of this book is to encourage the further growth of this field of scholarship.

THEORETICAL FRAMEWORK

This book seeks to answer the following question: What is the distinctive contribution that visual images make to persuasive communication, whether in commercial advertising, in political messages, or in social issue campaigns? An appropriate starting point for addressing this question is to ask a broader one: What are the fundamental characteristics that distinguish visual images from other modes of communication? If we can specify in what essential ways images differ from words or music or other vehicles of meaning, we can then go on to examine the implications of those differences for the persuasive uses of visual media.

Any mode of communication can be described in terms of either semantic or syntactic properties. A semantically oriented description focuses on how the elements of a particular mode (images, words, musical tones, or whatever) are related to their meanings. A syntactically oriented description is concerned with the interrelationships among the elements themselves as they combine to form larger meaningful units. Each mode of communication has its own characteristic combination of semantic and syntactic features.

The semantic properties of the various modes are a central concern of semiotics, the field of scholarship devoted to the study of "signs," defined by Danesi (1994) as "any mark, bodily movement, symbol, token, etc., used to indicate and to convey thoughts, information, commands, etc." (p. xi). Semioticians have developed a variety of schemes for classifying the relationships between signs and their meanings (or, more precisely, between "signifiers" and "signifieds"). By far the most widely used of these schemes is a triadic classification proposed by the American philosopher Charles Sanders Peirce (1839-1914), whose writings have been receiving renewed attention by communication scholars in recent years (Dahl & Buhl, 1993; Jensen, 1995; Moriarty, 1994). Peirce's system, one of many he created during his lifetime, entails three categories: the icon, the index, and the symbol. *Iconic signs* are characterized by some form of similarity or analogy between the sign and its object. For instance, a scale model of a building is an iconic representation of certain features of the real building: its shape, perhaps its color, but not its size. *Indexical signs* are a complex category, but for present purposes, a partial definition is sufficient. According to this definition, a sign is indexical if it is actually caused by its object and serves as a physical trace pointing to the object's existence. Peirce (1991) illustrates this type of sign with the example of a bullet hole, which signifies that a shot was fired (pp. 239-240). Finally, Peirce's third type of sign, the *symbol*, involves neither similarity nor physical causation but, instead, an arbitrary convention on the part of the symbol's users. Words are the typical example here. With the rare exception of onomatopoeia, they are connected to the things they refer to only by virtue of a social convention.

Semantic Properties of Images

How do visual images fit into this system of classification? Representational pictures that resemble some aspect of reality are particularly clear examples of iconic signs. Indeed, the term *icon* is derived from a Greek word for picture, and Peirce (1991) originally had referred to iconic signs as "likenesses" (p. 30), a word that also suggested pictures in 19th-century English. It must be emphasized, though, that in Peirce's scheme of things, an iconic sign need not provide a particularly close replica of its object's overall appearance. For instance, the line depicting a river on a map is an iconic representation of the course of the real river, although the line may not look very much like the river (e.g., in terms of color) even when the latter is viewed from an airplane. Likewise, a child's stick figure drawing of a person could qualify as an iconic sign by virtue of matching the basic structure of the person's body, despite the absence of realistic details.

Actually, even full-color photographs cannot duplicate certain features of the appearance of reality, such as the sense of three-dimensional space that we get when we look at the real world with both eyes. Although 3-D movies, holograms, and virtual reality are moving us ever closer to the totally lifelike experience that has traditionally been considered the ultimate goal of visual imaging technologies (Bazin, 1967), the inevitable discrepancies between ordinary pictures and reality have led many writers to emphasize the artificial aspect of pictorial representation and, occasionally, to reject the notion of iconicity altogether (see Eco, 1975; Goodman, 1976; Krieger, 1984). However, as I have argued in detail elsewhere (Messaris, 1994), the available evidence does not support such an extreme view. In fact, recent research on cognition and perception suggests that even a very rudimentary match between image and reality (e.g., a simple sketch or stick figure) is enough for the brain to be able to employ its real-world processes of visual interpretation.

In addition to iconicity, there is another semantic characteristic that has distinctive implications for the way in which we react to certain images. Any picture made by photographic means, whether on film or video, fits Peirce's notion of a sign produced as a physical trace of its object. Therefore, aside from being iconic, such pictures are also indexical signs. The indexicality of photographic images (i.e., the fact that they are, in certain respects, direct physical imprints of the reality recorded in them) plays an important role in some forms of visual persuasion, which will be outlined presently. For the moment, it should be noted that, as far as semantic features are concerned, it is the indexical and iconic properties of visual images that most clearly set them apart from language and other modes of communication. It is true that some kinds of visual representations (e.g., technical diagrams or maps) are arguably based at least in part on arbitrary conventions, and in that sense, they can be said to entail the type of semantic relationship that Peirce labeled symbolic. However, symbolic signs are, if anything, even more characteristic of language and the other major modes. Conversely, iconicity is only a minor feature of verbal communication, and the type of indexicality exemplified by photographic images is entirely absent from most of the primary means of human communication, although it is certainly a defining feature of such secondary forms as fingerprints or plaster casts.

Syntactic Properties of Images

When it comes to the syntactic aspects of images, the theoretical literature is less systematic and less developed than it is in the case of visual semantics. However, several writers have touched in a variety of ways on a conceptual distinction that is particularly pertinent to the topic of visual persuasion (Arnheim, 1969; Gombrich, 1972; Jamieson, 1984, 1992; Worth, 1982). Whereas movie directors and other people who work in visual communication have developed relatively precise conventions for indicating spatial or temporal relationships among two or more images (more accurately: among the objects or events portrayed in those images), visual communication is characterized by a lack of explicit means for identifying other ways in which images might be related to each other. In particular, what visual communication lacks most crucially is a so-called propositional syntax. What do we mean by this term? Consider some of the kinds of verbal statements that might be made in an advertisement. The product being sold might be compared with another product and proclaimed the better of the two. A politician might claim that her presence in Congress had led to the lowering of taxes. An antiabortion leaflet might argue that abortion is equivalent to murder. These are all propositions about types of connections between two entities—Product A *is better than* Product B; the politician *caused* lower taxes; abortion *equals* murder—and a distinctive characteristic of verbal language is the fact that it contains words and sentence structures (a propositional syntax) that allow the user to be explicit about what kind of connection is being proposed in such statements. An equally distinctive characteristic of visual images is the fact that they do not have an equivalent of this type of syntax. Whereas spatial or temporal connections can be presented quite explicitly through images, visual communication does not have an explicit syntax for expressing analogies, contrasts, causal claims, and other kinds of propositions.

This is a complicated point that is best appreciated through a concrete example. We will examine a short scene from *A New Beginning*, a much-analyzed political video used in the 1984 Reagan reelection campaign. In this video's opening sequence, a shot of Ronald Reagan's first-term inauguration is intercut with early-morning images of people around the country going to work (see Figures I.1-I.6). We see a tractor entering a field, a truck driving off from a farmhouse, and then the Reagan inauguration; a cowboy moving horses out of a corral, a man in a hard hat directing a crane, and the inauguration once again; a commuter getting into a car, workers at the gates of a factory, the inauguration; and so on. This kind of cross-cutting between two parallel streams of images is an established convention of narrative cinema. If this had been a fictional film or TV program, the parallel editing most likely would have been employed to signify a fairly straightforward spatiotemporal connection between the two sets of events: at the same time that Ronald Reagan was being inaugurated, people elsewhere were setting out to work. In other words, as an indicator of narrative space and time, parallel editing has a relatively fixed meaning: "same time, different place."

In the context of a political campaign video, however, the juxtaposition between Ronald Reagan and the scenes of workers was surely intended mainly, or even entirely, as a means of suggesting other kinds of connections between the two. For instance, this juxtaposition could be seen as implying analogy or similarity: the president is a man of the people, and he is ready to work hard just as they are. The juxtaposition also could be taken as a sign of causality: Ronald Reagan's presidency has revived the economy and put people back to work. These interpre-

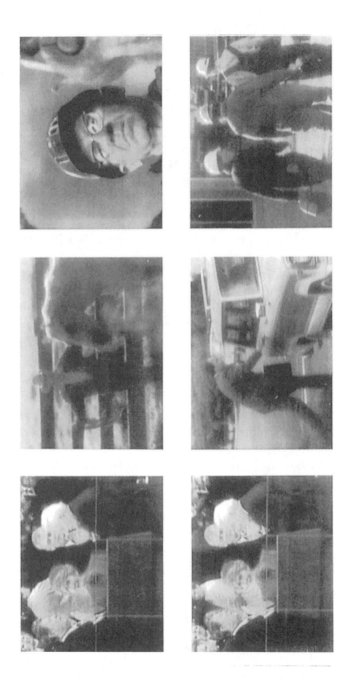

Figure I.1, Figure I.2, Figure I.3, Figure I.4, Figure I.5, and Figure I.6

tations are not mutually exclusive, nor do they exhaust the possibilities. In fact, that is precisely the important point about this example for our purposes. There is nothing in the editing itself that would allow us to say that one of these interpretations is more correct than the other. The very same syntactic device, parallel editing, is compatible with a variety of different meanings: analogy, causality, or whatever else an inventive viewer might imagine.

So, as soon as we go beyond spatiotemporal interpretations, the meaning of visual syntax becomes fluid, indeterminate, and more subject to the viewer's interpretational predispositions than is the case with a communicational mode such as verbal language, which possesses an elaborate set of explicit indicators of analogy, causality, and other kinds of connections between two or more concepts. It will be argued below that this relative indeterminacy of visual syntax plays a central part in processes of visual persuasion. In fact, in the context of advertising, this seeming "deficiency" of visual syntax is arguably one of its principal strengths. Accordingly, for our purposes, it will be appropriate to say that the characteristic syntactic property of visual syntax is precisely this indeterminacy.

Implications of Iconicity

Iconicity, indexicality, and syntactic indeterminacy: These three properties of images will be the starting points for our examination of the distinctive attributes of visual persuasion. Each of these properties has a particular set of consequences for the persuasive uses of images. In examining the implications of iconicity, we can begin with the following simple observation. When we look at the real world that surrounds us, the sights we see do not register in our brains as neutral, value-free data. Rather, each visual feature, from the smallest nuances of people's facial expressions to the overall physical appearance of people and places, can come with a wealth of emotional associations. These associations stem from the unique experiences of each individual in addition to the common, shared influence of culture and, to some extent, biology. So, the fact that images can reproduce the appearance of reality (or selected aspects of that appearance) also means that they can call forth a variety of "preprogrammed" emotional responses. By drawing on their intuitive understanding as well as a growing body of research concerning the relationship between vision and emotion, advertisers are able to elicit strong, sometimes primal reactions—desire for a particular type of sexy model; respect for a certain look that makes a politician appear dignified; pity for the pathetic appearance of a famine victim—that might not be as easily accessible through other, nonpictorial means. In short, iconicity gives advertisers access to a broad spectrum of emotional responses that can be enlisted in the service of an ad's cause.

An example from the world of fashion advertising illustrates just how subtle some of the applications of iconicity can be. In a TV program dealing with the computer manipulation of images of female fashion models (part of the TV series "The Human Animal"), Desmond Morris points out that one of the targets of computerized alteration is the size of the pupils of the women's eyes. Because an increase in pupil size can be a real-world sign of sexual excitation (Landau, 1989, p. 156), the pupils in fashion images are sometimes artificially enlarged to enhance the allure of the women in the images. In this context, therefore, pupil size is a good example of a pictorial element that derives both its cognitive meaning and its emotional resonance from an equivalence to a real-world perceptual stimulus.

Morris describes a number of other computer-manipulated features of fashion imagery, including such things as skin tone or the length of models' thighs, that appear to function in the same way. More generally, it could be argued that any advertising image that makes use of an attractive model or spokesperson derives at least part of its appeal from the capacity of pictures to act as surrogates for real-life visual encounters. This aspect of the appeal of persuasive imagery was exemplified all too vividly in the response of my niece and her friend to the image of Luke Perry in the Mars Bar ad. In fact, the crowning act of that response—pretending to kiss Luke Perry's face on the screen—may be seen as an implicit acknowledgment of the TV image's efficacy as a surrogate.

This ability of pictures to conjure up real-world optical experience is the central driving force of a cluster of visual devices having to do with the placement of the viewer vis-à-vis the people or other objects in an image. These devices include the implied distance at which the viewer is positioned (close-up, long shot, etc.), the image's orientation (head-on, three-quarter view, etc.), the angle of view, and the use of subjective point of view, among others. As Meyrowitz (1986) has argued, the effectiveness of these devices appears to stem from the fact that their conventional uses are typically modeled on people's real-world experiences of inter-personal space, orientation, angle, and point of view. For instance, politicians being interviewed on television will often make a deliberate effort to orient themselves toward the camera, and therefore toward the viewer, in order to mimic the real-world appearance of a direct, nothing-to-hide approach and, conversely, to avoid the negative implications of not looking someone straight in the eyes. Similarly, when they engage in televised debates, politicians typically insist on an equal number of close-ups for all participants. This practice is presumably motivated by the conventional use of close-ups as a means of increasing attention and eliciting stronger engagement on the part of the viewer, and this convention in turn is presumably based at least in part on the real-world association between interpersonal closeness and involvement.

As these examples may suggest, the iconicity of visual images is not just a matter of content. Whereas the appearance of the people or places in a picture may be its most obvious iconic element, the picture's formal or stylistic features (e.g., whether it is a close-up or a long shot) also may bear an iconic relationship to our real-world visual experiences. The iconicity of visual form is of special interest for persuasive communication because many viewers tend to be less aware of form or style than of the content of images (Kraft, 1987; Messaris, 1981). Thus, form can be used as a relatively more subtle or indirect way of suggesting certain meanings and evoking viewers' reactions to them.

This aspect of iconicity has played a substantial role in ads dealing with sexual or gender imagery. Especially in the area of print advertising, whose single images are often designed much more meticulously than the multiple shots of TV commercials, the creators of ads have traditionally attempted to build gender or sexual connotations into the formal or stylistic features of images, rather than just the manifest content. So, for example, ads for certain feminine products might be displayed against backgrounds containing soft contours and flowing curves, whereas ads aimed at men might feature more angular or hard-edged shapes in the background (Baker, 1961). These conventions are based to some extent on the idea of a loose visual analogy between the shapes in the ads and the physical characteristic's of men's and women's bodies. At the same time, though, the conventions also reflect a more abstract analogical link between these shapes and traditional views of masculinity and femininity. As we will see when we discuss this topic in detail, there is evidence that even very young viewers are responsive to the messages contained in such stylistic conventions and, furthermore, that these stylistic elements are capable of conveying meaning over and above the more overt content or message of an ad.

The iconicity of visual images is a topic with special relevance for contemporary developments in the world of commercial and social issue advertising. With increasing frequency, commercial advertising is being designed to cross national and cultural boundaries. This trend is receiving added impetus from the growing inclusiveness of the reach of satellite services, a development made possible to a large extent by the promise of advertising revenues. The globalizing aims of advertisers have led to a special emphasis on advertising's visual aspects, which, precisely because of their iconicity, may be assumed to travel across cultures more easily than words do. A similar assumption also motivates much of the work of people and organizations interested in using visual images to promote greater understanding between members of different cultures or subcultural groups. Such efforts are often premised on the belief that images can replicate some of the positive consequences, such as increased tolerance or even empathy, that may result from direct encounters between people of different backgrounds. However, the notion that iconicity necessarily leads to cross-cultural transparency of meaning has come into question not only by scholars and critics but also by the creators of ads. Indeed, in recent years, the latter have become keenly sensitive to the possibility that cultural differences in the nuances of an image's meaning may undermine an ad's effectiveness. A full examination of these issues must therefore lead us beyond the advantages conferred on images by iconicity to an appraisal of its limits.

Implications of Indexicality

In addition to being iconic signs, all images produced by photographic means are also indexical, in Peirce's sense of the term. Indexicality is a critical ingredient in the process of visual persuasion whenever a photographic image can serve as documentary evidence or proof of an advertisement's point. The case of celebrity endorsements is a simple illustration of this situation. The verbal statement, "Luke Perry likes Mars Bars," or a drawing of the actor holding the candy may in themselves be effective ways of appealing to the tastes of his fans. However, a video clip of Luke Perry with a Mars Bar does something that neither the words nor the handmade picture can do. By providing a photographic record, it actually documents the actor's endorsement of the product.

The documentary aspect of photographic images is an implicit or explicit component of a wide variety of persuasive formats, ranging from "man-or-woman-in-the-street" interviews with consumers or voters to visual campaigns for such social causes as famine relief or rainforest preservation. In all these situations and in many others, at least part of the persuasive power of the images in question stems from their indexicality. Yet photographs can, of course, lie. The picture of a model in a fashion ad can be made more attractive through airbrushing, and voter interviews or product demonstrations can be staged. In principle, therefore, it could be argued that a viewer's faith in the documentary properties of any image ought to depend not on the medium itself but on the trustworthiness of the person using that medium. Some media critics are predicting that society as a whole is, in fact, moving in the direction of such an attitude toward photography as a result of growing public awareness of two relatively recent developments: the use of computers to manipulate images and the proliferation of TV programs that blend staged and "authentic" video footage. It may well be that this predicted shift in public attitudes is beginning to take place. Nevertheless, the logical culmination of such a trend—the point at which the documentary value of photographs is seen by the broad public as no higher than that of paintings or drawings—seems a long way off. For the moment, then, it is surely safe to say that indexicality should still be counted as a distinctive feature of visual persuasion, even if the precise status of this feature is becoming increasingly problematic.

Implications of Syntactic Indeterminacy

Both indexicality and iconicity may be thought of as "positive" characteristics of visual communication: These two semantic properties are qualities that images possess and that other modes of communication do not. As far as syntax is concerned, however, it was argued earlier that the most pertinent characteristic of visual communication for present purposes may actually be its lack of a certain property, rather than its possession of others. As we have seen, what visual syntax lacks, especially in comparison to verbal language, is a set of explicit devices for indicating causality, analogy, or any relationships other than those of space or time. This lack of a propositional syntax has an important implication for the persuasive uses of images. Making a causal claim, drawing an analogy, or expressing other kinds of logical connections between ideas are all integral aspects of the process of argumentation. The fact that visual syntax cannot be explicit about such connections means that the process of visual persuasion cannot include explicit arguments. Any argument can, of course, be spelled out in words on the soundtrack of a TV commercial or in the text of a magazine ad, but attempts to express arguments through the images themselves in either TV or print ads must necessarily fall short of complete explicitness.

On the face of it, this characteristic of visual communication may appear to be a deficiency. In fact, however, it can be argued that in certain respects, it is actually a strength. There are at least two reasons why this might be so. First of all, because a visual argument cannot be entirely explicit, making sense of it may require of the viewer a greater degree of mental participation than would otherwise be the case. In a way, there-fore, the viewer's interpretation of a visual argument is more of a product of her or his own mind than it would be if the argument were completely explicit to begin with. Indeed, each viewer's interpretation is likely to contain nuances of meaning that literally will make it her or his own creation. If there is any truth to the traditional assumption that, other things being equal, people are more likely to adopt a proposition that they themselves have been induced to construct, then the implicitness of visual syntax and argumentation can be seen as a potential strong point of the process of visual persuasion.

A concrete demonstration of this possibility is provided by the 1984 Reagan campaign video described earlier. It was suggested that the editing in this video's opening sequence could be interpreted either as a causal claim ("Ronald Reagan's handling of the economy put people back to work") or as an analogy ("The president is ready to do the job, just as any other citizen is"). The former interpretation places greater emphasis on Reagan's qualities as a strong and effective leader, whereas the latter is more focused on a view of Reagan as a man of the people. Both interpretations have some relationship to facets of the broader persona cultivated by Ronald Reagan during his time in office: on one hand, the powerful ruler who revived earlier traditions of pomp and display; on the other hand, the folksy middle-American. This blend of images may have contributed to Reagan's exceptional popularity with the electorate by appealing simultaneously to somewhat contradictory feelings about the appropriate degree of separation between the people and the president. Similarly, the open-endedness of the editing in the campaign video may have been a factor in its success by allowing each individual viewer to tailor the message to his or her own predispositions about these matters. People inclined to look up to political power may have seen in the editing a somewhat different meaning from that derived by viewers with more egalitarian tendencies. One way or the other, though, a viewer's interpretation of this kind of editing seems more likely to be a personal construction than would be the case with a totally explicit argument.

The implicitness of visual syntax has a second major consequence for the persuasive uses of visual images. Because of the notion that images alone cannot express an explicit argument, the verbal claims made in advertisements tend to be held to much stricter standards of accountability than whatever claims are implicit in the ads' pictures. This ability to imply something in pictures while avoiding the consequences of saying it in words has been considered an advantage of visual advertising since the earliest days of its development as a mass medium. A case in point is the advertising of cigarettes. It would be unthinkable nowadays for the text of a cigarette ad to resurrect the kinds of preposterous claims of health benefits that were made in the early days, before the medical consequences of smoking were fully understood; but—for the moment, at least—it is still common practice for cigarette manufacturers to advertise their products by juxtaposing them with images of vigorous outdoor activity.

As the example of cigarette advertising may suggest, the implicitness of visual syntax is arguably a potential mechanism for avoiding the legal implications of certain kinds of advertising claims. For the most part, however, the purposes served by using visual arguments are unrelated to legal concerns. Rather, what is left unspoken by resorting to images is often some assumption or expectation that the ad's audience itself may not want to confront directly. This aspect of visual argumentation is especially likely to be found in connection with two of the major themes of commercial advertising: sex and social status.

For a convenient illustration of this point, let us return once more to the example of Luke Perry's Mars Bar commercial. The juxtaposition of the actor's image with the picture of the product conforms to a standard syntactic convention in celebrity endorsement ads. However, the meaning of such a juxtaposition can vary widely from one ad to another. For instance, if the Mars Bar had been juxtaposed with the image of a famous athlete, this combination could have been interpreted as implying that Mars Bars provide an energy boost. If, less plausibly, the person in the ad had been a famous chef, the combination of images could have been taken as a suggestion that Mars Bars are equal in quality to the chef's own creations. But what are we to make of the ad as it actually was, with Luke Perry's image next to the Mars Bar?

Judging from the reactions of my niece and her friend, one might be tempted to conclude that this juxtaposition was just one more instance of an advertising practice that critics often complain about—namely, using sex as a lure to create an artificial desire for some product that may be totally unrelated to sex. Along the same lines, a knowledgeable media critic might also point out that the specific combination of sex and food is encountered quite frequently in commercial advertising (a point to which we will return later). However, in this particular case at least, these standard criticisms of advertising seem to be somewhat off-target. The idea that visual syntax creates unconscious sexual associations and turns products into implicit sex substitutes may be a valid description of some forms of advertising, but in this instance, it is probably too simple-minded. Instead, the following alternative interpretation may be closer to the mark.

As is true of much of advertising (whether commercial, political, or social issue-oriented), this ad appears to be concerned with social identity. By publicly linking a product with a certain image, the ad makes it possible for users of the product to draw on that link as a means of making a public statement about how they themselves wish to be viewed. In the specific case of preadolescent girls responding in each other's company to an ad featuring an attractive male actor, the connections established through the ad's visual syntax can evidently provide the opportunity for implied comments about their own evolving gender identities. Because this is a sensitive topic and, indeed, a topic for which they might not even have an explicit verbal vocabulary, the visual connection supplied by the ad—Mars Bars as an indicator of a burgeoning sexual interest in men—allows them to express an idea that they might not wish (or be able) to deal with if they had to do so through the analytical medium of language.

So, in the kind of response exhibited by my niece and her friend, a Mars Bar—or whatever the product might be—is not an imaginary substitute for an illusory goal; rather, by virtue of the advertising, it becomes a shared vehicle for the all-too-real process of social identity display. Furthermore, if this account is correct, what was true of this specific incident may also be true more generally of a wide range of situations in which advertising serves as the basis of social display. For example, for a person aspiring to upward mobility, ordering a brand of vodka whose advertising includes original works of art may be a way of signaling good taste and refinement; for a married, middle-aged man, smoking a brand of cigarettes advertised by cowboys may be an attempt to proclaim that he is still one of the boys himself; and, for a girl about to enter adolescence, buying any product endorsed by a handsome man may serve as a signal that she no longer wants to be considered a child. In all of these cases, and others like them, the visual syntax of specific advertisements may endow products with certain tacit associations that are broadly recognized in the social circles in which the products are used. At the same time, however, the kinds of associations involved in such instances are things that many people might not want to spell out explicitly. Upward mobility may be a common personal goal, but open efforts to display it are often considered gauche. Likewise, explicit attempts to put on an appearance of virility or to act in age-inappropriate ways are likely to meet with contempt or disapproval. In situations of this sort, then, the tacitness of the associations created by advertising may allow the users of the products to benefit from these associations while avoiding the consequences of making them explicit. In short, the implicitness of visual syntax may make it possible for people to have their cake and eat it too.

*   *   *

We have taken an introductory look at three characteristic properties of persuasive images: iconicity, indexicality, and lack of an explicit propositional syntax. These three topics will serve as organizing principles for the discussion that follows. By virtue of their iconicity, the images in ads can simulate the visual appearance of reality, and they can be used to elicit attitudes and emotions associated with real-world people, objects, and places. These aspects of visual persuasion will be examined in the first section of this book. In the first chapter of this section, we will analyze some of the basic pictorial devices (such as camera angles or image size, as well as the physical characteristics or facial expressions of people in images) through which iconicity does its work. Chapter 2 will extend the concept of iconicity to the formal and stylistic aspects of images (e.g., their abstract shapes, colors, or overall design). This chapter will include a review of disguised, so-called "subliminal" imagery in advertising images. In Chapter 3, our discussion of iconicity will conclude by examining its implications in the increasingly important area of cross-cultural advertising. In addition to looking at advertising that crosses national boundaries, we will also review efforts to use images as bridges between people of different ethnic or racial backgrounds in a single nation.

Part 2 is devoted to indexicality and contains a single chapter on visual truth and falsehood. The indexicality of photography (including film and video) makes it possible for photographic images to serve as evidence in support of the claims of commercial or political advertisers, as well as organizations using images for social advocacy. Because of the automatic nature of the photographic process, its results appear more trustworthy than words or handmade images. And yet there are numerous ways, including powerful new computer techniques, through which the apparent documentary quality of photographic images can be subverted. These issues will be our concern in Chapter 4.

The book's final section, comprising two chapters, is devoted to the complex topic of visual syntax and its lack of explicit means for making causal claims or expressing other types of propositions. Because of this lack, there is an open-ended quality to visual arguments, and a corresponding fluidity and adaptability to the meaning of persuasive images. Chapter 5 will examine these matters in detail and will include a review of research on viewers' responses to visual syntax in ads. Finally, in Chapter 6, we will analyze the ways in which the implicit quality of visual propositions can make it possible for images to convey messages that advertisers are reluctant to put into words. The book will conclude with a brief epilogue on certain ethical ramifications of the uses of images in advertising.

PART 1

IMAGE AS
SIMULATED REALITY

1

◀◉▶

PICTURES
AND REALITY

◀◉▶ If there is one property that most clearly distinguishes pictures from language and from the other modes of human communication, that property is iconicity (to use the Peircian terminology that was described in the introduction). Through combinations of lines and shapes and colors on a piece of paper or a movie screen or a video monitor, pictures are able to recreate the kinds of visual information that our eyes and brains make use of when we look at the real world. Note that iconicity does not necessarily entail a precise match between the appearance of a picture and the appearance of reality. There are many kinds of pictures—for instance, cartoons, sketches, or black-and-white photographs—whose visual characteristics are superficially quite different from those of real-world objects or places. Nevertheless, all of these kinds of pictures are capable of capturing and conveying to our eyes the distinctive features that our brains need in order to be able to figure out what we are looking at. And that is what counts.

Our goal in this chapter is to address the following question: What are the implications of iconicity for the uses of pictures in ads? An important first step toward an answer comes from recent work by

Damasio (1994), Grodal (1994), and Shepard (1990). Although it may seem natural to think of visual perception as an autonomous psychological process, these writers stress the fact that real-world vision is intimately connected with emotion, which, in turn, is tied to our functional needs as biological and social creatures. When we look at the world, we are strongly predisposed to attend to certain kinds of objects or situations and to react in certain kinds of ways. These predispositions reflect the influence of culture, but—as all three of these writers emphasize—they have also been shaped to a certain extent by biological evolution. In short, real-world vision comes with a set of built-in response tendencies. Consequently, to the extent that a picture can reproduce the significant visual features of real-world experience, it may also be able to exploit the response tendencies that are associated with those features.

How do advertising images, in particular, take advantage of this possibility? In principle, we can distinguish between two kinds of roles that real-world visual cues typically play in advertising: on one hand, drawing attention to the ad; on the other hand, eliciting a certain emotion on behalf of whatever it is the ad is selling. One of the simplest examples of the former occurs in advertising images in which someone looks directly at the spectator. This ubiquitous device, used by spokespeople in TV commercials and models in magazine ads, draws its attention-getting power from our real-life tendency to look back when we are looked at. A well-known example of the latter can be found in some political images. On the assumption that looking up at someone can be associated with feelings of respect or awe, portrayals of politicians in ads or posters occasionally adopt a low (upward-looking) angle of view. Because the primary purpose of this convention is to create a certain feeling toward the person in the image, the use of low angles in this context can be considered an emotion-eliciting device.

However, because low angles are less common than straight-on views, it could be argued that they also function as attention-getters; and, conversely, there are some situations—such as the famous recruiting poster of Uncle Sam saying "I want you . . ."—in which looking into the viewer's eyes could be considered a means of intimidation or subordination and not just a way of attracting attention. In other words, whereas the distinction between attention-getting and emotion-eliciting devices provides a useful framework for thinking about the different dimensions of our responses to ads, in practice, any one visual device could conceivably serve both functions. The fact that we will discuss these two functions separately should not obscure this point.

ATTRACTING ATTENTION

In an analysis of the fundamentals of persuasive communication, Henrik Dahl (1993) argues that one of its central characteristics is the fact that it is typically *unwanted* communication. With the possible exception of those of us who have a professional interest in the subject, most people do not actively seek out exposure to advertising. Furthermore, the ability to avoid advertising on television has increased as a result of the proliferation of cable channels. To be sure, advertisers may develop ways of reversing this trend as they become more proficient at using the Internet and other new media. For instance, when television becomes more interactive, commercials may be offered as a precondition for receiving fee-free movies, and viewers may be required to indicate their reactions or provide other information during the course of the commercials as a means of ensuring that attention is paid to them. Even in such circumstances, though, most types of advertising will continue to face the problem of catching the viewer's eye through their intrinsic qualities. Ordinarily, this can be thought of as the advertiser's first task. The iconicity of visual images provides advertisers with a variety of tools for handling that task. Many of those tools are derived from the principles of real-world, face-to-face interaction, and that will be a major focus of our discussion. However, we will begin by looking at a very different form of visual attention-getting, a kind of visual manipulation that cannot occur at all in the real world.

Violating Reality

In a medium whose very essence is the ability to reproduce the look of everyday reality, one of the surest ways of attracting the viewer's attention is to violate that reality. Consider the case of a print ad produced by an organization called The Deciding Vote (see Figure 1.1). The ad's aim is to get more women to vote, and one of the ways in which it makes its case is through forceful verbal text: "Most politicians still think women should be seen and not heard. In the last election, 54 million

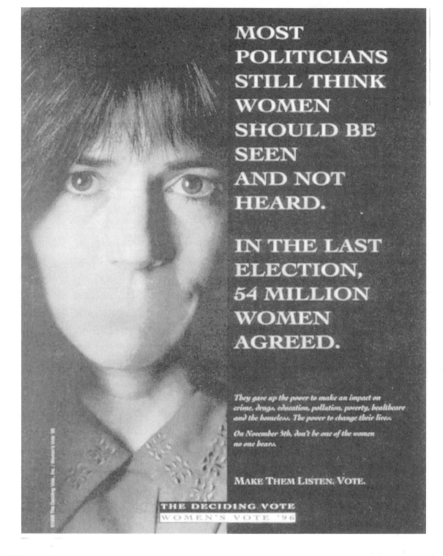

Figure 1.1.

women agreed." But the first thing that hits the viewer's eye is the striking photograph that accompanies this text. We see a close-up of a woman's face looking at us with troubled eyes. Her features are normal except for one glaring, one-of-a-kind aberration. Where her mouth should be there is no mouth; only a smooth, seamless continuation of the surface of her skin. This image is an excellent example of the critical role that iconicity plays in our response to pictures. Because of iconicity, we experience the image as a warp in reality, not just the manipulation of a symbol. It gives us a jolt, and it gets us to look.

The perceptual principles that are brought into play when we look at this kind of image have been adumbrated by the distinguished cognitive psychologist Roger Shepard (1990). In the course of a more general examination of how our brains deal with impossible figures, Shepard points out that the human perceptual system is finely tuned to pay special attention to unfamiliar objects when they are only slightly different from our expectations: "[A]n object that is novel and yet similar to an already significant object may especially warrant our close attention. We need to know how far something can depart from its usual or expected form and still have the consequences that we have found to follow from its 'natural kind'" (p. 202). In the normal course of visual perception, our brain figures out what it is that we are looking at as follows: For each shape that our eyes encounter, the brain attempts to find a match in a "dictionary" of previously encountered shapes that we build up over the course of our lives (Marr, 1982). If an unfamiliar shape is grossly different from anything else in this dictionary, it will either be ignored entirely or the brain may take the first steps in the construction of a new "entry." However, if the discrepancy between the unfamiliar shape and some preexisting one is only partial, the mental task of fitting in the new shape becomes more complicated. As a result, such partially strange shapes can cause us to pay closer attention.

An especially effective application of these principles can be achieved through the technique of "morphing," or using a computer to bring about a smooth transition between two different images—for example, a man and a woman, or a human and an animal. If the morphing process stops halfway between the two, the resulting hybrid can trap our brain in an unresolvable tug-of-war between two competing entries in our dictionary of shapes. As an attention-getting device, this kind of hybrid can be endlessly fascinating. Another way of approximating this effect involves the blending or merging of two different images without actual morphing. This technique is fairly common in advertising, but it has rarely been used as effectively as in a Saab ad from the 1980s, in which a

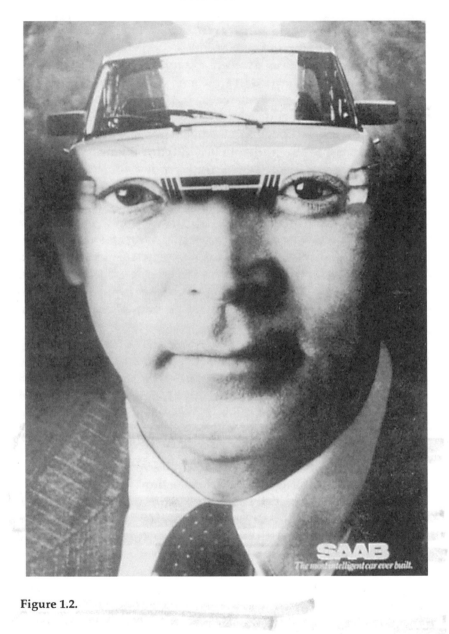

Figure 1.2.

man's face and the front of a car come together in one seamless whole (see Figure 1.2). From chin to nose, this object is distinctly human; but at the level of the eyes it begins to merge with the car's headlights, and from there on up, the car takes over completely.

Surrealism and Visual Metaphor

To viewers who are familiar with the history of art in the 20th century, this man/car image may be somewhat reminiscent of paintings by the surrealist René Magritte, who was fond of such mind-bending constructions. Both surrealism in general and Magritte in particular have provided continuing inspiration to the creators of advertising images, partly because of the effects we are discussing here, but also for other reasons that we will consider in Chapter 6. Strictly speaking, though, there is an important difference between traditional surrealism and the kind of thing that we see in the Saab ad or in the image of the mouthless woman from our earlier example. Surrealism is sometimes thought of as a representation of dream imagery and, therefore, as a source of various hidden meanings. However, attempts to read such meanings into the works of the traditional surrealists very quickly run into the problem of overinterpretation. As practiced by artists like Magritte or Salvador Dali, surrealism was mainly an art of eye-grabbing visual paradoxes. When we look at our Saab/man or mouthless woman, on the other hand, we see visual paradox but we also see something additional. Both of these ads have a very definite metaphorical dimension, and we would be missing much of the ads' impact if we ignored it.

In the case of the mouthless woman, the first line of the ad's text ("Most politicians still think women should be seen and not heard") guides us toward a political interpretation of the image. The erasure of the woman's mouth represents the suppression of women's opinions by the political system as well as by their own failure to vote (as the second line of text suggests). The intended meaning of the Saab/man juxtaposition is also indicated textually. The smooth meshing of the man's features with those of the car is evidently meant as a representation of the car's perfect responsiveness to its driver, who is made to feel as if the car is an intelligent extension of his own body. In each of these ads, then, an image of a concrete physical event or situation (erasure, merger) is used as a means of evoking an analogous abstract concept (political silencing, automotive responsiveness). Because of the analogical connection between each image and its corresponding concept, these images can be considered visual metaphors.

The topic of visual metaphor has been examined by several writers, including Green (1985), Hatcher (1988), Hausman (1989), Johns (1984), Kaplan (1990, 1992), Whittock (1990), and, most notably, Kennedy (1982, 1990, 1993) and Kennedy and Simpson (1982). On the whole, these writers tend to use the term *metaphor* rather expansively, encompassing some types of visual devices that we will be examining under different headings in later chapters. For the purposes of this discussion, we can define visual metaphor somewhat more narrowly as the representation of an abstract concept through a concrete visual image that bears some analogy to that concept. Note, however, that this definition still covers a wider range of images than the specific types with which we are concerned here, because it includes cases in which there is no distortion of the physical object or event portrayed in the image. For instance, according to this definition, a plain, ordinary, undistorted picture of an eagle can serve as a visual metaphor for the concept of freedom because of the analogy between defying gravity and casting off social restrictions. It should be understood, therefore, that our car/man and mouthless woman images belong to a subcategory of visual metaphor as defined here and are not representative of all possible applications of that term.

This subcategory of visual metaphor, involving some violation of physical reality, is a very common convention in advertising, and there are any number of examples that we could have chosen in place of the two that we have looked at up to this point. As far as the distortion of bodies is concerned, an even more extreme case than that of our mouthless woman can be found in an ad for the New York Life Insurance Company. The caption reads, "If choosing between life insurance and competitive interest rates is putting you through the wringer . . . get them both" (see Figure 1.3). The photograph above this caption shows a man literally going through two immense rollers, which squeeze his legs into a pair of flat, undulating ribbons. Another ad by the same company contains a slightly different caption: "If you're torn between life insurance protection and competitive interest rates . . . get them both" (see Figure 1.4). These lines are accompanied by a photograph of a man's body split in half. Similar techniques can be applied to nonhuman objects, of course. An Absolut Vodka ad, labeled "ABSOLUT ATTRAC-TION," shows a martini glass next to a bottle of Absolut; the glass is bent

Figure 1.3 and Figure 1.4.

Figure 1.5.

in the direction of the bottle, as if being drawn toward it by some invisible force (see Figure 1.5).

The kind of merging or blending of two objects that we encountered in the Saab ad is also a common advertising practice (Wolf, 1988, Chap. 1). Another noteworthy example occurs in an antismoking poster put out by the Health Education Board of Scotland (see Figure 1.6). As in the Women's Vote ad, the central image here is of a young woman gazing at the viewer with a vaguely uneasy expression. This woman's facial features are all intact. However, in place of hair, she has a dense, tangled mass of disintegrating cigarette stubs. The caption reads, "Perfume won't hide it." Less dramatically, the merging of two or more images that do not belong together has become a staple device in ads featuring landscapes or cityscapes. In such cases, the point of the impossible juxtaposition is typically to demonstrate how easily a travel agency or airline or other mode of transportation can move a passenger between different locations. A recent Ford Explorer ad, for instance, contains a background photograph in which we see the skyline of Manhattan on the right, a Southwestern landscape (Monument Valley, Utah) on the left, and a gradual shift from one to the other in between (see Figure 1.7). The point of this composite is to show that the Ford Explorer is equally at home in both kinds of environments. Likewise, other ads have merged Monument Valley and London (Figure 1.8), or Manhattan and Paris, or various other locations to demonstrate ease of travel.

In many of these examples, particularly the ones involving human bodies, the images can be seen as serving both of the functions we discussed in the introduction to this chapter: On one hand, the violation of reality attracts attention; on the other hand, the image's metaphorical dimension gives rise to an emotional response: resentment at the exclusion of women from politics; admiration for the precision of Saab's engineering; anxiety about life insurance; loathing of cigarettes; and so forth. As we have already noted in our initial discussion of these two functions of images, it is quite common for them to occur together as a result of a single visual device. In fact, when an ad uses the violation of reality as a means of attracting attention, it is highly unusual for that ad *not* to have an additional metaphorical dimension—although of course, not all visual metaphors are as emotional as the ones above. As a rule, advertisers avoid reality violations or any other kinds of visual oddities whose sole purpose is catch the viewer's eye without any further mean-

Figure 1.6.

Figure 1.7.

15

Fly in the U.S. See more of Europe.

Because USAir is now part of British Airways Executive Club® Frequent Traveller Programme, you can apply the miles you've earned on USAir towards both international and domestic travel awards on British Airways and its partners. Now you can see a lot more of the world. *It's the way we make you feel* that makes us the world's favourite airline.

BRITISH AIRWAYS
The world's favourite airline

Figure 1.8.

ing. As one agency chief has put it, "You are wrong if, in your ad, you stand a man on his head just to get attention. But you are right if you have him on his head to show how your product keeps things from falling out of his pockets" (quoted in Marra, 1990, pp. 38-39). Presumably, if an unusual image is used gratuitously and does not contain any message about what it is the ad is selling or promoting, the viewer may come away from the ad not remembering anything beyond the image itself.

As far as reality violations are concerned, the one situation that may appear to break this rule is the case of advertising imagery that attempts to replicate the spirit, and not just the outer form, of surrealism. As we have already noted, traditional surrealistic art is not metaphorical in the sense in which we have been using that term, and it may therefore seem that surrealistic ads must fall into the category of gratuitous attention-getting. However, when it appears in commercial advertising, surrealism makes up for its lack of a metaphorical dimension by conveying a different type of message about the product. As we will see in Chapter 6, there is evidence that viewers associate this visual style with sophisti-

Figure 1.9.

cation and superior social status. Consequently, even if it does not contain any direct representation of the product, a surrealistic image is capable of imbuing it with upscale connotations. In that sense, the attention-getting aspects of surrealism are anything but gratuitous.

In general, both surrealistic images and metaphorical violations of reality are particularly well-suited to the requirements of visual advertising precisely because of their ability to combine an eye-catching first impression with a more substantive message. As a parting look at the latter technique, let us briefly examine an ongoing campaign for Duracell batteries. The TV commercials in this campaign feature a variety of Duracell-powered humanoid robots (see Figure 1.9). The situations depicted in these ads are strange enough in their own right, but the most remarkable thing about the ads is the appearance of the humanoids. These are actually human actors wearing semitransparent masks and moving with robotic stiffness. The uncanny results of this transformation—creatures that seem not-quite-human and yet not really anything else—can keep a viewer's eyes glued to the TV screen even after the content of the commercials has become thoroughly familiar. It would be hard to find a better illustration of Shepard's principle that *slight* deviations from familiar objects are the most arresting forms of visual distortion.

Figure 1.10.

Visual Parodies

But visual distortions and violations of reality are not the only kinds of pictures that can trap the brain's "dictionary search" between a familiar object or situation and a new or unfamiliar one. This feat can also be accomplished by another major category of advertising imagery, namely, visual parodies. Both in the United States and elsewhere, the visual culture of the mass media is perpetually engaged in producing new variations on well-known images from the past, including such subjects as the somber-faced rural couple in Grant Wood's "American Gothic" (see Figure 1.10); God giving life to Adam in Michelangelo's Sistine Chapel ceiling fresco; the "Great Wave" by the Japanese artist Hokusai; and any number of movie scenes, ranging from *Casablanca* to *Star Wars*. The aspect of this phenomenon that most directly concerns us here is illustrated in an ad based on the image of the Mona Lisa, whose protean features seem to provide inexhaustible inspiration to parodists (Strumwasser & Friedman, 1992).

In this particular ad, we actually have two versions of her image, side by side (see Figure 1.11). In one version, she is holding a bottle of Prince Spaghetti Sauce; in the other, a bottle of Prince Chunky Homestyle. This difference in the product is matched by her face and figure: in the first version of the image, she appears in her familiar form (although this image is actually an artist's copy, not the original painting by da Vinci); in the second version, she has gained a considerable amount of weight. Both versions contain departures from the original (most notably, of course, the bottles), but for our purposes, it is the "chunky" version that is of particular interest. This is a good example of an image that would mean very little to a viewer who did not have the original as a reference point. This does not mean that it was absolutely necessary to have the first version (which is much closer to the original) right there in the same ad, as it is in this one. In fact, an alternative ad featuring just the chunky version might have been quite effective in its own right—for viewers who are already familiar with the Mona Lisa (i.e., probably most mass media consumers). But for those few people who have somehow not yet been exposed to the original (or, rather, to its reproduction in the media), a chunky-only ad would have been of little interest.

As in the case of visual distortions, then, what we have here is an eye-catching departure from the appearance of a previously familiar

Figure 1.11.

object, and our response to it is one more illustration of the value of such disparities as a means of attracting attention. The chunky image is not the Mona Lisa as we know her, but on the other hand, she is also not an entirely new person. Placed side by side with her old self, she excites some of the same kind of curiosity that can arise when we compare before-and-after photographs in weight-loss and other personal transformation ads. To be sure, this side-by-side comparison is a relatively unusual feature in parodies. In other respects, though, the type of mental response elicited by this ad's second image is characteristic of the fascination that most parodies seem to exert on their viewers. Of course, this fascination has other important sources too. A major reason for the increasing use of parody in advertising is the assumption that its self-referential quality and often-ironic tone can give viewers a flattering sense of being hip and media conscious (Savan, 1994, pp. 302-303). There is clearly more to be said about visual parodies, and it will be said in due course, but first we must go on to the next topic in our examination of techniques for attracting the viewer's attention.

Direct Eye Gaze

We have already discussed the fact that having a model or spokesperson look into the viewer's eyes is a standard attention-getting device. We have also discussed in passing one of the best-known examples of this device, the image of Uncle Sam saying "I want you . . ." (see Figure 1.12). As it happens, this is another one of those images that is constantly being parodied, and in fact, the original World War I recruiting poster in which this image first appeared was itself a parody of an earlier British design. The enduring hold that the Uncle Sam image has exercised on the visual culture of the United States may be partly due to his archetypally craggy physiognomy (although most parodies do not preserve that aspect of the original). But another important reason for the image's popularity is surely the way in which Uncle Sam seems to reach into the viewer's space and actively get him or her to pay attention. This effect is due not only to Uncle Sam's direct gaze but also to his pointed finger, which is literally aimed at the space of the viewer. In an alternative version of the poster, in which Uncle Sam looks but does not point, the illusion of entering the viewer's space is considerably diminished (see Figure 1.13).

These aspects of the image's appeal illustrate a broader observation about the attention-getting process in advertising. Because of the iconicity of visual images, much of that process is modeled on elements of real-world interpersonal interaction. This modeling is abundantly obvious, of course, when it involves a person in an image displaying facial expressions or gestures patterned on real-world facial and bodily cues (looking in the eyes, pointing). But as we shall see presently, the modeling

Figure 1.12 and Figure 1.13.

22

of real-world interaction can also take more indirect forms involving camera positioning that reproduces the distances and orientations of interpersonal interaction.

Despite the significance of the pointed finger in the Uncle Sam example, when it comes to advertising as a whole, it is probably the nature of a spokesperson's gaze, together with his or her general facial expression, that plays the most important role among the various attentional cues that are directly modeled on real-world behavior. This point is in accord with data suggesting that in our interactions with other people, we tend to be especially responsive to visual cues coming from relatively narrow zones encompassing their eyes and their mouths. Studies of where people look when they are interacting with each other have found that we spend more time focusing on those zones than elsewhere (Solso, 1994, pp. 136-137), and there is some evidence (accompanied by some controversy) to the effect that this behavioral tendency is innate, and that neural circuitry in our brains may be genetically predisposed to process the kinds of visual information contained in those zones (Fridlund, 1994, pp. 65-68).

As in the case of the attention-getting devices examined earlier, eye gaze and other facial cues often serve additional functions beyond catching the eye of the viewer. A typical illustration of this possibility comes from the world of political image-making. When politicians appear in interview shows, debates, or other televised forums, they tend to orient themselves toward the camera, even though in such circumstances they are ostensibly interacting with an interviewer or political opponent. Facing the camera serves the purpose of engaging the TV viewer's interest and attention more directly, but it is also an attempt to inspire trust. By appearing to look the viewer squarely in the eyes, the politician may also appear to be an aboveboard, nothing-to-hide kind of person. The classic demonstration of these aspects of eye gaze was given by John F. Kennedy in the presidential debates of 1960, an event that has been of enduring interest for students of visual communication because of its provocative outcome: People who listened to the debates on the radio were more likely to consider Richard Nixon the winner; in the eyes of TV viewers, however, the perceived winner tended to be Kennedy. Clearly, some aspect of the TV images must have had a substantial impact on viewers' judgments. According to retrospective analyses, what made the difference was Kennedy's appearance. Compared to Nixon (who had recently been ill), Kennedy looked more youthful, he acted more vigorously, and—most importantly, from our perspective—he spent more time looking directly into the camera.

Of course, much has changed in the public's view of politics and media since the debates of 1960. What may have worked for JFK in 1960 should not be assumed automatically to work for candidates today. If people are more knowledgeable and skeptical about the workings of the media, as many advertisers think they are, it may be that the practice of deliberately turning away from one's interlocutor and toward the camera—an action that many politicians find unnatural and have to be trained carefully to perform—is seen by some viewers as slick and manipulative, rather than a sign of honesty. So, in this one area at least, the benefits that come from the attention-getting potential of the direct gaze may be undermined by its other implications. But there also may be situations in which the function of attention-getting itself is served better by abandoning the direct gaze in favor of some alternative strategy.

Rear Views

The most radical alternative to the direct gaze is a 180-degree shift in the spectator's point of view. In other words, what we are talking about now is an image in which we see the back of some person instead of her or his eyes and face. In our real-world interactions with others, this view from the back can imply turning away or exclusion. Is there any conceivable reason to prefer such a view to a frontal one? As it happens, there is at least one genre of advertising in which this view is a common practice. In many travel ads, we see an enticing landscape in the background and one or two people in the foreground. Very often, the foreground person or people are facing directly away from the spectator, so that all the spectator sees is a rear view. What could be the purpose of this convention?

The first thing to note in answer to this question is that the convention seems to take a somewhat different form, depending on the nature of the landscape that is being advertised. In ads for mountainous areas (e.g., Alaska), we tend to see people at some distance (see Figure 1.14). In ads for seaside resorts or cruises, we typically get a much closer view (see Figure 1.15). The first of these two kinds of images is reminiscent of the conventions of 19th-century Romantic landscape painting, and, because

Figure 1.14.

the people who work in advertising are often highly knowledgeable about art history, this resemblance is surely no coincidence. In its original

Figure 1.15, Figure, 1.16, Figure 1.17, and **Figure 1.18.**

context, the convention of the person(s) facing away from the viewer of the painting was intended as a comment on the otherworldly beauty of nature. The person in the picture turns away from society (i.e., the picture's viewers) and becomes absorbed in the grand spectacle of mountains, canyons, etc. This aspect of the meaning of the rear view appears to be present in both versions of the contemporary travel ad. One of the reasons for heading for either mountains or beaches is to get away from it all, and the rear view may be a way of making that point. But in those ads that feature seascapes, there is another aspect to this convention, and it is this latter aspect that comes closer to our present concerns.

Not surprisingly, the models in seascape ads usually have very little clothing on and are often nearly naked (see Figures 1.16-1.18). Consequently, in such ads, the meaning of the view from the back is likely to acquire a sexual dimension. Whereas the exposed flesh of the person in the image may arouse the viewer's sexual curiosity, the rear view denies that viewer a fuller look. In this context, then, the rear view becomes a means of attracting the viewer's eye through the power of suggestion. Even in an age in which complete nudity is becoming increasingly acceptable in the mass media, this strategy appears to retain its effectiveness, and the rear-view convention has made several appearances in other areas of advertising, including ads for Jaïpur (a perfume by Boucheron of Paris) and Chivas Regal Scotch Whisky (see Figures 1.19 and 1.20). Both of these ads feature women, and both add a new twist to the more traditional rear-view convention. The women have their hands behind their backs, and that is where the product is displayed. In the Jaïpur ad, the woman is naked, and the unusually shaped perfume bottle actually encircles her hands, imparting a hint of kinkiness to the image. The woman in the Chivas Regal ad is in a dark dress that exposes much of her back but also provides a contrasting background color for the silver, gift-wrapped box of Chivas that she cradles in her hands. In both cases, therefore, there is a suggestion of an interaction with someone whom we do not see. So here, the rear view becomes doubly intriguing. It creates interest not only in the women but also in the men with whom they are presumably interacting, and yet it gives us a limited view of the former and no view of the latter.

Viewing Distance

In addition to illustrating some of the possibilities of the rear or blocked view, travel ads also provide a simple demonstration of the importance of distance as a visual variable. It was noted earlier that seascape ads typically give us a closer view of the people in them than ads about mountain travel do. This difference is not accidental, of course. If a person in a seascape ad is meant to attract attention through her or his sexual qualities, that effect can be magnified by a closer viewing position. The underlying logic of this usage (process) has been analyzed

Figure 1.19 and Figure 1.20.

in detail by Meyrowitz (1986), who argues that viewing distance in visual media (close-up, medium shot, long shot, etc.) operates by analogy with interpersonal distance in real-world interaction. In real life, greater proximity is generally associated with heightened attention and more intense involvement; the same should hold true of our reaction to people in images. These propositions have been tested by Byron Reeves and his associates, who have found that tighter close-ups, as well as larger TV screens and shorter distances between the viewer and the screen, do indeed lead to increases in both attention and involvement (Lombard, 1995; Reeves, Lombard, & Melwani, 1992), although the large-screen effect does not occur consistently (Reeves, Detenber, & Steuer, 1993). Furthermore, a study by Donsbach, Brosius, and Mattenklott (1993) has found that zooming in for a tighter close-up can also enhance the perceived importance of a person on TV.

Subjective Camera

If closer views can get us to pay more attention, does it follow that all advertising images should be shot in close-up? Or, to put this question differently, are there any reasons why an ad might benefit from a longer view? The most obvious and common reason is that an attention-getting close-up may leave out information that could enhance other aspects of the ad's appeal, such as a flag flying behind a candidate in a political ad or an impressive mansion in an ad for a luxury car. Moreover, Fiske (1987) has argued that very tight close-ups can actually incite hostility, which would be counterproductive in most areas of advertising. But what if hostility is indeed the goal? Consider two photographic-product ads based on the same theme, a confrontation with a big, carnivorous, hostile animal. In one ad, for Tamron lenses, the animal is a wolf (Figure 1.21). The other ad, for Nikon cameras, features a grizzly bear (Figure 1.22). Both animals are photographed head-on, with their eyes focused straight at us and their fangs bared, but the wolf appears in a much tighter shot than that of the grizzly. It may seem that here we have a clear case for the tighter close-up. Grabbing the viewer's attention is the main point of both of the images, and, in contrast to most other kinds of ads, these two would clearly stand to gain if, as Fiske assumes, too-tight close-ups can create a hostile appearance. Nevertheless, the wider view in the Nikon ad is no accident, and a good argument can be made that it is an effective

Figure 1.21.

Figure 1.22.

attention-getter in its own right. What the ad accomplishes by eschewing a tighter close-up is the inclusion of the photographer's legs in the picture. We see that he has been treed by the grizzly, which is snapping at his feet. So the wide view has the effect of putting us in another person's shoes as he or she goes through a hair-raising encounter. We participate vicariously in the experience, and that sense of entering another's life can in itself exert fascination and attract our interest.

The kind of perspective used in the Nikon ad is usually referred to as a subjective or point-of-view shot because it gives us the visual experience of seeing the world through someone else's point of view and participating in her or his subjectivity (Messaris, 1992, pp. 185-188; Zettl, 1990, pp. 219-221). In advertising, subjective shots are often used to heighten the interest and impact of action scenes, as in our Nikon example or in many ads featuring the driver's perspective in a speeding car (see Figure 1.23). Occasionally, subjective shots can also be found in conversation scenes, where they are used to draw the viewer into an exchange of persuasive information (Gable, 1983). For instance, during a TV commercial in which one neighbor tells another about the superior properties of a new laundry detergent, the camera might shift to the point of view of the person receiving the advice or, more rarely, the person offering it.

The effectiveness of action-scene subjective shots has been tested by Orton, Reeves, Leshner, and Nass (1995) in an experiment involving two simultaneously produced videotapes of the same event, recorded from both a subjective and a nonsubjective perspective. Using a similar method, Galan (1986) has tested viewers' responses to subjective and nonsubjective versions of a TV commercial about two students discussing a new brand of potato chips. In both studies, the subjective versions received better evaluations and higher scores on measures of viewers' involvement. These findings support the central idea behind the use of the subjective shot, that is, the assumption that this device can serve to draw the viewer into the situation portrayed in an image. Because the entire basis for this effect is the image's simulation of someone's visual experience, subjective shots can be considered the ultimate example of iconicity. They provide an appropriate point at which to conclude this discussion of attention-getting devices and proceed to an examination of what comes after attention.

Figure 1.23.

ELICITING EMOTION

Beyond attracting the viewer's attention, the image(s) in an ad are typically meant to give rise to some emotional disposition toward the product, politician, social cause, or whatever else the ad is about. The iconicity of visual images serves this process by making it possible for images to draw upon the rich variety of visual stimuli and associated emotions to which we are already attuned through our interactions with our social and natural environments: facial expressions, gestures, postures, personal appearance, physical surroundings, and so on. Moreover, as we have already seen, visual images are capable of simulating certain aspects of those interactions by means of the variables that control the viewer's perspective: degree of proximity, angle of view, presence or absence of subjective shots, and so on.

Vertical Camera Angle, Power, and Status

A convenient starting point for our discussion is the visual variable that is sometimes referred to as "vertical camera angle" (Kepplinger, 1987, Chap. 3; 1991, pp. 180-181; Kepplinger & Donsbach, 1990; Zettl, 1990, pp. 216-219). This variable has to do with whether the person or object in an image is shown from below (low angle), from above (high angle), or in a level view. The effects of low and high angles have been tested extensively in a series of experiments and other studies ranging over a period of two decades. The assumption that a low angle can make someone appear more powerful has been supported in experiments by Mandell and Shaw (1973) and by Kraft (1987). These researchers were concerned directly or indirectly with the political applications of this device ("Grinnell prof," 1987). To the extent that people's political attitudes are motivated by feelings of vulnerability and desires for powerful leadership or protection, low angles in campaign imagery should be able to enhance a politician's standing with her or his public. This is a common assumption in discussions of political imagery (e.g., Diamond & Bates, 1984, p. 296). And yet, in the United States at least, political ads or posters do not use this device very often. While individual examples are certainly not hard to find, they constitute the exception, rather than the norm. Why should this be?

A hint at an answer to this question is provided by another pair of studies that dealt with the relationship between camera angle and viewers' reactions to a filmed persuasive message (McCain, Chilberg, & Wakshlag, 1977; Tiemens, 1970). In the first study, in which the viewers were students and the spokesperson was a professor, there was some evidence of a positive relationship between low angles and persuasiveness (Tiemens, 1970). But this relationship was reversed in the outcome of the second study, whose spokesperson and viewers were all students. The discrepancy between these two results suggests that viewers may respond well to low angles when the person depicted in them is someone of recognized authority (as teachers are supposed to be in the educational context), but that low angles are rejected when the viewers and the person viewed are of equal status. If this is a valid interpretation of the findings, it implies that the effects of low angles in political imagery will depend on the degree of status inequality that people are willing to accept between themselves and their political leaders. In an authoritarian climate, in which hierarchical relationships are taken for granted, the unambiguous enhancement of status through low-angle imagery may find an appreciative viewership. But where egalitarianism is the norm, level-viewed portrayals may be more appropriate, as seems to be the case in the United States.

These conclusions are consistent with the relative scarcity of pronounced low angles in political ads and other promotional portrayals of politicians in the United States. Americans have traditionally been ambivalent about according superior status to political figures, and any obvious attempt to display authority or power is a risky move for an American politician—hence, the success, in American political life, of people who are able to combine the look of leadership with convincing evidence of being just plain folks in other ways. This skill was surely a major factor in the phenomenal popularity of Ronald Reagan, whose example demonstrates the aspect of this issue that is most relevant for our purposes: The primary instrument through which this skill is expressed is typically the politician's own appearance. It was in his finely modulated demeanor, more than anywhere else, that Ronald Reagan was able to display the seamless continuity between his status as vanquisher of the Evil Empire and his identity as a man of modest, small-town origins. Conversely, Reagan's successor, George Bush, whose candidacy for national office was handicapped by his upper-class background, had to be trained not to betray that background through his facial expressions and other mannerisms. His trainer, Roger Ailes, has written an entire book emphasizing the centrality of personal appearance in politics and public life (Ailes, 1988). By extension, iconicity—the property of pictures that makes it possible for most of a politician's constituents to be exposed to that appearance—can be considered the central ingredient of mediated political image-making.

While low-angle views may not play as large a part in politics as one might expect, they can be found more frequently in the now-obsolete genre of war-mobilization posters and other related images (Paret, Lewis, & Paret, 1992; Rhodes, 1976). Two examples of this genre from World War II give us a revealing demonstration of the difference between low angles and physical appearance as means of conveying a sense of strength and heroism. The first poster, produced in 1943, was used in the Philippines to strengthen resistance against the Japanese occupation (see Figure 1.24). It shows a young Filipino fighter holding a flag aloft and hurling a grenade. In the second poster, also from 1943, we see three Chinese, a man, a woman, and a child, looking straight at us with determined looks on their faces (see Figure 1.25). This poster was used in the United States to support fund-raising for the Chinese war effort. For our purposes, the main technical difference between the two images is that the first employs a low angle, whereas the second gives us a frontal view and therefore depends only on the appearance of the people in it to create the intended impression. Both images successfully convey feelings of power and resolve, but, in my eyes at least, the second image also manages to blend those feelings with a sense of stoically endured suffering. This latter aspect of the image's meaning is not simply a result of the fact that the woman in the image is wounded, because the young man in the first poster also has a wound. Rather, it is the second poster's facial expressions that most pointedly communicate its double message. Once again, therefore, we see that the ability to reproduce the appearance of people's physical features gives images access to nuances of emotional expression that may not be available through other means. Furthermore, because these posters were drawn by hand, the second image, by the artist Martha Sawyers, is a reminder that the effects of iconicity do not depend on photographic fidelity to the real world. The image's emotional tone

Figure 1.24 and Figure 1.25.

is the product of a few handmade lines that manage to capture the distinctive features of human expressive physiognomy.

Before we leave the topic of low angles, the two posters we have just examined can be used to illustrate one final point. In contrast to the image of the Chinese family in the second poster, the Filipino man in the first one is looking away from the viewer. Because the man is throwing a grenade, in this particular case a direct frontal view would have sent an ambiguous message. However, even in the absence of such complications, whenever low angles are used with the intention of creating a positive impression—whether in military imagery, in politics, or elsewhere—side views are generally more common than frontal ones. This convention may reflect an intuitive assumption that a low angle combined with a frontal view can actually look overbearing, even menacing, rather than noble or heroic. We see an illustration of this possibility in an ad by the R. J. Reynolds Tobacco Company arguing that stricter enforcement of existing laws would reduce underage smoking dramatically while avoiding the burden of additional regulatory bureaucracy (see Figure 1.26). The accompanying low-angle image of a judge peering down at us from the bench complements this message by conveying a sense of the potential onerousness that comes with the powers of the law. Having someone look down at us can be intimidating.

The Look of Superiority

Whether in combination with frontal views or not, low angles are not very common in commercial ads, despite some evidence that they can positively affect viewers' perceptions of inanimate objects and therefore can be used to create more favorable impressions of consumer products (Meyers-Levy & Peracchio, 1992). When it comes to facial expressions of superiority, though, there is one area of commercial advertising in which looking down on the viewer *in a figurative sense* is the norm. Anyone who has looked at ads for clothes and other fashion items will have noticed a striking difference between the images in high-fashion magazines, on one hand, and ads for less-expensive products, on the other. This difference can also be observed in a comparison between the demeanor of haute couture runway models and the facial expressions of their counterparts in such venues as the Home Shopping Network. Models who display moderately priced clothing usually smile and strike ingratiating

Figure 1.26.

39

poses. But high-fashion models are generally unsmiling and sometimes openly contemptuous. So pronounced is this contrast that it is tempting to formulate it in a simple rule: the higher the fashion, the more sullen the expression.

Of course, things are not really so simple. To a certain extent, the absence of conventionally pleasing poses in high-fashion ads may stem from a reaction against explicit "salesmanship" that has also occurred in other areas of advertising (Goldman, 1992, chap. 7). All the same, the major reason why these ads, in particular, have come to feature this haughty look is surely a matter of social status (Barthel, 1988, chap. 6; Berger, 1972, pp. 132-133). The supercilious expressions on the models' faces serve to increase the desirability of what they're selling by evoking status anxiety in the viewer. Or, to put this another way, we could invoke Groucho Marx's famous joke about not wanting to belong to any club that would accept him as a member. By looking down on their viewers, the models in high-fashion ads offer reassurance that the world displayed in the ad is indeed superior to the one inhabited by the upwardly mobile consumer.

Looking Down, Nurturance, and Subservience

Up to this point, we have been concerned with visual conventions that literally or figuratively put the viewer in the position of looking up at someone. What about the opposite situation? Although high angles as such are not a major advertising convention, imagery that invites the viewer to respond to weakness most definitely is. More specifically, such a reaction is likely to be evoked whenever an ad resorts to either one of those two clichéd subjects, the child or the cute animal. Testifying to the enduring appeal of these clichés, a veteran advertising expert gives the following advice to the creators of ads:

> If your [selling] proposition has anything to do with kids and/or dogs, or if you have any logical reason to use pictures of them, spend the money for the best casting agency and the most talented photographer. If the two produce as they should, you will have a photograph that can get increased attention for the *most* Routine Proposition with which anyone ever had to work. (Antin, 1993, p. 189)

The strong feelings of affection that such images bring out in most people are almost certainly the result of innate predispositions. As Konrad Lorenz (1970) showed in a classic study, humans appear to be genetically designed to experience a nurturing tendency in response to certain specific facial features that distinguish the juvenile from the adult forms of many species (e.g., relatively higher foreheads, larger eyes, smaller noses, etc.). This predictability of people's responses has made pictures of children a reliable ingredient of commercial ads (e.g., for food and drinks, medications, automotive safety, financial services, etc.) as well as nonprofit appeals for a variety of causes (e.g., children's aid organizations, environmentalism, international development, etc.) (see Figure 1.27).

But pictures of children or young animals are not the only advertising images that use juvenile characteristics as part of their appeal. In a widely cited and enduringly relevant analysis of the portrayal of women in magazine ads, Erving Goffman (1976) found that the poses of models in these ads included a variety of actions or gestures that could be described as both submissive and childlike: coyly lowering one's eyes or head, playfully lying on the floor, and so on (see Figure 1.28). (For the most part, the images in which such behavior occurs belong to a different category from the kind of upper-class, high-fashion ads discussed above.) Goffman interprets these childlike poses as a reflection of the subservient or dependent role that women have traditionally had to play in society vis-à-vis men. Accordingly, it is not surprising to find such poses in ads actually directed at men. However, it turns out that the very same kinds of female poses are often encountered in ads addressed primarily to women. Because the models in these ads frequently display this behavior directly toward the camera—that is, they treat the lens as a substitute for the eye of an imaginary male onlooker—it could be argued that when women look at the ads, they are actually seeing themselves as a man might see them.

Identification

This last point is especially noteworthy. In effect, by giving female viewers a male perspective on the models in the images, these ads are creating visual conditions that can lead to cross-gender identification. But, on the other hand, we can also take it for granted that the primary inclination of most female viewers will be to identify with the female

Sponsor a Child for Only $10 a Month.

At last! Here is an affordable $10 sponsorship program for Americans who are unable to send $20, $22, or $24 a month to help a needy child.

And yet, this is a full sponsorship program because for $10 a month you will receive:

• a 3 1/2" x 5" photograph of the child you are helping.

• two personal letters and an updated photo from your child each year.

• a complete Sponsorship Kit with your child's case history and a special report about the country where your child lives.

• issues of our newsletter, "Sponsorship News."

You can really make a difference!

$10 a month may not seem like much – but as a sponsor, your monthly support will help provide so much:

• emergency food, clothing and medical care.

• a chance to attend school.

• help for the child's family and community, with counseling on housing, agriculture, nutrition, and other vital areas to help them become self-sufficient.

All this for only $10 a month?

Yes! This is possible because each child has more than one sponsor, and so, despite worldwide inflation...

...you can personally help make a dramatic and compassionate impact on the life of a needy child. And at a cost that is truly affordable.

A child needs your love!

Here is how you can sponsor a child immediately for only $10 a month:

1. Fill out the coupon and tell us if you want to sponsor a boy or a girl, and check the country of your choice.

2. Or mark the "Emergency List" box and we will select a child for you who most urgently needs your love and support.

3. Send your first $10 monthly payment in right now with the coupon to Children International.

Then, in just a few days, you will receive your child's name, photograph and case history.

May we hear from you? We believe that our Sponsorship Program protects the dignity of the child and the family and at the same time provides Americans with a positive and beautiful way to help a needy youngster.

Carlos lives in a one-room shack with a dirt floor and no furniture. He needs nutritious food, clothing, and an education. Won't you help a child like Carlos?

Sponsorship Application

☐ **Yes, I wish to sponsor a child.** Enclosed is my first payment of $10. Please assign me a ☐ Boy ☐ Girl ☐ Either.

Country preference: ☐ India ☐ The Philippines ☐ Thailand ☐ Chile ☐ Honduras ☐ Dominican Republic ☐ Colombia ☐ Guatemala ☐ Ecuador ☐ Special Holy Land child program

☐ **OR, choose a child who most needs my help from your EMERGENCY LIST.**

NAME _____

ADDRESS _____

CITY _____

STATE _____ ZIP _____

☐ Please send me more information about sponsoring a child.
☐ I can't sponsor a child now, but wish to make a contribution of $_____

Please forward your U.S. tax-deductible check, made payable to:

Children International

Joseph Gripkey, Chief Executive
2000 East Red Bridge Road • Box 419413
Kansas City, Missouri 64141

A worldwide organization serving children since 1936. Financial report readily available upon request.

Figure 1.27.

Figure 1.28.

models. In fact, encouraging viewers' identification with the people in images may be the most common way in which visual advertisements exploit their iconic relationship to our real-world visual and psychological experiences. In our real-world social interactions, our psychological capacity to identify with other people enhances our ability to predict their actions toward us, and it also allows us to learn through observation. By identifying with someone else, we turn the observed consequences of her or his actions into lessons for our own lives. Much advertising is patterned directly on this aspect of our real-world experiences. By presenting us with models whose sexual or financial or other types of success we may wish to emulate, advertising images draw upon our tendencies for identification in order to strengthen our emotional involvement with ads. However, as we have just seen, ads can also give the viewer the visual experience of someone who is interacting with the model in an image, and this visual positioning can split the direction of the viewer's identificational tendencies. Because of these complications, as well as the fundamental importance of the very phenomenon of identification, it is worth examining the visual aspects of this phenomenon in some detail. We will begin by looking at identification in the cinema, the area in which it has received the greatest amount of attention from visually oriented scholars (see, especially, the literature on identification in thrillers and horror films, which is discussed in Messaris, 1994, Chap. 5).

If the argument presented earlier is correct, the ads discussed by Goffman would appear to imply a male point of view, even though the intended viewer is often a woman. So the women who look at these ads are being invited to identify both with the person being viewed and with an implicit, opposite-sex viewer. There is some similarity between this situation and the circumstances in which female viewers often find themselves at the movies. Film scholars have argued that, traditionally at least, the stories of Hollywood movies have tended to be male-centered and have therefore put female spectators in the position of viewing the women on the screen through a man's perspective (Mayne, 1993). However, it must be emphasized that, unlike these movies, the ads we are most concerned with are addressed mainly, if not exclusively, to women. What happens when we compare these ads with movies that actually have a female protagonist and, presumably, are targeted more heavily toward a female audience?

In movies, the visual device that is most unambiguously associated with identification is the subjective shot. Film directors who are concerned about maintaining the viewer's identification with a single character throughout the course of a movie will generally avoid using subjective shots from any other character's perspective. That avoidance has a consequence that may seem counterintuitive. Of all the characters in a movie, the protagonist is the only one who cannot be shown from a head-on perspective, looking directly into the camera. Why? Because, in most types of fictional movies (with some exceptions that need not concern us here), a head-on, eyes-into-the-camera view ordinarily implies that the on-screen character is interacting with someone who is located off-screen and whose point of view coincides with that of the camera. In other words, eyes into the camera ordinarily indicate that the shot is subjective, and such a shot will therefore be avoided when the on-screen character is the protagonist, precisely because of the more general avoidance of subjective shots from nonprotagonists' points of view. As a result of these conventions, the movie viewer's identification with an on-screen character typically occurs in the presence of a side view, rather than a direct frontal one. This principle may have originated historically in a cinema whose protagonists were overwhelmingly male, but it extends to movies with female protagonists as well. In that respect, therefore, these movies give us a very different view of women from the one we get in the ads with which we are concerned. As a deliberate strategy, the eye-to-eye view of someone with whom we are intended to identify is a distinguishing characteristic of ads aimed at women but is not a common ingredient of female-protagonist movies.

Direct views into the camera have also tended to be the exception rather than the rule in some ads aimed at men. Historically, ads for men's clothing, grooming aids, and other appearance-enhancing products have been more likely to feature side rather than head-on views of their subjects, and this convention can also be found in other male-oriented ads in which masculine appearance is part of the ad's theme. The Marlboro man, for instance, is rarely shown looking into the viewer's eyes. On the other hand, however, during the past two decades or so, there has been a notable countertrend in male-oriented advertising, featuring men whose poses contain some of the same elements—including the direct view—traditionally associated with women. Perhaps the clearest examples of this countertrend are the Calvin Klein jeans ads that

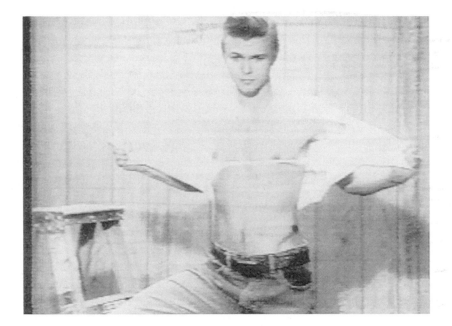

Figure 1.29.

created a media controversy in 1995 (see Figure 1.29). In the TV versions of these ads, several young men were shown looking into the camera and displaying their bodies in a variety of poses. The viewer's sense of direct interaction with these models was enhanced by the audible presence of an off-screen interviewer, who asked them personal questions and directed their actions. As was noted in the press when these commercials were shown, the fact that this interviewer was a man who expressed admiration for the men's appearance underscores the presence of a gay sensibility in these commercials (Lippert, 1995a, 1995b), and others have pointed out that there is a broader tendency in male-oriented advertising to acknowledge the existence and the interests of gay consumers (Kahan & Mulryan, 1995). Consequently, the more direct self-display that is evident in some recent male-oriented ads may be partly due to these considerations, rather than indicating a more explicit concern about how men look in the eyes of women. (This does not mean that one possibility precludes the other, of course.)

We have seen, then, that both women's ads and, increasingly, some ads for men solicit the viewer's identification in a manner that is more complex than the one traditionally associated with movies. In the typical movie, we are invited to *identify* with the protagonist (shown in a side view) and to *interact* vicariously with other characters (shown occasionally in subjective shots). In ads, however, identification and interaction are often conflated because the same-sex model (with whom we are inclined to identify) is shown to us in a direct view (implying interaction). Despite this complexity, though, there is some reason to believe that it is these ads, rather than the movies, that exploit most effectively the visual cues that lead to identification in our real-world interactions with other people. In a study mentioned earlier, Galan (1986) examined viewers' identification with characters appearing in a commercial. Although the study's primary objective had been to investigate the difference between subjective and nonsubjective shots, some of the data also have a bearing on the effects of direct, face-to-face views in comparison with views from the side. These data suggest that the direct views were more conducive to identification than were the side views and may even have been more effective than the subjective views in this respect.

The idea that direct views should be especially effective at eliciting identification is also consistent with a theoretical argument developed by Cappella (1993). Summarizing a large body of research, Cappella demonstrates that human beings probably have an inherent predisposition to react empathically to emotional displays in other people's faces. Because these displays are most evident when we are facing someone else directly and looking into her or his eyes, direct views should enhance the likelihood of empathic reactions and, hence, identification. Taken together, Cappella's theoretical argument and Galan's empirical findings lead to a conclusion that may come as a surprise to some scholars concerned with the phenomenon of identification in visual media. Despite the fact that the visual elicitation of identification has been studied and thought out much more intensively in movies than in ads, it may well be the case that the complex visual positioning created in so many ads aimed at women—and, increasingly, men—is actually the most effective visual method for tapping into our real-world identificational tendencies.

Sexual Appearances

In addition to functioning as foci of same-sex identification, images of men and women in advertising can also be used to attract the opposite sex, of course. It is sometimes assumed that men are more responsive to the visual aspects of sex than women are, and several biologically oriented writers have attempted to provide an evolutionary explanation for this putative gender difference (Ellis & Symons, 1990; Wright, 1994, pp. 43ff.; see also Buss, 1989). However, existing data on women's and men's actual reactions to ads do not conform to this assumption. Although there is some evidence that female nudity by itself may make female viewers feel uncomfortable (LaTour, 1990), both women and men have been found to react favorably to ads in which a man as well as a woman appear naked (Severn, Belch, & Belch, 1990), and women's responses to physically attractive male models do not appear to differ notably from men's responses to females (Baker & Churchill, 1977). Indeed, in recent years, some advertisers seem to have made a deliberate point of emphasizing women's sexual interest in men's looks (Reichert, Morgan, Callister, & Harrison, 1995), perhaps as an implicit response to criticisms of ads' traditional focus on sexy women. One of the clearest examples of this trend toward male sexual display was the TV commercial in which women gather at a window to ogle a shirtless, well-muscled male construction worker while he downs a can of diet soda. Even more explicitly, print ads for such fashion designers as Valentino and Versace have featured clothed female models embracing totally naked men.

While biologically based theories may not fit the facts about overall patterns of male and female responses to opposite-sex images (in ads and, perhaps, elsewhere), one of the more specific details of this kind of theory does have some relevance for our present concerns. Arguing that sexual attractiveness is based to a significant extent on the external bodily signs of reproductive fitness, researchers working within this theoretical framework have developed a number of hypotheses about innate aspects of human sexual response to physical appearance. For example, it has been argued that biological evolution has endowed men with an innate tendency to desire full lips in women, because this facial characteristic is a sign of high estrogen levels and, therefore, high fertility (Horgan, 1995, p. 177). For somewhat similar reasons, it has also been argued that men's sexual responses to women's bodies should be based mainly on the narrowness of the waist-to-hips ratio, and should be relatively indifferent to overall weight (Ridley, 1993, pp. 291-293). As it happens, this particular hypothesis has received consistent empirical support. For example, in ratings of the physical attractiveness of women in pictures, men have tended to give higher scores to heavier women with narrower waists than to thinner women with narrower hips. This finding comes as a direct challenge to the traditions of fashion advertising, which has tended to feature extremely thin women with very small hips—in other words, the exact opposite of the pattern that the men in this research tended to find most attractive.

Superficially, this preference for thin models among fashion advertisers may seem to be a perverse, and persistent, miscalculation. But of course, that is not the case. The fashion industry's predilection for thinness does not stem from a misreading of real-world sex cues; rather, it represents a deliberate suppression of those sex cues to heighten the sense of the female body as pure status display. In other words, this situation could be described as a conflict between sexual and social status cues, with the latter coming out on top.

More generally, though, sex and status tend to work together. Aspects of physical appearance and behavior that function as sexual signals also convey messages about social standing. For example, a study of editors of women's magazines found that these professionals routinely distinguish among several different types of female looks, including such categories as "classic beauty," "sensual/exotic," and "girl next door" (Solomon, Ashmore, & Longo, 1992). The authors describe these categories as different dimensions of physical beauty, defined by such visual characteristics as color and style of hair, shape of nose and cheekbones, and so on. But the categories have class connotations as well—for example, "girls next door" are more respectable and middle class than "sensual/exotic" types, but less upper class than "classic beauties"—and these connotations are conveyed through the same physical characteristics that distinguish one category from another. Furthermore, these physical characteristics also have ethnic associations. In particular, as the second part of its name implies, the "sensual/exotic" category tends to be more strongly associated with those ethnic groups that traditionally have held a lower status in American society.

Environmental Imagery

Because of the central role that sex and status play in commercial advertising, up to this point our examination of iconicity has dealt almost entirely with images of people—that is, images whose appeal to the viewer comes from their ability to replicate the meaningful features of faces, bodies, gestures, expressions, and so on. In order not to come away from this discussion with a completely one-sided view of our topic, let us now take a brief look at what happens when we remove people from the picture altogether. One place in which this is especially likely to occur is the landscape imagery that appears in environmentalist advertising. Because of the environmentalist movement's very heavy—and very successful—reliance on visual media such as posters, illustrated publications, greeting cards, and videos, as well as regular TV and print ads (see Brower, 1991), the visual rhetoric of environmentalist advocacy has been a particularly inviting topic for visually oriented researchers (Bouse, 1991; Canter, 1990). A major goal of this research has been to investigate the visual features that determine people's preferences for certain kinds of natural environments over others, and here the researchers have drawn on a large body of theoretical work by Jay Appleton and other writers influenced by his approach (Appleton, 1990; Jakle, 1987; Nasar, 1988). Appleton has advanced the hypothesis that our preferences for some kinds of landscapes may be shaped by biology rather than just culture. This hypothesis assumes that evolutionary forces may have predisposed all humans to favor certain environmental features that are beneficial to survival—or at least *were* beneficial to survival during the past evolution of our species.

The types of features that Appleton and his followers have investigated most thoroughly are two: high points in a landscape, from which a viewer would be able to survey the surrounding terrain and assess its opportunities and dangers; and places of shelter or concealment, from which a person could look out without being seen. These two features are usually referred to as "prospect" and "refuge" in the literature. According to this literature, an innate human interest in places of prospect or refuge may be part of the reason that landscapes with hills or mountains are often preferred to flat ones, landscapes containing stands of trees or bushes are often preferred to those lacking any tall vegetation, and so forth. These assumptions, together with others based on the same type of reasoning, are consistent with the conventions of environmentalist advertising, and they have been supported by empirical tests of viewers' reactions to pictures (Heerwagen & Orians, 1993; Ulrich, 1993). Of course, the possibility that landscape preferences may have a bio-evolutionary basis does not negate the fact that people's attitudes toward the natural environment are also shaped very powerfully by culture. For our purposes, the primary value of Appleton's theory lies not so much in its biological components as in its demonstration that even fairly abstract aesthetic choices (e.g., a preference for hilly rather than flat terrain in landscape images) can ultimately be traced back to concrete, real-world circumstances. By virtue of iconicity, environmental advocates and other advertisers are able to tap into the emotions associated with those circumstances.

*   *   *

We have examined a broad spectrum of iconic devices through which the images in ads are able to attract our attention, engage our emotions, and shape our attitudes toward products, political figures, or social causes. By means of iconic representations of people's physical appearance and interpersonal behavior, advertising images reproduce real-world visual cues that are associated with a variety of emotional responses, such as sexual interest, status envy, submissiveness, or nurturance. But images can also simulate our real-world visual experiences by manipulating our point of view. By analogy with various aspects of our everyday interpersonal interactions, devices such as close-ups, low or high angles, and frontal or reverse orientations can enhance our engagement with an image, accentuate feelings of inferiority or superiority, elicit trust or curiosity, and so on. Furthermore, point of view can also be used as a means of eliciting identification, either by simulating a subjective perspective or by manipulating the positioning of a person in an image.

This overview of applications of iconicity is by no means a complete list of all the ways in which iconic devices can be harnessed for advertising purposes. Indeed, such a list would be unthinkable even in principle. As our brief look at environmentalist imagery may have suggested, and as should be evident in any case, the real world of visual experience offers unlimited opportunities to advertisers in search of "prepro-grammed," emotion-laden responses to visual cues. Consequently, the goal of this chapter has been to analyze some of the most common applications of these cues and, more generally, to give a concise illustration of how iconicity works in advertising.

2

◄O►

VISUAL FORM
AND STYLE

◄O► While I was writing this chapter, the Microsoft Corporation began the advertising campaign that launched its new operating system, Windows 95. One of Microsoft's ads had to do with the system's ability to perform multiple tasks at the same time. This ad was produced in two versions, one for print media, the other for TV. The print version's principal visual content is a set of four squares patterned after the Microsoft Windows logo (see Figure 2.1). Superimposed on this design are the words "Walk & chew gum," while the ad's body copy spells out the message more literally: "Windows 95 makes multitasking on a PC easy. So now you can print while you write while you run an old DOS program while you cruise the Internet while you do whatever." In other words, the print ad's basic point is conveyed mainly through the verbal text. The TV commercial, on the other hand, takes a decidedly more visual approach. Although it too features the four squares of the Windows logo as its central image, these squares are used actively to provide a graphic demonstration of the message. The commercial opens with a voiceover announcer listing the various tasks that an operating system needs to perform. As each task is mentioned, one of the four windows goes into a little routine: blinking on and off, fluctuating in size, and so on. Then the announcer goes on to talk about the desirability of performing more than one task at the same time, and suddenly all four of the windows begin to demonstrate their routines simultaneously. Voilà: multitasking.

This TV commercial illustrates an intriguing aspect of the process by which human beings make sense of visual images. The ad conveys a visual impression of multitasking purely through abstract images, without any concrete content. We do not see a person using a computer. We do not see what actually happens on a computer screen during multitasking. In fact, we do not see a computer at all. And yet, despite all this—or perhaps precisely because of it—we get an immediate sense of what multitasking is all about. How do our eyes and brains make this inference? The key to the process is analogical thinking: the ability to perceive a structural similarity between two objects or situations that may be completely different in other respects. In this particular example, our minds are able to perceive the essence of multitasking even though the actual content of the image on the TV screen (namely, a bunch of squares going through various motions) is a totally abstract entity. By virtue of analogical thinking, we extract the essential feature from this display—the simultaneity of varying tasks—and associate it with the real-life situation of working on a computer.

The fact that we can make such analogical connections between abstract features or elements of a visual display and corresponding features or elements of the real world has a noteworthy implication for the concept of iconicity. As Sebeok (1979) has pointed out, it is often assumed that iconicity is simply a matter of similarity between the content of an image and whatever it is that the image represents; but this view is too narrow. We have already seen in the introduction that iconicity need not entail a complete surface similarity between a picture and reality, so long as the picture reproduces the visual cues that we use in real-world vision. Now, in view of the Windows 95 example, we are confronted with a second extension of the concept of iconicity. In effect, what this example demonstrates is that iconicity is not confined just to the content of images but can also be characteristic of their formal or stylistic qualities. Even a highly abstract image such as the one in this commercial can have iconic properties if its formal or stylistic aspects have some analogical connection to aspects of reality. However, it should

Figure 2.1.

be emphasized that iconicity of form is not found only in abstract images. As we shall see below, formal or stylistic iconicity also can be present in highly representational pictures, and it can be used occasionally as a way of conveying messages that are not contained in the pictures' manifest content.

In this chapter, we will examine three kinds of uses of formal/stylistic iconicity in advertising. To begin with, we will discuss the iconic properties of individual formal features, such as shapes or colors. This is the aspect of formal iconicity that has received the most attention from visual theorists and also from advertising critics. To people in the latter category, the main reason for being interested in this topic is the possibility that formal iconicity can be used for purposes of sexual symbolism. We will examine the validity of this assumption, and we will then go on to consider a second, closely related topic, namely, subliminal persuasion. In the area of advertising, this term refers primarily to the use of disguised or camouflaged imagery, usually of a sexual nature, that supposedly affects a viewer without registering on his or her consciousness. Our review of this topic will look at pertinent evidence on the effectiveness of subliminal imagery and on public awareness of its existence. We will then proceed to an examination of a third topic, entailing a shift in focus away from individual formal elements and toward the overall compositional style of a picture. Specifically, we will discuss such stylistic dimensions as simplicity versus complexity and order versus disorder. Drawing on theoretical perspectives from art history, we will consider the role of visual style in ads as a signifier of gender, social status, and youth.

INDIVIDUAL FORMAL ELEMENTS

A print ad for the 1991 Toyota Camry V6 provides an excellent introduction to our first topic. The ad's main goal, stated clearly in the text, is to emphasize the car's power (see Figure 2.2). "Going from zero to traffic speed in the length of an on-ramp can be a real test of nerve," the text tells us, and it goes on to describe the features that make this an easy test for the powerful Camry V6: "Four-Cam, 24-valve, electronically fuel-injected engine" and "156 horsepower and 160 ft.-lbs. of torque." The ad's image, a Camry zooming up a ramp to an expressway, gives us a graphic demonstration of what these facts and figures mean. The

Figure 2.2.

intended sense of power is conveyed by the action itself, and it is enhanced by a trailing streak of red created by the car's taillights. In other words, this image is essentially a visualization of the situation referred to in the text's opening sentence. However, over and above this direct rendition of the text, the image also contains another noteworthy element. In the background, behind the car, the line of the on-ramp and the line of the expressway come together to form a V-shape pointed in the direction of the car's travel. We can be sure that this formal feature was deliberate. Visual ads are generally among the most meticulously composed images of our mass-mediated culture, and this ad is clearly no exception. We can take it for granted, then, that the abstract V-shape behind the car was intended as a contribution to the ad's overall message. But what is the nature of that contribution?

This type of question, an inquiry into the meaning of an image's abstract design elements, has been asked and answered countless times by art historians and other people interested in the meaning of visual form. The most comprehensive and sustained theoretical treatment of this topic is surely the work of Rudolf Arnheim, spread over a lifetime of relevant publications (see especially Arnheim, 1954, 1969, 1988). But the most compact summary of Arnheim's position is probably the following statement by one of his disciples, Molly Bang (1991), who is also a practicing artist:

> This word *associate* is the key to the whole process of how picture structure affects our emotions. . . . We feel differently looking at different pictures because we associate the shapes, colors, and placement of the various picture elements with objects we have experienced in the "real" world outside the picture. (p. 102)

How does this notion apply to the Toyota Camry ad? Bang herself provides the answer: "We associate pointed shapes with real pointed objects" (p. 102). In other words, the basis of these associations is a formal similarity or analogy. In the context of this ad, the V-shape conjures up a number of possible associations, including spikes, wedges, and knife-points, although the most relevant connection is probably with arrowheads. By virtue of these associations, all of which imply an ability to slice through obstacles, the V-shape becomes an echo of the ad's main theme of power, reinforcing the image of a car that can fight against gravity.

The central idea in Arnheim's theory and Bang's statement—that is, the idea that analogy of shape, color, and so on is the key to the meaning of abstract design elements—has a long history in the fine arts (see Homer, 1964) as well as in the literature about visual advertising and graphic design (Baker, 1961). Although the Toyota ad may have been a particularly skillful attempt to integrate an abstract formal analogy into a concrete representational image, it is not hard to find other examples of ads using the same type of arrowhead shape for very similar purposes. A print ad for Canyon Ranch resorts shows a man jumping up to put a ball through a basketball hoop (see Figure 2.3). The dramatic low angle of this photograph enhances the sense of soaring into space, which also may have been meant to resonate with the ad's headline, "Proof of reincarnation." The feeling of escaping gravity is heightened further by the photograph's unusual frame, a triangle pointing upwards. It is evident that the design of this frame must have been based on the same assumption that led to the V-shape in the Toyota ad. But is there any evidence that viewers actually do respond to these shapes according to the presumed analogical associations?

This question has been addressed systematically in unpublished research by Hartmut Espe and Martin Krampen, which I recently replicated in part. Espe and Krampen were interested in viewers' perceptions of the meanings of simple shapes, presented individually rather than as parts of larger compositions. In common with other writers who have dealt with this issue, these researchers were particularly concerned with three general categories: shapes with sharp angles (a triangle and a star); shapes with right angles (a square and a rectangle); and curved shapes (a circle and an ellipse). College students were asked to rate each of these six shapes on a series of semantic-differential scales (i.e., adjective pairs such as "weak-strong"). For present purposes, the most relevant of these were two clusters dealing with perceived *potency* (weak-strong, soft-hard, potent-impotent) and *activity* (passive-active, slow-fast, calm-excited).

Each of the three categories of shapes received a distinctive rating on these two dimensions of meaning. Sharp-angled shapes were rated high on both potency and activity. Right-angled shapes were also rated high on potency, but they were rated medium on activity. Curved shapes were rated low on both dimensions. In my replication of these findings, the average ratings (measured on a 7-point scale, with 132 viewers) were as follows:

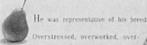

Figure 2.3.

TABLE 2.1

	Potency	*Activity*
Triangle	5.5	5.0
Star	5.6	5.8
Square	5.5	3.9
Rectangle	5.5	3.6
Circle	3.6	2.6
Ellipse	2.8	2.6

The high numbers for the triangle and the star speak directly to the question of how viewers react to the V-shaped visual devices found in the Toyota Camry and Canyon Ranch ads. These numbers support the assumption that sharp-angled shapes do indeed appear powerful and dynamic in the eyes of viewers. At the same time, the findings for the other two categories of shapes provide broader support for the notion that visual design elements are interpreted according to analogical associations with real-world objects. Presumably, right-angled shapes are interpreted by a relatively straightforward analogy with the formal features of our architectural and carpentered environment; hence, the connotations of solidity and stability. The case of curved shapes, on the other hand, is somewhat more complicated. Whereas there is a wide range of specific objects with which one could associate a circle or an ellipse, it is also likely that the most salient aspect of such shapes—when they are viewed out of context—is a more abstract quality of gentleness or smoothness. This latter view appears to fit the findings cited above, and it also serves to illustrate an important point: that formal iconicity is not always confined to a one-to-one correspondence between pictorial elements and individual, real-world objects. We will return to this point in more detail later.

The examples and data examined above are just the tip of the iceberg as far as the possibilities of formal iconicity are concerned. Much more could be said about other aspects of shape, as well as other visual variables such as color and size, not to mention the placement of visual elements within an overall design. Still, the material that we have looked at so far does provide an elementary introduction to the basic logic through which formal analogies can give rise to meaning. Taken together, the ads and the data suggest that the abstract ingredients of a visual composition can be effective means of imbuing an image with such qualities as dynamism, excitement, and so on. However, it is probably fair to say that, if such general concepts were the only kinds of connotations to which visual analogies could give rise, people who write about advertising would not find formal iconicity as interesting as some of them seem to. The reason that this topic has attracted a fair share of attention from such writers lies in a somewhat different direction from the one we have pursued up to now.

Sexual Imagery

What that direction might be is made clear enough in a satirical ad for *Penthouse* magazine that appeared in advertising trade publications (see Figure 2.4). Aimed at potential advertisers who might consider placing their ads in *Penthouse*, this ad makes the point that the magazine's readers have a variety of interests and are not just fixated on sexy pictures. The headline says, "STOP THINKING ABOUT US THAT WAY." The ad's only image is a large close-up of a ripe apricot, whose bulging curves and tight grooves are obviously meant to suggest a woman's buttocks. Just as obviously, the sexual connotation in this picture is a joke. In addition to lampooning the idea that *Penthouse* is only about sex, this visual device is also a parody of a practice of which advertisers have often been accused: embedding sexual allusions in images that are superficially nonsexual. Critics have pointed to the presence of such sexual symbols in a wide variety of advertising images, including pictures of cars, lipstick, perfume bottles, cigarettes, pool cues, and, of course, fruit (Dyer, 1982, p. 123; Moog, 1990, pp. 143-144, 147, 154-155; Savan, 1994, p. 201; Wernick, 1991, pp. 41, 60-61, 76-77).

Examples of this kind of thing are not hard to find. A billboard for Newport cigarettes shows a woman leapfrogging over a fire hydrant while a man looks on from behind (see Figure 2.5). The hydrant's sprinkler is on, sending a spray of water over the woman's body. In another Newport billboard, we see a man holding up a saxophone to a woman's mouth. Her lips are curled around the tip, and her cheeks are distended. It does not take much imagination to detect phallic symbols in these images. Indeed, in all likelihood, the sexual symbolism was deliberately designed to be relatively obvious to knowledgeable viewers. As in the case of the *Penthouse* ad's buttocks imagery, the penis

Figure 2.4.

analogues in these ads are almost certainly spoofs. The message is not just about sex but also about being media-savvy and hip. In other words, these ads can best be seen as part of the growing trend toward reactive advertising, which acknowledges the viewer's sophistication and seeks to engage her or his interest through self-mocking parody. One of the

Figure 2.5.

most frequently cited examples of this trend is the cartoon character Joe
Camel, whose prominent snout is commonly seen as yet another parody

of a phallic symbol (Ewen, 1991; Savan, 1994, pp. 103-106). In fact, awareness of this particular case is so widespread that it has given rise to anti-ads in which Joe Camel appears with an actual penis dangling from his proboscis ("Adbusters spoof ad contest," 1995, p. 55). The trend toward parodies of body-part symbolism is not confined to Western advertising. In 1994, an agency of the Taiwanese government halted the airing of a TV commercial that "demonstrated the benefits of a high-tech water-spurting toilet by using carefully selected peaches to represent the human bottom" ("Cheeky ad," 1994, p. 22). Apparently, an industry group had expressed concern that the commercial might hurt the sale of peaches.

SUBLIMINAL ADVERTISING

In critical discussions of advertising, the kind of sexual symbolism that we have just examined is sometimes considered an example of subliminal imagery. This term is often used rather loosely to refer to any type of covert visual message (Nebenzahl & Secunda, 1993; Rochelle, 1983; Rogers & Seiler, 1994). For instance, Mark Crispin Miller (1990) applies the term to the case of "product placement," that is, the insertion of product names, logos, advertising billboards, and so on in the middle of movie scenes. He gives as an example a shot from the movie *Murphy's Romance* (1985) in which a Coca-Cola sign is displayed prominently on the door of a drugstore. Because the sign's appearance coincides with the first meeting between the film's heroine and hero, it could be argued that the Coca-Cola brand name benefits from the scene's positive aura. Another notable case of product placement occurred in *E.T.* (1982), whose child protagonists were shown eating Reese's Pieces candy; in the 3 months following the movie's premiere, sales of the candy went up 66% (Nebenzahl & Secunda, 1993). Among more recent movies, both *Jurassic Park* (1993) and *Forrest Gump* (1994) contain examples of this practice. The former includes a scene in which *Jurassic Park* spin-off merchandise is shown in a gift shop, whereas the latter features a logo for Nike running shoes. Because filmgoers' attention is likely to be focused on a movie's plot, they may be influenced by such inserted images without paying much conscious attention to their presence. It is this assumption that leads Miller and others to label product placement a covert technique.

Strictly speaking, however, not all cases of covert advertising imagery can be considered genuine examples of subliminal advertising. In its more technical sense, the label subliminal imagery applies to two distinct situations, namely, "tachistoscopic" presentations and "subliminal embeds." The term *tachistoscopic* means "rapidly viewed." A tachistoscopic presentation is a visual display (either pictorial or verbal) that is flashed on a screen so briefly that the viewer's conscious mind cannot register its presence. Therefore, any effect it has on the viewer must occur "subliminally," or below the threshold of her or his awareness. In advertising, the classic example of this technique was a 1957 news story about a movie theater in which the words "Eat Popcorn" and "Drink Coca-Cola" were covertly flashed onto the screen for 1/3,000th of a second at regular intervals (every 5 seconds) while movies were being projected. Over a period of 6 weeks, the experiment reportedly led to an 18.1% increase in the sales of popcorn and a 57.5% increase in the sales of Coke, and for some time thereafter, this story was cited as a dramatic demonstration of the impressive powers of subliminal advertising (Haber, 1959; Saegert, 1979). However, it was subsequently revealed that the experiment had never really taken place at all and that the story was either a fabrication or the result of a misunderstanding (Rogers, 1993).

Subliminal embeds are pictures or words that are inserted in an ad in such a way as to blend in unobtrusively with the rest of the image. In other words, this type of subliminal advertising involves deliberate camouflage of some sort. Perhaps the best known example of a subliminal embed was a verbal insert that occurred in a Gilbey's London Dry Gin print ad in 1971 (Key, 1973, pp. 3-8) (see Figure 2.6). The ad featured a tall glass containing liquid and ice cubes. Inscribed in three of these cubes were the letters S-E-X, formed by the cracks and ripples on the surface of the ice. The existence of this ad was originally publicized by Wilson Bryan Key, whose four books (1973, 1976, 1981, 1989) have been the major catalysts of public concern about subliminal advertising. Most of the cases described by Key involve sexual imagery that is concealed in patterns of shadows, reflections, surface undulations, and so on. For instance, in his most recent book, he invites the reader to scrutinize an ad for Tanqueray gin that appeared in *Time* magazine and other national publications. The ad portrays a stream of gin flowing into a glass. According to Key, if one isolates a certain section of this design, one notices that a "formidable, erect, male genital has been embedded in the

Figure 2.6.

gin stream" (Key, 1989, p. 15). Similarly, he makes the following obser-vation about the icing in an ad for Betty Crocker Super Moist cake mix: "Any standard anatomy text will confirm that the shape painted into the icing is an accurate tumescent female genital. 'Super Moist,' at the portrayed state of excitation, constitutes a normal physiological event" (p. 17). Because the presence of these embedded images is disguised to some extent by the surrounding visual pattern, they can be considered more covert than the *Penthouse* ad and the other sexual symbols discussed above. Furthermore, it must be emphasized that, despite the surrounding camouflage, the sexual imagery described by Key tends to be relatively realistic, whereas the kinds of sexual symbols we encountered in the Newport ads (the fire hydrant and saxophone) are much more approximate.

Does subliminal advertising work? In general, scholarly opinion on this topic tends to be skeptical (Moore, 1982; Pratkanis & Aronson, 1992, pp. 199-205; Theus, 1994; Zanot, 1992), but some of the negative evidence on which this skepticism is based comes from areas that do not concern us directly, such as subliminal sound recordings. There are still relatively few direct tests of the kinds of subliminal images that are most likely to be used in advertising, partly because of the difficulty of manipulating such images for experimental purposes. Therefore, it is probably fair to say that for the moment, the issue remains open.

The persuasive use of tachistoscopic presentations has been tested in an experiment by Cuperfain and Clarke (1985). This study was based on a somewhat contrived situation, the showing of a film about the care of woolen products to students who were subsequently questioned about this topic. At five points during the course of the film, images of laundry detergents were flashed on the screen for 1/60th of a second. The duration and intensity of these flashes had been previously adjusted so as to yield an image just below the threshold of conscious perception. Two different laundry detergents were tested, with two groups of viewers, and there was also a control group. After the film screening, all viewers were asked to indicate their choice of detergent. Although no viewer was aware of having seen any of the tachistoscopic presentations, preference for one of the two detergents was affected significantly by the experimental manipulation. In short, this study provides at least partial confirmation of the efficacy of tachistoscopic imagery.

The most straightforward and systematic investigation of Wilson Bryan Key's claims about subliminal embeds was conducted by Kelly (1976), who tested a sample of seven subliminal ads discussed by Key and a matching set of nonsubliminal ads with similar images. By combining each of these two sets of ads with a number of magazine articles, Kelly created two versions of a fake magazine. The two versions were shown to two different groups of students, who were instructed to read a certain article and were then given time to browse through the rest of the contents. In subsequent tests of the students' recall of the advertised products and of the accompanying images, there was no difference between the subliminal ads and their nonsubliminal counterparts. This failure to find any effect of subliminal embeds was echoed in a study by Gable, Wilkens, Harris, and Feinberg (1987), who inserted subliminal sexual imagery in a number of product photographs and asked students to compare the original versions with the altered ones side by side. The sexual embeds did not produce any notable effects on attitudes toward the photographs.

In contrast to these two studies, though, research by Kilbourne, Painton, and Ridley (1985) did yield some positive evidence on the effects of concealed sexual imagery. This study was based on two subliminal ads that reportedly had appeared in national magazines. One of the ads was for Chivas Regal whisky and contained an image of a nude woman embedded in a reflection on a whisky bottle. The other ad, for Marlboro Lights, had a picture of a penis embedded on the surface of a rock. The authors emphasize that these were "actual anatomical representations," and were "clearly identifiable" once their existence had been pointed out, but hard to spot otherwise (p. 50). Each ad was altered by a professional artist in such a way as to remove the subliminal image. The original and altered versions were then tested on two different groups of students (including both men and women). Whereas the embedded penis failed to enhance the appeal of the Marlboro ad, the nude woman in the Chival Regal ad resulted in higher ratings for the subliminal version. Furthermore, these findings were subsequently confirmed through GSR measurement, a standard physiological indicator of arousal.

On the whole, then, there may be some reason for supposing that subliminal advertising can work occasionally, although the evidence is by no means unequivocal. Regardless of its effectiveness, though, there is another set of facts about subliminal advertising that might temper the fears of anyone who is overly concerned about it. Three government agencies (the U.S. Treasury Department's Bureau of Alcohol, Tobacco, and Firearms; the Federal Communications Commission; and the Federal Trade Commission) have issued strong statements against the use of subliminal techniques in commercial advertising, and the practice has been explicitly proscribed by the advertising and broadcasting industries' internal codes of ethics. Consequently, even if the examples discussed by Key and other researchers are all authentic, the overall frequency of subliminal advertising in mainstream media is not likely to be very substantial. In fact, when it comes to tachistoscopic advertising, it is more than likely that we are talking about a phenomenon that is nonexistent outside the research laboratory. Because the briefest image duration that can be attained on television—that is, 1/30th of a second, equivalent to a single TV frame—is well above the limits of conscious perception, the medium is technically incapable of transmitting tachistoscopic imagery by itself. The same goes for movies, whose minimum image duration is even longer: 1/24th of a second. Of course, a determined advertiser could pay to install special tachistoscopic projectors in movie theaters, but the likelihood of such a move should be judged in the light of its undoubted obtrusiveness.

In an attempt to get a quantitative estimate of how often mainstream commercial advertisers use subliminal techniques, Rogers and Seiler (1994) conducted an anonymous survey of advertising industry practitioners and their clients. Out of 256 respondents to this survey, a total of 24 (9.3%) indicated that they either had used subliminal techniques themselves or knew of others who had used them. However, in response to a follow-up question about the nature of the practices to which they were referring, only one member of that group of 24 described an actual case of visual concealment, the embedding of the word "sex" in the background cross-hatching of a bank ad. According to the authors, the remaining respondents were evidently using the term "subliminal" more loosely, as a catchall label for any kind of visual subtlety, such as the use of youthful models as a device for appealing to young consumers. A similar conclusion had been reached by the author of a previous survey (Haberstroh, 1984), who investigated the use of subliminal embedding by advertising agency art directors. Two out of the 47 respondents to this survey indicated that they had used subliminal embeds themselves or were aware of their use by others. But, as in the case of Rogers and Seiler, Haberstroh concluded that the ads described by these two respondents did not fit the technical definition of subliminal advertising.

If these survey findings are valid indicators of the incidence of subliminal advertising, it does indeed seem to be a rare occurrence. But that is not how the general public views this phenomenon. Three surveys have assessed public attitudes toward subliminal advertising among residents of Washington, DC (Zanot, Pincus, & Lamp, 1983), Honolulu

(Synodinos, 1988), and Toledo, OH (Rogers & Smith, 1993). Despite the differences in the places and times of these studies, the findings were remarkably consistent. First of all, about three fourths of the respondents expressed some familiarity with the concept of subliminal advertising. Second, between half and three fourths professed a belief in its effectiveness. Third, roughly half of the total number of respondents said that they thought subliminal techniques are used "often" or "always" in commercial advertising. It must be added immediately that these findings are subject to the same reservations that were cited above in connection with the surveys of advertising industry professionals. If those professionals were stretching the term "subliminal advertising" beyond its technical definition, it is reasonable to assume that members of the general public do so too. Still, the sizable percentages in the data from these public surveys are certainly suggestive of widespread suspicions concerning the use of covert advertising practices. It is instructive to compare these attitudes with the findings of a fourth survey (Block & Vanden Bergh, 1985), which assessed public beliefs about the efficacy of subliminal techniques for self-improvement (e.g., weight loss, improved study habits, etc.). In contrast to the data we have just considered, respondents' attitudes toward subliminal self-improvement were mostly doubtful. This additional finding reinforces the image of a mistrustful public that is hinted at in the other sets of results. Many people apparently feel that they are being manipulated effectively by hidden forces— but that those forces cannot be used for their own benefit.

Advertising professionals are well aware of the jaundiced eye with which much of the public looks upon subliminal persuasion (Cook, 1993). In the mid-1980s, the American Association of Advertising Agencies put out a flier with a picture of ice cubes and this statement: "People have been trying to find the breasts in these ice cubes since 1957. . . . Well, if you really searched, you probably *could* see the breasts. For that matter, you could also see Millard Fillmore, a stuffed pork chop and a 1946 Dodge" (quoted in Levine, 1991, p. 134). Similarly, David Ogilvy (1983) has observed that "The British Institute of Practitioners in Advertising solemnly banned the use of subliminal advertising—which did not exist" (p. 209), whereas John Gruen, a creative director at the Ogilvy & Mather agency, has made the following point about subliminal embeds: "It's tough enough to get across an obvious message like 'toasty oats are crunchy.' To be deliberately obscure is crazy" (quoted in Levine, 1991, p. 134).

More recently, though, advertisers have taken a different approach to the problem of public suspicions about covert persuasion. As in the case of other controversial advertising practices, a number of ads have featured deliberate parodies of subliminal techniques ("Ads mocking subliminal advertising," 1991; Garfield, 1994a, 1994b; Hinsberg, 1991; Savan, 1994, pp. 61-64). In a 1991 print ad for Seagram's Extra Dry Gin (see Figure 2.7), two martini glasses, arranged symmetrically on the page, contain two halves of a tiny image of a man and woman, each half embedded in swirling liquid. The ad's headline reads, "Refreshing Seagram's Gin has hidden pleasure. Welcome into the fold," and this hint at the presence of the embedded image is followed by a more explicit instruction about how to join the image's two halves together: "Fold so 'A' meets 'B.'" A 30-second TV spot for Toyota's Paseo, also from 1991, starts out with an announcer declaring that "We think you'll like the 1992 Paseo so much we don't have to use cheap advertising tricks to play on your emotions." The images of the car that follow are punctuated by brief flashes of such words as "SEXY," "WILD," and "BUY IT." More enigmatically, a 1994 print ad for Colombian Coffee (see Figure 2.8) shows a single coffee bean against a shadowy background in which viewers whom I quizzed have claimed to detect female breasts and other anatomical features; beneath this image is a singles ad that reads as follows:

Single male bean, rich, good taste. Seeking intimacy in steamy relationship, willing to stir things up. GRAB LIFE BY THE BEANS. Send photo.

Finally, in a 1994 ad for Kahlua Cafe instant coffee, the steam rising out of a coffee cup forms a romantic image of a woman and man embracing under a palm tree (see Figure 2.9). Clearly, none of these advertisements is actually meant to work on viewers' minds subliminally. The Kahlua Cafe ad's image and the Paseo ad's words are plainly discernable, and the other two ads' verbal copy makes it obvious that they are both spoofs. The real purpose of these ads' "subliminal" imagery is to attract attention by engaging viewers in visual detective work. At the same time, the ads may also give viewers a flattering sense of being in the know about the tricks of advertising.

REFRESHING SEAGRAM'S GIN HAS HIDDEN PLEASURE.
WELCOME INTO THE FOLD.

Figure 2.7.

THE OVERALL STYLE OF IMAGES

Most of our discussion so far has been concerned with one-to-one analogies between individual visual forms in pictures and specific,

Figure 2.8.

similarly shaped objects in the real world. The most obvious exceptions to this rule are the two curved shapes that we discussed in connection with the research of Espe and Krampen. The viewers' responses to those

Figure 2.9.

shapes suggest that they were probably seen in terms of abstract qualities such as gentleness or smoothness, rather than any specific association with a concrete object. In other words, here we have a somewhat different order of formal analogy, and the time has come to consider it in more detail.

When a certain type of shape or any other kind of formal element is intended as a covert representation of individual objects, such as breasts, buttocks, or genitalia, it is likely that that shape will occur as an isolated element in specific locations within an overall image. For instance, a phallic symbol might be placed between a woman's legs, as in the Newport fire-hydrant ad. But if the meaning of a shape or any other kind of formal element is meant to be more abstract or general (e.g., sexuality or passion, instead of discrete body parts), then that shape is less likely to be used as a single pictorial element and more likely to become a diffuse ingredient of the picture's overall style. For example, the connotations of gentleness in circular shapes are sometimes used, by extension, to symbolize traditional notions of femininity; in such cases, an image is less likely to feature a single circle and more likely to feature curved lines throughout. This point is illustrated in a print ad for Aveda Plant & Flower Pure-fumes that appeared in a woman's fashion magazine (see Figure 2.10). The ad displays a tight close-up of flower petals. Although some parts of this composition may suggest individual objects, the ad's aura of femininity is surely intended to flow as well from the smoothly curving lines of the image's overall design.

Style and Gender

The notion that visual style can have gender connotations in and of itself is a traditional assumption in advertising and, even more so, in graphic design. In a book written in 1961, Stephen Baker, at that time a creative director at an advertising agency, gives the following explanation of the basic reasoning behind this assumption: "The harsh, angular edges of square objects . . . suggest masculine temper while the round shape of a circle implies the gentleness of a woman" (p. 50). Note that Baker is not suggesting a strictly visual analogy between squares and circles, on one hand, and the physical characteristics of male and female bodies, on the other. That route would certainly have been feasible, as a two-page print ad for Neutrogena rainbath makes clear (see Figure 2.11). In this advertisement for shower and bath gel, the undulating curve of a woman's reclining body appears under the following headline: "the rain makes everything clean. and soft. and smooth." The tight framing

Figure 2.10.

of the woman's torso gives it an abstract quality, allowing the viewer's mental image to oscillate between two interpretations: on one hand, a curved shape; on the other, femininity. (Additionally, the verbal headline suggests one possible explanation for Espe and Krampen's findings

the rain makes everything clean.

and soft.

and smooth.

Neutrogena
rainbath
shower and bath gel

Figure 2.11.

about the ratings of circular shapes.) But this kind of physical similarity is not what Baker appears to have in mind. As his explicit reference to "masculine temper" indicates, he is associating shapes with conventional conceptions of men's and women's behavioral styles—their "temperaments"—not their actual looks. In short, he is dealing in abstract connotations of style, not the direct analogues of visual form.

Style is not just a matter of shape, of course. In the Aveda ad, the connotations of the gentle curves are echoed by the picture's consistently soft focus. This feature, too, is an analogical device, as implied by the term "soft." The fact that the Neutrogena ad is also in soft focus underscores this point, as well as a related one: Because of the variety of analogical devices through which any particular abstract concept can be expressed, mutual reinforcement of stylistic connotations is a common feature of advertising images. Continuing his discussion of masculinity and femininity, Baker (1961) argues that virtually any visual quality—size, color, texture, and so on—can give rise to gender connotations in the appropriate circumstances (pp. 45-54).

An especially revealing example of this principle is contained in a well-known study by Welch, Huston-Stein, Wright, and Plehal (1979). The study's overall aim was to investigate the stylistic characteristics of children's TV commercials. As part of this investigation, the researchers looked at the speed or pace of the editing and the nature of the editing transitions. In particular, the researchers made a distinction between straight cuts, which create an instantaneous transition from one shot to the next, and dissolves or fades, both of which entail a more gradual replacement of one shot by another. All of these aspects of editing are usually considered means of making a scene more or less exciting, tranquil, and so on (Penn, 1971). But Welch and her colleagues made the assumption that the editing styles of the commercials would also differ according to the gender of the children at whom they were aimed. An analysis of a sample of Saturday morning TV ads found support for that view. Commercials aimed at boys were characterized by faster editing and greater use of straight cuts, whereas girls' commercials had a slower editing pace and were more likely to employ fades or dissolves. The researchers label these stylistic characteristics as "subtle sex-role cues." In other words, the commercials' editing styles had evidently been conceived as analogical representations of conventional conceptions of masculinity and femininity: on one hand, speed and abruptness; on the other, a more measured and gentle way of being.

Of course, just as style can be used as an analogue of traditional gender qualities, so too can it be deployed as an instrument for challenging those traditions. An ad for Compaq's LTE 5000 notebook computer is headlined "THE ULTIMATE NOTEBOOK FOR WHOEVER YOU HAPPEN TO BE" and contains a photograph of a woman sitting at a restaurant table with the computer in front of her (see Figure 2.12). Superimposed on her image is the word "hotshot," and the body copy beneath this label begins with the line "That's Ms. Hot Shot to you." The implications of these words are reinforced by the woman's powerful, self-confident appearance, and they reverberate in the image's style. Although the bottom of the image is out of focus, the hard-edged tone of the top—including her high-contrast, somewhat vampy make-up—leaves us in no doubt about the fact that this woman has little to do with the passive, delicate creature envisioned in Baker's principles and the children's TV commercials.

An obvious question raised by the Welch study is whether children are actually sensitive to such stylistic evocations of gender. This question was explored in a follow-up experiment by Huston, Greer, Wright, Welch, and Ross (1984), in which identical commercials were edited in two different ways, corresponding to the two stylistic tendencies observed in the previous study. Children were shown these commercials and asked to guess whether they were intended for girls or boys. The results showed that the children did indeed seem to have an implicit grasp of stylistic manipulations.

This finding could be seen as simply a result of the many hours that most American children spend in front of the television in the early years of their lives. However, there is some evidence that stylistic analogies can make sense even to completely inexperienced interpreters. The evidence in question comes from a remarkable series of experiments by John M. Kennedy (1993). The overall aim of these experiments was to test blind people's ability to interpret raised-outline drawings through their sense of touch. The experiments dealt with a broad range of pictures, including representations of space and motion. In one of the studies of motion perception, subjects were given drawings of wheels whose spokes were distorted in various ways: in one drawing they were all crooked, in another the lines were all wavy, in a third they were smoothly curved,

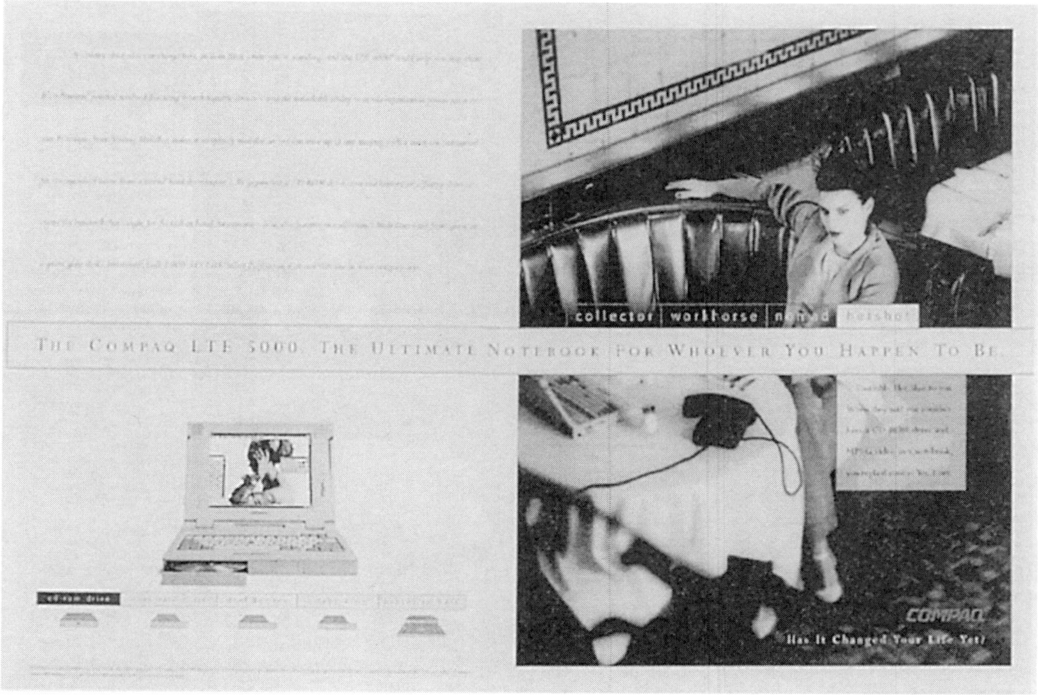
collector
workhorse
hotshot
THE COMPAQ LTE 5000. THE ULTIMATE NOTEBOOK FOR WHOEVER YOU HAPPEN TO BE.
COMPAQ
Has It Changed Your Life Yet?

Figure 2.12.

and so on. The subjects' task was to figure out how each wheel was supposed to be moving: was it spinning smoothly, was it wobbling, was its motion jerky? The experiment was conducted with two groups of subjects, one blind, one sighted. For every one of the stylistic distortions, agreement between the groups was overwhelming: almost everyone associated the crooked line with jerky movement, the wavy line with wobbly movement, the curved line with spinning movement, and so on (Kennedy, 1993, pp. 243-249).

In other words, these blind people, as well as their sighted counterparts, were able to make an analogical connection between a stylistic feature in one mode of experience (touch or visual shape) and an abstract quality in a different mode (motion). Evidently, formal iconicity can be meaningful even to people who have never seen a picture before. Taken together with the findings of Welch and her colleagues, Kennedy's study highlights the distinctive role that stylistic analogies can play in advertising images. As the title of Welch's study says, style is a relatively subtle way of conveying meaning—more subtle, certainly, than an explicit portrayal of sexual or gender imagery. Despite this subtlety, though, Kennedy (1993) emphasizes that, for most of the blind people in his study, the connection between style and meaning appeared to be "perceptual or intuitive rather than thought-out in a manner easy to make explicit" (p. 249). So, although style may be subtle, its meaning is readily accessible to our intuitions. We sense it, even if we cannot say how.

Style and Social Status

As Welch's study and Baker's comments suggest, a central function of visual style in advertising is to signal social identity and to convey a particular conception of that identity. Of course, both Baker and Welch were concerned exclusively with gender identity. But the style of visual advertisements is also a critical ingredient in the signaling and characterization of social status and youth. In fact, to a certain extent, the stylistic qualities that tend to be associated with these two aspects of social identity are mirror images of each other. Ads for high-status, luxury products occasionally feature a spare, tightly ordered style, whereas the style of youth-oriented ads is often deliberately loose and anarchic. But it would be a mistake to make too much of these generalizations. Although we will presently pursue them further, it must be emphasized from the outset that they represent only one part of a more complicated total picture.

For an example of an ad with high-status connotations, we turn to *The New Yorker*, a traditional venue for upscale advertising. On page 23 of the September 12, 1994 issue, we find two ads, one for the Malo Boutique, the other for the Tanino Crisci shoe emporium, both located on Madison Avenue within a short distance of each other. The addresses by themselves tell us all we need to know about the exclusive character of these establishments, but let us take a closer look at the Tanino Crisci ad's visual style (see Figure 2.13). Above the shop's name and a tiny drawing of a horse and rider (whose top hat and riding jacket are also clear upper-class markers), the ad features a black-and-white photograph of two shoes. Even if every other status signifier in the ad were removed, this simple photograph—just two shoes against a plain background, nothing else—would be enough to convey a sense of premium quality. In fact, it is precisely this reductive visual style—the image's rigorous symmetry, the lack of color, the complete absence of props or any other ornament—that most distinctively characterizes the photograph as an indicator of high status, although the rich, lustrous tones of the image as it appears in the glossy pages of *The New Yorker* add a dimension that cannot be reproduced on more ordinary paper.

Why should this kind of composition have upscale connotations? Stuart Ewen (1988, p. 86) has pointed out that ads for luxury goods often adopt a style that could be called classical, and that label may be a useful guide to an understanding of this particular case. Traditionally, art historians have tended to discuss classicism as the first phase in a recurring stylistic cycle that begins with simplicity, symmetry, and order and moves toward increasing elaboration and extravagance (Friedlaender, 1952; Sypher, 1955; Wolfflin, n.d.). But a more appropriate way of getting at the meaning of classicism is to look at its antecedents, that is, what it was reacting to. The artistic movements with which the label classicism is most closely associated have tended to coincide with historical periods defined by the consolidation of wealth and power (Dressler & Robbins, 1975; Espe, 1981; Panofsky, 1995). In this context, classicism represented the imposition of order and control where previously there had been greater fluidity. In other words, traditionally, it has been a style of exclusion and containment, and it is these aspects that appear to be most relevant to its current position as a status indicator in advertising. The

Figure 2.13.

Tanino Crisci ad's simple composition, its lack of props, and, above all, its eschewal of color are best understood as ingredients of a reactive classicism, a style that implicitly rejects the flashiness and the glitter of the social climber. If open display of wealth characterizes the status aspirant, the ad's classicism is the sign of an elite that is secure enough to hold back.

Although this ad's classicism may be unusually severe, the broader stylistic tendencies that it represents are typical of much high-fashion imagery. However, classicism is by no means the only stylistic marker of

Figure 2.14.

status in advertising. Consider a print ad for Pepe Jeans from the April 1995 issue of *Vogue* (see Figure 2.14). In this ad, a model's figure is superimposed on a background photograph of a neoclassical architectural facade, but the symmetry and regularity of the building's structure are not reflected in the photograph. The framing is strongly asymmetrical, the low camera angle causes the building's vertical lines to converge, and the image's baseline is decidedly off-kilter, producing a pronounced leftward tilt. Why such an eccentric composition? One likely reason is that contemporary art photography is also characterized by a rejection of traditional compositional principles. A photograph produced for sale in today's art market will often include features deliberately that traditionally were considered mistakes, such as off-balance compositions, blurs, double exposures, under- or overexposures, lack of sharp focus, and so on. Consequently, adoption of this iconoclastic style can give an advertising image some of the high-status aura that emanates from high art.

Style and Youth

At the same time, though, there is another side to the Pepe Jeans ad's stylistic eccentricity. In addition to being a marker of high-art style in contemporary photography, the violation of traditional visual conventions is also a distinguishing characteristic of much visual imagery aimed at adolescents and young adults. The underlying logic of this connection is presumably some analogy between stylistic rejection of tradition and youthful reaction against the constraints of the adult world. If adolescence is a time of antagonism toward conventions, then a style that overturns the old order may be an appropriate visual analogue of that aspect of the adolescent sensibility. Because the model in the Pepe Jeans ad appears to be somewhat younger than most of her counterparts in other *Vogue* ads, the ad's visual style can be seen as a means of enhancing a message that is already present in the ad's content.

More generally, then, there appear to be at least two relatively distinct ways of looking at the implications of a rule-violating style. One set of connotations points toward social status, the other toward youth. In the world of fashion imagery, both kinds of connotations are often present at the same time. But there are other areas of advertising, including TV commercials, in which the focus is largely or exclusively on the latter. The medium in which one is most likely to encounter youth-oriented visual rule-breaking is surely MTV. Since the advent of MTV in the 1980s, directors working on ads for such products as sneakers have developed a style that could be described as the negation of traditional Hollywood principles of composition and editing. Among other things, this style includes such devices as jump cuts, camera jiggle, swish pans, tilted framing, and eccentric cropping. As in the case of high-fashion still photography, there is some relationship here between advertising practices and the broader world of film and video art. The style of contemporary, youth-oriented advertising recapitulates the iconoclastic stance of two earlier periods in motion-picture history, the French New Wave and the American underground cinema. To a considerable extent, this similarity is intentional because the directors of today's TV commercials and rock videos are typically well-schooled in film history and well aware of these art-film precursors of their own iconoclasm (e.g., Rothenberg, 1994, pp. 210-211). However, whereas rule-breaking in print ads can connote both status and youth, in TV commercials, the emphasis is almost exclusively on the latter.

TV commercials that violate traditional stylistic principles also tend to contain rapid editing (Pals, 1995; Rosenberg, 1995). This too can be assumed to signify a youthful orientation, because editing speed has been shown to enhance the perceived energy level of motion pictures (Kraft, 1986; Penn, 1971), and high energy is conventionally considered an attribute of youth. How do young people respond to rapid editing and an antitraditional style in advertising? One of my studies examined college students' reactions to a 30-second MTV-style public service announcement (PSA). Produced in 1994 by the Rock the Vote Education Fund and directed by Jim Gable, the PSA was aimed at getting viewers to call an 800 number for information related to health care reform. This message was delivered on-camera by rock star Mike D of the Beastie Boys. The PSA's style could be described as a deliberate subversion of the traditional talking-head format. Although Mike D does appear in every single shot, the camerawork and editing consistently undermine traditional notions of continuity. There are sudden jumps from one side of his face to the other, there are occasional changes from a full-color image to a monochrome negative, and there are several points at which a hat appears on Mike D's head and then vanishes. At times, his face is framed in a super-tight close-up that distorts his features; at other times, the camera pulls back for a medium shot. All of this happens at a rapid-fire editing pace that is more than twice as fast as the average rock video and three times as fast as the average TV commercial. The PSA's 43 shots go by at the rate of 0.7 per second. As measured a few years ago by MacLachlan and Logan (1993), the corresponding averages for MTV music videos and for all 30-second commercials were 1.6 and 2.3 seconds per shot, respectively.

In an attempt to isolate viewers' responses to the PSA's visual style as opposed to its content, I produced an alternative version of the PSA consisting of a continuous talking head with no editing. This version was based on the PSA's original, unedited footage and contained the same spokesperson, Mike D, delivering the same verbal message as in the final product. The two versions were shown to two groups of undergraduates, who were then asked to indicate their reactions on a written questionnaire. For present purposes, three sets of findings are most noteworthy. First, the edited version received higher ratings on questions dealing with enjoyment and aesthetic appreciation. Second, it produced higher agreement with the statement, "I plan to go along with the PSA's message." Third, it got higher agreement scores on statements about its suitability for young audiences (e.g., "This PSA is aimed at people of my age group"). In short, the edited version of the PSA was liked more, it was judged more persuasive, and it was seen as more directly aimed at young people. Because the two versions did not differ in content, these findings indicate that the fast-paced, antitraditional style of MTV may indeed have youthful connotations in its own right.

Despite these findings, though, it should not be assumed that this style is necessarily a more effective way of addressing young people. There is one more factor that has to be taken into account. In addition to the responses described above, our study of the Mike D PSA also obtained measures of message comprehension, assessed through a multiple-choice question. Here, too, there was a difference between the two versions of the PSA. The frequency of incorrect responses was significantly higher for the MTV-style version than for its unedited counterpart. This result is in accord with earlier research on viewers' responses to editing (Geiger & Reeves, 1991; Lang, 1991; Thorson, Reeves, & Schleuder, 1985), and it suggests that the enhanced youth appeal of MTV's visual style may entail a concomitant sacrifice in clarity (Hitchon, Duckler, & Thorson, 1994). To be sure, an ad that is difficult to understand the first time can sometimes make up for that difficulty by generating interest in repeat viewing (Cox & Cox, 1988; Pechmann & Stewart, 1988). But such a response cannot be taken for granted. So, although fast, nonconformist editing may be a good way of making it clear to young viewers that an ad is meant for them, the overall appropriateness of such a visual style must also depend on how seriously it impedes comprehension of the rest of the message. As we have seen, style can be an important part of an ad's meaning, but it is rarely the only meaning.

3

◄○►

CAN PICTURES
BRIDGE CULTURES?

◄○► If images can bring us closer than words can to the appearance of reality, are they also an effective means of communicating across cultural boundaries? Does the iconicity of visual communication make it a vehicle for the sharing of meaning between people who are separated by linguistic or cultural differences? There are at least two aspects of advertising to which these questions are directly relevant. To begin with, because of the growing globalization of economic activity, commercial advertising is directed increasingly to a variety of linguistic and cultural communities. Among advertisers as well as researchers, this situation has led to a recurring concern about the degree to which it is necessary to tailor advertising messages to the characteristics of each specific community. Should different ads be produced for different languages and cultures, or can pictures be relied upon to transcend such differences? This is the first set of issues that we will address in this chapter.

The second section of the chapter looks beyond the commercial applications of visual communication. Because of their ability to simulate a direct encounter with other people and places, visual images have often been used in deliberate attempts to foster cross-cultural understanding. Through public service announcements (PSAs), educational films, children's television, and other means, the people involved in such efforts have tried to counteract prejudice by cultivating intergroup knowledge and empathy. Much of the research on this topic has dealt with full-length TV programs or films, rather than 30-second spots or other standard advertising formats. Consequently, in this part of the book, our own focus will often extend outside the conventional confines of the world of advertising.

ADVERTISING ACROSS CULTURES

Advertising that crosses national boundaries is not a new development. Products such as Coca-Cola have been marketed internationally since before World War II (Quelch & Hoff, 1986, p. 59), and discussions of the feasibility of standardized international campaigns have been appearing in scholarly journals for more than a quarter of a century (e.g., Dunn, 1966; Elinder, 1965; Fatt, 1967; Lorimer & Dunn, 1967). However, the growth of international advertising has accelerated considerably during the past two decades (see Hill & Shao, 1994; Rosenthal, 1994), in tandem with a 20-fold rise in the volume of world trade, to a current level of more than 4 trillion U.S. dollars (Brown, Lenssen, & Kane, 1995, pp. 74-75). Increasingly, advertisers have come to see their target audience as spanning entire regions—such as East Asia (Babyak, 1995; Javalgi, Cutler, & White, 1994) or western Europe (Halliburton & Huenerberg, 1993)—or, indeed, the entire globe. More than 10 years ago, a prominent observer of these trends was arguing that "companies must learn to operate as if the world were one large market—ignoring superficial regional and national differences" (Levitt, 1983, p. 92).

In response to these imperatives, a number of writers have argued that advertisers need to place greater emphasis on the visual aspects of ads. In an article subtitled "To globalize, visualize," Kernan and Domzal (1993) claim that "effective global ads are never predominantly verbal" because "anyone can interpret a visual execution" of an advertising theme, whereas "a verbal ad requires that the consumer understand the language in which it is written and, if the ad is ambiguous, the subtleties of that language as well" (p. 55). Similarly, Bourgery and Guimaraes (1993) make the following point:

Advertising agencies today are trying to create a "visual esperanto": a universal language that will make global advertising possible for virtually any product or service. The new visual esperanto is based on the idea that visual imagery is more powerful and precise than verbal description (which leaves too much room for personal interpretation). Moreover, all people can comprehend the messages of visual imagery. (p. 24)

But the central premise of these statements—the idea that anyone can understand a picture—is controversial. Academic writers have long insisted that the conventions of pictorial representation are culture-bound (Scott, 1990), and critics of international advertising can point to a variety of visual campaigns that did not travel very well from one culture to another. Ricks, Arpan, and Fu (1974) note that a picture of the emperor Nero in an Italian lipstick ad "struck no accord" when it was shown to Japanese consumers because "Nero was alien to them," while Exxon's famous tiger "failed to elicit favorable reaction in Thailand," where tigers are "simply not symbols of power and strength" (p. 49). More starkly, the director of a Russian advertising agency says that certain "Western" TV commercials "would be incomprehensible for us" (quoted in Wells, 1994, p. 89). Such difficulties have given rise to considerable skepticism about the efficacy of global advertising. An article in the trade journal *Advertising Age* declares that the "global village is fantasy land" (Hill & Winski, 1987, p. 22), and an academic analysis warns that a dedication to standardized global advertising is "not unlike being dedicated to committing economic suicide" (Onkvisit & Shaw, 1990, p. 110).

In addressing the theoretical issues raised by these arguments, it will be useful to distinguish between three different ways in which cross-cultural visual advertising could possibly go awry. First of all, it is conceivable—in principle, at least—that members of a culture to which an ad is exported might actually find the ad's images completely meaningless. In other words, in this situation, we would be dealing with an inability to perform the fundamental mental act of connecting the shapes on a page or TV screen to real-world objects. If, as some academic writers have assumed (e.g., Goodman, 1976), pictures were a language that had to be learned just as much as any verbal language does, then we certainly should expect images to mean nothing to viewers who were not familiar with the particular representational conventions through which those images were created. Although variants of this hypothesis are not uncommon in the academic world, this type of misinterpretation is not something that advertisers are concerned about (or even aware of), partly because a base-level exposure to "Western" visual media probably can be taken for granted in almost any culture today (Chaffee, Pan, & Chu, 1995; Hjarvard, 1994; Wasser, 1995). In any event, in keeping with the approach that was outlined in the introduction, we will proceed on the assumption that the iconicity of visual images makes them a relatively unproblematic medium for cross-cultural communication about the surface appearance of reality. Accordingly, our discussion of potential problems in cross-cultural advertising will look elsewhere. We will consider two possibilities: On one hand, a viewer might correctly perceive the contents of an image (people, objects, places) but misinterpret the intended cultural implications of those contents; on the other hand, a viewer might be aware of the cultural implications but unresponsive to the values behind them.

Cultural Allusions in Images

What kind of advertisement might lead to the former of these two potential scenarios? Consider a print ad for the film *Spring Break*, a 1983 Columbia production (see Figure 3.1). The ad portrays a group of young men raising a flag with the film's name on it. From that name and their appearance, we can infer that they are vacationing college students. They are standing on—and planting the flag in—a bikini-clad woman's thigh (depicted on a much larger scale than they are). This picture is clearly a visual metaphor, in the sense discussed in Chapter 1. It is also a parody. The men's poses and the position of the flag are based on a famous image from World War II, Joe Rosenthal's photograph of U.S. troops raising the Stars and Stripes on their way to victory during the battle of Iwo Jima. This photograph later became the model for a monumental statue honoring the U.S. Marine Corps at Arlington National Cemetery, and it has been the subject of numerous parodies both before and after its use in the *Spring Break* ad (Marling & Wetenhall, 1991). For example, during the prelude to the Gulf War, the *Philadelphia Inquirer* ran a cartoon in which the Marines hoist a banner with a picture of a gas pump and the words "High Test."

In the context of American visual media, the cultural references of the *Spring Break* ad are anything but abstruse. However, it is easy to imagine a viewer from another country missing some of those references. Although the Iwo Jima flag-raising has occasionally been featured in movies or other media with an international audience, its status as a recurring cultural symbol is confined to the United States. Furthermore, the concept of spring break as major party time is also distinctively American and has few direct equivalents in other parts of the world. So a viewer from abroad might well find the ad's meaning somewhat opaque, and this example would certainly seem to support the views of those writers who are skeptical about the viability of cross-cultural advertising.

But it is important not to overstate the case here. True, the *Spring Break* ad does contain layers of meaning that our hypothetical non-American viewer might not share. But this observation begs the question of how broadly those layers of meaning are shared by viewers within the United States itself (cf. Peebles, 1989). Even if we assume that the significance of spring break looms as large in the minds of all Americans as it does in those of some college students, when it comes to the Iwo Jima image, things are very different. In a test of visual-culture knowledge conducted with a class of 29 undergraduates (Messaris, 1994, pp. 179-180), only 14 students were able to give even an approximate place and time (e.g., a World War II battle) for Joe Rosenthal's original photograph of the flag-raising. Others mentioned Vietnam, Korea, and even the Civil War. Recognition rates were similarly low among U.S.-born graduate students in visual communication, some of whom placed the flag-raising as far back as the American Revolution or the War of 1812.

Furthermore, almost none of these students had any detailed knowledge about the actual circumstances memorialized in Rosenthal's photograph. Historians commonly describe Iwo Jima as one of the most horrific battles ever fought by U.S. troops, a relentless 36-day ordeal in which 6,821 Marines were killed, 19,217 were wounded, and some 20,000 Japanese lost their lives, many of the latter being buried alive in underground tunnels or incinerated by flamethrowers (Ross, 1985; Wheeler, 1980). It is hard to believe that anyone familiar with such details could find the *Spring Break* ad amusing—or, indeed, could have designed such an ad in the first place. On the other hand, it can be said that these historical circumstances are irrelevant to the ad's meaning. But that is precisely the point. What this ad demonstrates is that the *intended* cul-

Figure 3.1.

tural references in advertising are often relatively shallow. There may be a gap in relevant cultural knowledge between viewers in an ad's country of origin and their counterparts in other places, but in many, if not most, cases, that gap is not very profound.

These words of caution should be kept in mind as we proceed with our examination of cross-cultural interpretations of advertising. As we have just seen, the cultural knowledge required for the interpretation of an ad can involve both specific images (such as the Iwo Jima flag-raising) and more diffuse cultural practices (such as the rituals of spring break). This is not always a hard-and-fast distinction, but it provides a conven-ient framework for thinking about the potential sources of cross-cultural misunderstandings of visual advertising. When an ad incorporates an allusion to, or replica of, a specific earlier image, a viewer's ability to comprehend that part of the ad's message can come only from previous media experience. However, references to more general cultural prac-tices may make sense to viewers from other countries purely on the basis of cross-cultural parallels, without any prior exposure to the originating country's media or way of life. Because of this difference, we will discuss these two aspects of cultural content separately.

Allusions to Specific Images

In addition to testing students' knowledge of Joe Rosenthal's Iwo Jima photograph, the study mentioned above also assessed their famili-arity with two classic American images that were presented in the form of advertising parodies: James McNeill Whistler's "Arrangement in Grey and Black, No. 1" (commonly referred to as "Whistler's Mother") (see Figure 3.2) and Saul Steinberg's *New Yorker* magazine cover in which radically diminishing perspective is used to give a Manhattanite's view of the rest of the country (see Figure 3.3). In the parodies that were used in this study, the former image appeared in a newspaper advertisement for a department store sale under the caption "A sale to make a mother whistle," (see Figure 3.2) whereas the latter served as the template for a magazine ad about business opportunities in Pewaukee, Wisconsin (see Figure 3.3). With regard to the parody of Whistler's mother, the students were asked "Who is this?" (in a written questionnaire). In the case of the Pewaukee ad, the question was "What's the city in the original version of this picture?"

The study included a group of 12 international graduate students who were tested in tandem with 23 graduate students born in the United States. Only two of the international students were able to name Whis-tler's mother, and three knew that New York was the city in the original version of the Pewaukee image. (Likewise, only two had recognized the

Figure 3.2.

Iwo Jima flag-raising.) These numbers may appear to offer an unambiguous demonstration of the potential interpretational obstacles faced by advertising when it crosses cultural boundaries. Both the Whistler painting and the *New Yorker* cover are subjects of frequent parodies in the United States, and yet these highly educated international students were evidently almost completely unfamiliar with either of the original images. Once again, though, one should be cautious in one's interpretation of these facts. As it happens, substantial numbers of the U.S.-born students (7 and 10, respectively) were also unable to identify these two images.

As in the *Spring Break* case, then, these additional numbers remind us that when it comes to specific images, advertisers cannot take viewers' knowledge for granted even in the cultures from which those images originated, no matter how widely the images may have been reproduced. Of course, some kinds of ads deliberately use images that only a

Figure 3.3.

limited segment of the population can be expected to recognize. This practice is particularly common in advertising that incorporates references to high-art imagery to convey a sense of superior status. But when ads are addressed to a wider audience, the ability to make visual references that viewers can actually grasp will always be threatened by the fragmentary nature of visual culture and by the speed with which younger generations lose sight of the cultural imagery of the past.

Because advertisers are well aware of these circumstances, ads that borrow previously existing images are often designed to make some sense even to viewers who are not aware of the visual reference. This principle is clearly at work in a 1989 print ad for Schneider photographic lenses (see Figure 3.4). The ad's headline reads, "HANGING AROUND FOR THE NEXT STEP IN LENS TECHNOLOGY? CHECK OUT SCHNEIDER'S SUPER-SYMMAR SERIES." These words appear under a photograph of a man dangling precariously from the hands of a clock on the side of a building, high above a city street. Fans of silent cinema will recognize the inimitable Harold Lloyd in a scene from *Safety Last* (1923). Much of that film is taken up by Lloyd's gravity-defying stunts as he climbs up the outside of a building, and the image used in the ad comes from the culminating moments of this celebrated scene. So, for someone who has seen the movie, the ad serves as a trigger for a host of hair-raising memories, and those memories undoubtedly increase the ad's impact. At the same time, though, the ad's picture of Lloyd is surely an arresting image in its own right. A viewer who had never heard of Harold Lloyd or seen *Safety Last* could still find the ad enjoyable and should certainly be able to get the ad's point, because the relationship between the headline and the picture does not depend on any knowledge of the picture's source. Consequently, we can also imagine an image such as this crossing cultural boundaries with ease.

In fact, even though this image comes from a quintessentially American movie, it may seem strange to refer to it as an example of American visual culture. Unlike most photographs or paintings produced in the United States, Hollywood movies have achieved a certain universality, even when they deal with American society and American themes (Wasser, 1995). To put it differently: In most parts of the world, there is already a substantial transplanted visual culture composed of Hollywood movies. A particularly telling demonstration of this point occurred in a political campaign poster that appeared in Warsaw on June 4, 1989, the day of the elections that signaled Poland's transition from communism to democracy (Weschler, 1989, p. 66) (see Figure 3.5). Against a backdrop of the word "Solidarity," we see a tall man in Western garb

HANGING AROUND FOR THE NEXT STEP IN LENS TECHNOLOGY? CHECK OUT SCHNEIDER'S SUPER-SYMMAR SERIES.

Representing a remarkable breakthrough in large-format photography, Schneider's new Super-Symmar HM lenses are simply the sharpest, best-performing lenses made, with the kind of flexibility that will get you the shot you want . . . time after time. They deliver astonishing resolution and contrast, even at the edge of the field, whether you're shooting a large-product shot or at infinity.

If you're familiar with the 210mm and 150mm focal lengths, you'll be delighted to learn that Schneider is introducing the Super-Symmar HM 120mm f5.6 featuring a 211mm image circle at infinity. For 75 years, Schneider has been supplying photographers with leading-edge optics, with more than 14 million sold. And with every Super-Symmar lens from Schneider you get something you can't get from any other major manufacturer—our exclusive *LIFETIME WARRANTY*. Now, once again, we have combined the latest in design and engineering with precision German craftsmanship to produce a lens that opens up a whole new world of opportunity for large-format photographers.

Every photographer knows that inferior lens performance can leave you dangling. With Schneider you're always on solid ground. We're the best in the business. Schneider Corporation of America, 400 Crossways Park Drive, Woodbury, NY 11797. (516) 496 8500.

Super-Symmar
S E R I E S

● **Schneider**
KREUZNACH
SHOOT FOR THE BEST.

Figure 3.4.

striding confidently toward us. In place of a gun, he is holding a ballot. Except for that metaphorical substitution, this is a picture straight out of another Hollywood movie, *High Noon* (1952), and the man is Gary

Figure 3.5.

Cooper. Evidently, the image of the Westerner was as potent a symbol of freedom in postcommunist Poland as it is in the United States.

So, more generally, this example adds a further complication to our evolving view of the limitations of cross-cultural advertising. In principle, visual references to specific images, such as the Iwo Jima flag-raising, can make an ad difficult to understand when it is exported to another culture. In practice, however, this kind of difficulty is often counterbalanced by other factors. Ads that focus mainly on the surface meanings of borrowed images, as in the case of our *Safety Last* example, can appeal to viewers regardless of any previous knowledge of those images. But even when previous knowledge does make a difference, as in Solidarity's Gary Cooper poster, that knowledge can often come from the cross-cultural experience of Hollywood cinema, which has paved the way for a substantially common international visual culture.

Allusions to General Cultural Practices

Hollywood cinema and television can also provide a basis for cross-cultural interpretation of American ads that make references to more diffuse cultural practices or values, as opposed to specific images. For instance, international viewers who had seen such earlier Hollywood movies as *National Lampoon's Animal House* (1978) or *Porky's* (1982) presumably would have been in a better position to understand the values expressed in the ad for *Spring Break*, which appeared in 1983. Of course, being able to understand a certain set of values does not mean that one shares them, but that observation is as true of American viewers as of people in other countries. Indeed, it could even be argued that American movies and TV programs provide international viewers with an especially appropriate background for the understanding of American advertising, because the portrait of American culture on which ads are based is much closer to the fabrications of Hollywood than to the actual way of life of real Americans. But what about viewers who are not familiar with American media and are being exposed to American advertising for the first time? Although such viewers might not be able to make much sense of references to specific images, their ability to interpret more general cultural depictions cannot be ruled out a priori. In the absence of either firsthand or mediated experience, a person may still be able to form an intuitive understanding of selected aspects of an unfamiliar culture through extrapolation from the known features of familiar ones.

In an attempt to address this topic, Anne Dumas (1988) performed a study with two groups of graduate students attending a university in the United States. One group consisted of students who had grown up in China and were recent arrivals in the United States. The other group consisted of U.S.-born students. At the time of the study, students coming to the United States from China were still relatively unfamiliar with American mass media. Consequently, although the Chinese students in Dumas's study were certainly not first-time viewers of American advertising, their previous experience was quite limited compared with that of the U.S.-born group. The participants in the study were all interviewed individually regarding their responses to a set of print ads taken from American magazines. Initially, each ad was shown with all text and other product information masked in order to assess the viewer's interpretation of the image by itself.

The students' responses to these images were open-ended and are presented by Dumas in considerable detail, but for our purposes, the following general findings stand out. To begin with, the Chinese respondents made it clear that they found most of the social situations depicted in the ads culturally remote from their own experiences. Their interpretations of these social situations were based explicitly on conjectures rather than immediate recognition of familiar circumstances. It turned out, though, that these conjectures often coincided with the interpretations of the American respondents. In particular, the Chinese students' guesses about family relationships (or their absence) were generally similar to the guesses of the U.S.-born students. On the other hand, the one aspect of the ads that the Chinese respondents were consistently unable to interpret along American lines was the display of social status.

One of the clearest examples of an image that appeared culturally alien to the Chinese was an ad for Bulova watches (see Figure 3.6). The ad portrays a tight embrace between a man in a military uniform and a woman. The text, which was withheld from the respondents until the end of the interview, explains that this is a homecoming scene from the Vietnam War era and that the man's watch had been a parting gift. This image drew immediate and warm praise from most of the U.S.-born students, who lauded its emotional power and its authenticity (e.g., "it really shows a moment of reality," "it's very genuine, I can believe it"). Among the Chinese students, however, the first reactions were very different. Virtually all of them expressed some form of puzzlement or difficulty

On Feb. 23, 1971,
Corporal Bert Moss
came home after
thirteen long months
at 2:32 p.m.
Bulova watch time.

Every minute of every day
is special to someone.
Bulova has been
measuring the minutes
of our lives, large and small,
for over 100 years.

BULOVA.
IT'S AMERICA'S TIME.

Figure 3.6.

in making sense of what they were seeing (e.g., "it's hard to see what's happening," "it's hard to understand who is what"). And yet, despite this sharp discrepancy in the initial responses, the Chinese students' interpretations of what was going on in the image were closely parallel to the interpretations of their U.S.-born counterparts. Both groups were much more likely to view the scene as a homecoming than as a departure (a judgment that was subsequently confirmed by the text), and both groups were evenly divided in seeing the woman (whose face was hidden from the viewer) as either a mother or a wife/lover. Dumas (1988) notes that the percentages for these various responses were just about identical in the two groups (p. 46).

If the Chinese students' view of what was actually happening in the image was not substantially different from the view of their American counterparts, what are we to make of their initial statements of puzzlement or confusion? The students themselves provided the answer to this question. In part, what they were reacting to was the fact that the faces of the people in the image are not clearly visible, something that no U.S.-born viewer complained about. But the need to see the faces may have been largely symptomatic of a more fundamental lack of familiarity with the situation depicted in the image. In particular, what evidently seemed remote from the experiences of many of the Chinese viewers was the image's open, very physical display of emotion. As one viewer put it, "Chinese people wouldn't express their feeling like this, they're very quiet people. Until maybe five or even two years ago, nobody could have done that" (quoted in Dumas, 1988, p. 49).

This kind of response to emotional expression was a recurring theme in the Chinese students' interviews, and the Bulova ad was not the only image that elicited such remarks. Similar comments were made about a Korbel champagne ad featuring a romantic couple strolling on a beach, as well as a Cutty Sark whisky ad in which a younger man affectionately places his hand on an older man's shoulder (see Figure 3.7). With regard to the former case, the Chinese students noted that the public display of affection between a man and a woman would have been frowned upon in China (at the time of the study, 1988). As for the latter image, students pointed out that it would have been considered unusual in China because of its violation of traditional standards of formality in interactions between fathers and sons. This point was expressed as follows by one of the male respondents:

> Friendship between a father and a son! I like this relationship [i.e., the image in the ad] very much, it's very different from what one sees in China! In China, fathers give serious faces to their sons, they think they're superior. Usually they just give orders or advice, but their relationship is

Figure 3.7.

not like friends. Here, they're not just father and son, [they] can talk to each other, [they] can have a drink, [they] can be happy. . . . I like this, but this is not something I see too much in China. (quoted in Dumas, 1988, p. 24).

Note the implied divergence between traditional Chinese cultural norms and this respondent's own professed values. This, too, was a recurring feature in the Chinese students' statements about the ads. Speaking of the romantic couple in the Korbel ad, a female respondent observed that such behavior outside of marriage would have been considered unseemly back home, and she went on to complain about the status of unmarried women in China:

> Here in America, if you're a single woman, it's fine, people don't blame you. People say, "It's a career woman, that's O.K." But if I go back to China and I don't get married before I'm thirty, people'll say, "Oh, she must have some problems, mental or maybe . . . physical." Sometimes, it's really that they care about you, but sometimes, that kind of care, you don't want it! (quoted in Dumas, 1988, p. 41)

Another aspect of this tension between received norms and personal inclinations was voiced by a young woman who was commenting about the emotional embrace in the Bulova ad:

> This reminds me of my leaving. . . . In China we usually don't hold each other too much, but when I leave, I hold my mother. . . . Or when I see her again. . . . I can't help! [rising intonation] This is the first time I left her! (quoted in Dumas, 1988, p. 50)

These remarks are arguably one of the most important aspects of Dumas's findings. In talking about culture, we sometimes tend to think of it as a uniform set of practices or beliefs that everyone in a society subscribes to unquestioningly. But the statements quoted above remind us that the range of behavior that people view as natural or desirable can be considerably broader than the norms prescribed by their traditional culture. So, for many of Dumas's Chinese respondents, incompatibility between the advertising images and the canonical culture of their homeland was ultimately not an obstacle to comprehension. In fact, as these quotations suggest, the Chinese students often were highly receptive to the values implied in the images.

This is not to say that there were no instances whatsoever in which the Chinese missed some message that seemed perfectly obvious to the U.S.-born respondents. One situation in which this kind of thing happened repeatedly was the display of social status. Both the Cutty Sark and the Korbel ads featured men wearing tuxedos. To most of the U.S.-born viewers, this attire was a clear symbol of superior wealth and status. Many of the Chinese students, however, were apparently uncertain about, or even unaware of, these upper-class connotations. The Chinese respondents also differed markedly from the U.S.-born viewers in their inferences about a man in jeans, who was shown explaining a toy to a little boy in a Fisher-Price ad (see Figure 3.8). Whereas the overwhelming majority of the U.S.-born viewers saw this man as a member of the upper-middle class (e.g., "He is probably a yuppy, like the rest of us"—from Dumas, 1988, p. 66), every one of the Chinese students assigned the man to the working class, and half of them explicitly cited the jeans as evidence. As Dumas (1988) points out, the American concept of jeans as casual leisure wear was evidently unfamiliar to these Chinese respondents; instead, they treated the man's clothes as a sign that he was a manual laborer (p. 63). Despite these interpretational differences, though, the two groups of respondents were both very enthusiastic about the Fisher-Price ad. As in the Cutty Sark case, they applauded the ad's positive father-son image, and this time, many of the Chinese respondents said that the scene was typical of their own culture as well, because the ad's emphasis was on the father as teacher.

More generally, then, Dumas's findings point to a somewhat bifurcated conclusion about the possibilities for cross-cultural comprehension of advertising images. As our discussion of jeans and tuxedos demonstrates, and as some other studies have shown (e.g., Farley, 1986, p. 20; Tansey, Hyman, & Zinkhan, 1990, p. 32), there can be no doubt that individual cultural symbols may be meaningless or may have discrepant meanings outside their original settings. However, when it comes to the fundamental relationships from which social bonds are constructed (nurturance, sexuality, etc.), the cases we have discussed here suggest that there is greater scope for cross-cultural empathy and understanding, even when the conventional values of two cultures differ considerably. Cultures may selectively sanction one mode of social interaction or another (intimacy vs. reticence, privacy vs. display, etc.). But the range of relational tendencies within a society as a whole and within a single person's psychological repertoire is inevitably broader than the confines of any one culture. Where such breadth exists, cross-cultural communication may be possible, as Dumas's data indicate.

The Fisher-Price Power Workshop is so realistic, it's perfect for any job junior carpenters have in mind.

They can work with a drill that seems to pop through pretend wood. Or feel like they're using a real power saw. Or even level, bolt and buff.

Then, when the workday's over, they can pack everything neatly away inside the portable tool caddy.

The Power Workshop from Fisher-Price. It's just one of over 300 toys we make that make childhood a little more special.

Because you're only young once.

Figure 3.8.

Cross-Cultural Differences in Values

Our examination of Dumas's findings has already given us a preview of our concluding topic in this discussion of potential interpretational barriers in cross-cultural advertising. It was noted earlier that many of Dumas's Chinese respondents not only understood but also approved of the cultural values implied in some of the ads they were shown. However, the connection between comprehension and approval is by no means inevitable. A viewer could understand these ads perfectly and yet be unmoved or even repelled by the values in them. It is this aspect of miscommunication (i.e., lack of receptivity to implied values) that we will examine next.

This topic has been the primary concern of much of the formal research on communicational problems in cross-cultural advertising. Typically, studies in this area deal with samples of ads from two or more countries. On the basis of systematic analyses of the strategies employed in these ads, the researchers look for differences in the implicit values behind the strategies. A common theme of these comparisons is the contrast in advertising styles between the United States and other parts of the world. According to a study by Han (1990), for instance, U.S. ads are more likely to use individualistic appeals and less likely to use collectivistic appeals than are ads from Korea. Han interprets these findings as reflections of a more fundamental cultural difference between Koreans' emphasis on group responsibility and Americans' emphasis on personal independence. Applying a similar analytical framework to a comparison between the United States and Japan, Hasegawa (1995) argues that the collectivist tendency of the Japanese culture makes Japan an unsuitable venue for comparative advertising (i.e., direct references to competing brands), whereas such ads are quite common in the United States. Hasegawa's argument has been supported in research by Mueller (1987, 1992) and Gross (1993), who have found that Japanese advertising is less likely than U.S. advertising to contain hard-sell techniques, including direct brand comparisons.

The greater prevalence of comparative advertising in the United States has also been the focus of studies that have examined the differences between the United States and various European nations (Appelbaum & Halliburton, 1993; Cutler & Javalgi, 1992; Nevett, 1992). An additional finding of these studies has been that U.S. advertising is relatively more likely to convey information about the product, whereas European advertising has a relatively greater tendency to take an indirect approach, entertaining rather than explicitly informing the viewer. In general, then, both the Asian and the European comparisons lead to a characterization of U.S. advertising as more direct and openly commercial than the advertising of other countries. However, it should not be assumed automatically that these differences are reflections of irreconcilable disparities in cultural outlook. Especially with respect to Europe, diverging advertising styles may not correspond to any fundamental underlying cultural divergences. In fact, a related point has even been made with regard to Japan. According to Johansson (1994), the soft-sell approach, which is characteristic of Japanese advertising, may be a product of institutional arrangements in Japanese advertising agencies (i.e., the fact that a single agency commonly handles ads for competing brands), rather than a direct result of Japanese culture.

Even where advertising strategy does stem from culture, though, it would be premature to conclude that the differences recorded in this kind of research are necessarily impediments to the cross-cultural reception of ads. A small example: Biswas, Olsen, and Carlet (1992) have found that French advertising contains more sex than U.S. advertising; it can be argued that this difference mirrors a more relaxed attitude toward sex on the part of the French people (p. 75); but that does not mean that consumers in the United States are unresponsive to sexual appeals. For the most part, systematic research on cross-cultural advertising has focused exclusively on the content of ads, without analyzing viewers' responses, and the few studies that have actually looked at viewers have tended to investigate general attitudes toward advertising (e.g., Andrews, 1989; Somasundaram & Light, 1994), rather than responses to specific strategies. However, considerable information on the cross-cultural reception of ads is available in the form of anecdotal evidence.

Perhaps the most comprehensive source of this kind of information is David Ricks's (1993) *Blunders in International Business,* a book-length compilation of stories illustrating various things that can go wrong when a company tries to conduct business in an unfamiliar culture. Many of Ricks's stories are about the pitfalls of incompetent translation, as when the Frank Perdue Company's slogan, "It takes a tough man to make a tender chicken," was turned into the Spanish equivalent of "It takes a sexually excited man to make a chicken affectionate" (p. 74). Not surprisingly, such anecdotes have attracted a great deal of attention in advertising circles. An earlier edition of Ricks's book has become a standard reference in discussions of cross-cultural advertising errors, and advertising agencies are now much more likely to check verbal copy for possible cross-cultural double meanings, especially sexual ones.

Although Ricks's emphasis tends to be on verbal malapropisms rather than visual ones, his book describes a substantial number of cases involving visual material, and it is instructive to look at some of these in search of an overarching pattern. The following incidents are representative of Ricks's major themes. A refrigerator manufacturer trying to do business in the Middle East unwittingly offended local viewers by including a chunk of ham—forbidden to Muslims—in a picture of the product (pp. 60-61). An airline was almost banned from Saudi Arabia when its ads showed passengers consuming alcoholic drinks, which are also forbidden to Muslims (p. 61). Another airline managed to generate irate newspaper headlines in Japan when it inadvertently omitted a major Japanese island from a promotional map publicizing a new route (pp. 50-51). Some customers in other (unnamed) Asian countries object to a red circle on product labels because it reminds them of the Japanese flag (p. 31). Protests by citizens' groups in Ontario led to the termination of an advertising campaign that had used the Canadian flag in an attempt to create a local image for a new imported beer (p. 55). An aircraft manufacturer attempting to make sales in India experienced difficulties with a promotional brochure whose images of turbaned men turned out to be old *National Geographic* photographs of Pakistanis (p. 50). An ad highlighting the fact that a certain brand of toothpaste whitens teeth was received poorly in some regions of Southeast Asia, where the local population valued darkly stained teeth as a mark of prestige (p. 60). An Irish-themed beer ad featuring a man in a green hat was ridiculed in Hong Kong because the green hat is allegedly a Chinese symbol for a cuckold (p. 62). A U.S. corporation's efforts to promote its name through fake billion-dollar currency bearing the company logo backfired at a German trade show because "the Germans felt that the company was trying to show off American wealth, and they resented this impression" (p. 48).

What do these tales tell us about potential impediments to cross-cultural communication in advertising? With one or two exceptions, these episodes are not about viewers' lack of knowledge concerning the cultures in which the ads or other promotional materials were originally produced. (For example, Muslims know all too well that nonbelievers eat pork and drink alcohol.) Instead, the problem in most of these cases has to do with cultural ignorance in the opposite direction, that is, the advertiser's lack of awareness regarding the culture to which the ad is addressed. This ignorance can give rise to ads that inadvertently offend the target audience's cultural values—such as religious restrictions, patriotic sentiments, and so on—but it is not just culture clash that accounts for the problems described in Ricks's anecdotes. Rather, it is likely that viewers' negative reactions to culturally inappropriate advertising are exacerbated by resentment at being treated with indifference by the advertiser. For instance, whereas a Japanese citizen might realize that the omission of a Japanese island from a U.S. airline's promotional map was not deliberate, she or he could still feel insulted at the thought that the airline did not bother to learn more about Japanese geography or consult with a Japanese viewer before issuing the map.

The problem of potential resentment of the advertiser raises a related issue. As the Japanese example may suggest, a viewer's response to a culturally insensitive ad undoubtedly depends to a large extent on the ad's specific country of origin. The same geographical error that angered the Japanese when it was committed by Americans might not have caused as much resentment if its perpetrators had been of some other nationality. But the role of country of origin as a factor in viewers' responses is not confined to cases of cross-cultural misunderstanding. The place in which a certain product is made is frequently a significant aspect of the way in which that product is perceived by people in other countries (Parameswaran & Pisharodi, 1994; Suzuki, 1980). When country of origin is an asset, ads are likely to feature it. In the United States, French fashions, cosmetics, and fragrances (but not cars) are routinely advertised with pictures of Parisian street scenes (see Figure 3.9). Conversely, in France and elsewhere, ads for American cars, liquor, and cigarettes commonly feature Western scenery or other images with an American flavor (see Figure 3.10). To a certain extent, these national emblems may serve as certificates of quality, but their meaning clearly goes beyond that. When an American consumer buys a French perfume, we can probably take it for granted that "Frenchness" itself is part of the appeal. Likewise, to some people in some countries outside the United States, the Marlboro man is not just a representation of masculinity; he also represents America.

Figure 3.9.

In other words, nationality itself is often an important part of the meaning of international advertising. How an ad from one country will be received in another may depend to a large extent on the economic

FOUR ROSES. AMERICAN BOURBON

Figure 3.10.

and/or ideological relationships between the two countries. In many parts of the world, images of the United States are potent symbols of political freedom and material well-being (Messaris & Woo, 1991). These perceptions affect people's attitudes toward American ads and products, and, by extension, they also can be appropriated in local advertising. We have seen already how the picture of Gary Cooper from *High Noon* was put to use in a Polish election poster. Similarly, Shay Sayre (1994) describes several importations of "Western" imagery into Hungarian political ads, including a Tom and Jerry cartoon clip that was used as a metaphor for the triumph of democracy over communism. A somewhat different use of "Western" images can be found in Japan and some other Asian nations. There, ads for local products sometimes incorporate pictures of Americans (mostly white, but occasionally also black) in connection with themes of innovation, individualism, and freedom from traditional social constraints (Creighton, 1995; Larrabee, 1994).

Of course, even within a single country, reactions to such images are bound to vary widely. It has been argued that international advertising originating in the United States or other "Western" countries is particularly likely to find a receptive audience among younger, more fashion-oriented consumers (Domzal & Kernan, 1993). By the same token, however, people with a more traditional orientation often see American advertising as a threat. This kind of concern is expressed very poignantly in a letter to an Indian business journal quoted by Simon Chapman (1986):

> What advertising genius . . . decided that "the all American" was a suitable copy-line to promote Chesterfield cigarettes in India? How are the connotations relevant here? All-American, the blonde, blue-eyed six-footer raised on grandma's apple pie . . .? Presumably [the advertiser is] counting on the good old Indian sense of inferiority in the face of anything foreign. . . . I am wondering why this sort of self-demeaning message should be deemed a likely winner by one of our advertising agencies. . . . Can we not take ourselves seriously? . . . The homogenization of the world by American multinationals is hardly a new phenomenon, but . . . this particular assault of Americanization is one of its crudest manifestations yet—in India. (p. 124)

There is some evidence that such concerns are having tangible consequences. Both in India and elsewhere in the non-Western world, some observers have noted a reactive trend toward greater use of local models or actors in ads as well as in other media (Landler, 1994; Oyeleye, 1990, p. 204). And there is another side to this coin. The United States itself is going through a period of increasingly negative attitudes toward the outside world and, in particular, toward those countries that are perceived as posing an economic threat. As a result of this trend, some foreign corporations doing business in the United States have felt a need to resort to advertising that attempts to overturn negative perceptions and to create a more welcoming attitude. For example, the Fuji Corporation (which, at the time of writing, is engaged in a trade dispute with Kodak) has run ads that featured its sponsorship of the U.S. Olympic team; ads by Toyota have used the map of the United States to show all the places where the company is hiring or buying from Americans; and an ad for Mitsubishi contains a photograph of the Statue of Liberty as a reminder of the contributions that immigrants (including, by implication, immigrating companies) have made to the United States (see Figure 3.11).

How effective are such deliberate attempts to change cross-cultural perceptions through advertising? That is the topic of our next section. For the moment, though, we can summarize what has been said thus far as follows. On one hand, there are several factors that can pose barriers to the cross-cultural reception of advertising images. These factors include the presence of culture-specific imagery (e.g., the Iwo Jima flag-raising); references to local cultural practices (e.g., the use of jeans as leisure wear by affluent Americans); and incompatibility of cultural values (e.g., American individualism vs. the more collectivist orientation of many other cultures). On the other hand, however, the impact of these factors is often mitigated by countervailing circumstances. When images are appropriated for advertising purposes, they are often used in such a way as to facilitate comprehension even by someone who is unfamiliar with the original context (e.g., the shot of Harold Lloyd in *Safety Last*). Moreover, the global distribution of Hollywood movies and TV programs has created a substantial basis of shared images in parts of the world that differ considerably from one another with respect to current social conditions (e.g., the picture of Gary Cooper that was used as an election poster in Poland). Receptivity to images from other cultures can also be heightened by conflicts between individuals' personal beliefs and their society's official values (as in the case of some of Anne Dumas's Chinese respondents). Finally, acceptance or rejection of transnational advertising images can be affected crucially by general attitudes toward the ads' country of origin (e.g., American admiration of French sophistication vs. resentment of Japanese economic success).

Figure 3.11.

CAN PICTURES IMPROVE
INTERGROUP ATTITUDES?

Early in this century, W.E.B. Du Bois (1903) made a prophetic proclamation: "The problem of the Twentieth Century is the problem of the
color line" (p. 1). As this century approaches its end and we prepare for

the beginning of another one, we can state with equal confidence that a central task for all of us in the years ahead will be to find ways of erasing the many lines that still divide people of different colors, cultures, and nationalities. What, if anything, can visual media contribute to this task? As a first step in answering this question, let us look at a specific study of the relationship between media exposure and attitudes toward people of different racial groups.

Beginning in 1977, a team of researchers led by Norma Forbes and Walter Lonner began to study the impact of TV viewing on children living in Alaska (Forbes & Lonner, 1980; see also Lonner, Thorndike, Forbes, & Ashworth, 1985). In 1977, satellite transmission brought TV broadcasts to areas of Alaska that previously had had no regular TV service. Accordingly, Forbes and her colleagues were able to test children both before and after the introduction of the new medium. The children were all Native Alaskans (i.e., members of ethnic groups that had been living in Alaska before the arrival of Europeans). They were tested on a variety of attitudinal and cognitive measures. For our purposes, the critical portion of these tests had to do with the children's attitudes toward people of three different racial groups: black people, white people, and Native Alaskans. These attitudes were measured through a battery of bipolar rating scales. So, for each of the three groups that the children rated, the researchers were able to compare ratings from before and after the introduction of television and to look for any changes that might have come about during that period.

In two of the three cases—ratings of Native Alaskans and white people—there were no appreciable before-after differences. Ratings of both groups had been relatively favorable before television, and they remained so afterwards. Perhaps the children saw nothing on television that contradicted their initial views. On the other hand, perhaps these findings are a result of the children's extensive real-life experiences with whites and, of course, Native Alaskans before the advent of television. Attitudes based on direct experience may be relatively impervious to media influence. In contrast to these findings, the ratings of black people did change appreciably after the introduction of TV. The children in this study had little, if any, personal familiarity with blacks in their everyday lives, and television evidently did have some impact on their perceptions.

Before we take a look at what exactly happened to the children's ratings of black people, it may be useful to pause for a moment so that the reader can take a guess about the likely direction of the change. Did the ratings improve, or did they get worse? Many people who hear about this study for the first time pick the latter alternative. In fact, however, the findings were in the opposite direction. Before TV, the children's ratings of blacks had tended to be unfavorable. After TV, there was a pronounced movement toward the favorable side of the rating scales. In other words, television's effect was positive.

This result may seem surprising. We often think of the mass media as sources of negative images of African Americans and other groups with a minority status in the United States (Friedman, 1991). But, as far as fictional TV programs and movies are concerned, this conception of the media may be more of a historical reality than a current fact. When one takes a long view of the history of American cinema, it is indeed sobering to be reminded that the first feature film to become a major box-office success, *Birth of a Nation* (1915), was a celebration of the rise of the Ku Klux Klan, and that "the most popular American historical film ever made" (Clinton, 1995, p. 132), *Gone with the Wind* (1939), contained so demeaning a portrayal of a black woman (Prissy) that the actress who played her (Butterfly McQueen) was often reduced to tears. However, since at least as far back as World War II, there has been a notable countertrend in media images of black people as a result of a number of factors, including many years of protests by the NAACP and other organizations; the federal government's efforts to absorb blacks into the military during that war; and, subsequently, the civil rights movement of the 1950s and 1960s (Cripps, 1983, 1993). Fiction film and TV portrayals have become considerably more positive during this period, and, in fact, a critic recently complained that some current movies are painting such a prettified picture of race relations in the United States that white viewers may be losing sight of the less rosy underlying reality (DeMott, 1995).

Where does the Alaska study fit into this picture? The authors point out that, at the time the study was conducted, the most likely sources for the Native Alaskan children's impressions of black TV characters were three series, "All in the Family," "Barney Miller," and "Sanford and Son." Interestingly enough, whereas the three principal black characters in these shows (George Jefferson, a black detective on "Barney Miller," and Fred Sanford, respectively) were portrayed in a much more nuanced and multilayered fashion than was typical of the older screen images of black people, none of these three portrayals could be considered overwhelmingly positive. This is an important point because it has crucial implications for our interpretation of the study's findings. If these three black characters had been a bunch of goody-goodies, the children's positive reactions would have been perfectly predictable. But the fact that irascible George Jefferson and cantankerous Fred Sanford made nonblack children think better of blacks is much more noteworthy. What this finding suggests is that mere exposure to people of another race (or culture, or nationality, etc.) may be enough to bring about a positive change in attitudes, even if the portrayals of those people are not uniformly positive (and, of course, assuming that they are not clearly negative, either).

If this interpretation of the Alaska study is correct, it fits in with a commonly held belief about the sources of racism and other forms of intergroup prejudice. Such attitudes can have a variety of interacting causes, of course (Rex & Mason, 1986), but one possibility is that sheer lack of familiarity with people of other races or cultural backgrounds may be a contributing factor. From this assumption about the etiology of prejudice, it is a short step to a conception of the potential role of visual media in prejudice reduction. Because of their ability to simulate an encounter with other people, images might be able to make up for a viewer's lack of direct experience with those people, and, as in the Alaska study, this mediated familiarity might suffice for the reduction of negative attitudes.

This conception of how visual media might improve intergroup attitudes has been tested, explicitly or implicitly, in several studies performed over a number of years. An experiment by Gorn, Goldberg, and Kanungo (1976) provides a particularly straightforward picture of the characteristic features of this area of research. The experiment was conducted in Canada. With the support of the Canadian Broadcasting Corporation, the researchers produced a pair of brief scenes that were inserted into an episode of "Sesame Street." Both scenes showed groups of children playing together. In one scene, the children were Japanese-Canadian, and in the other, they were Native American. The entire "Sesame Street" episode, including these inserts, was shown to a group of white English-Canadian preschoolers, whereas a control group saw an animated cartoon instead.

After the screening, each child was shown a pair of photographs; one contained white children, and the other contained nonwhite children from the same racial backgrounds that had been featured in the "Sesame Street" inserts. Each child was asked to choose the children from one of the two photographs as playmates. In the control group, 79% of the children picked the picture of whites. In the group that had watched the "Sesame Street" episode, the choices were just about even: 52% white, 48% nonwhite. In short, simple exposure to nonwhite children on television was enough to bring about a significant increase in these white preschoolers' preferences for nonwhites.

The type of effect demonstrated in this experiment has been found repeatedly in other research on the relationship between visual images and children's intergroup attitudes. Studies in this area have used a variety of visual media and have explored the attitudes of English-Canadians toward French-Canadians (Goldberg & Gorn, 1979); Inuit-Canadians toward other cultural groups (Caron, 1979); whites toward blacks (Cantor, 1972; Katz & Zalk, 1978); and members of various groups toward Indochinese (Gordon, 1983) and toward each other (Lovelace, Schneier, Dollberg, Segui, & Black, 1994; Mays et al., 1975). Similar results have also been found in some research with adults, including studies on German attitudes toward dark-complexioned Europeans (Scherer, 1971); white U.S. soldiers' attitudes toward their black comrades (Kraemer et al., 1975); and black and white viewers' attitude changes in response to the TV series "Roots" (Ball-Rokeach, Grube, & Rokeach, 1981; Howard, Rothbart, & Sloan, 1978). However, there is an important difference between these studies of adults and the research done on children. In at least three of the four cases, the material viewed by the adults was explicitly concerned with prejudice, whereas the images shown to the children were simply presentations of members of various groups, without (for the most part) any overt mention of negative attitudes. What happens when adult viewers are exposed to more ambiguous material?

A fairly direct attempt to answer this question has been made in an experiment by Kindem and Teddlie (1982). This study investigated white college students' reactions to two films with black central characters. Half of the students were shown the film *Nothing but a Man* (1962), a serious exploration of race in America. The other half saw a farcical comedy, *Blazing Saddles* (1974). The students' attitudes toward blacks as well as other ethnic groups were measured both before and after the screenings. The effects of the two films differed considerably from each other, and there was also a pronounced variation in students' responses depending on what their initial attitudes had been. *Nothing but a Man* had a strong positive effect on the attitudes of students whose level of prejudice toward blacks had been low to begin with; however, in the case of students who had initially shown some prejudice, this film's effect was negligible. Conversely, however, students in this latter category became significantly less prejudiced after viewing *Blazing Saddles*, whereas students with little initial prejudice actually exhibited a significant increase in response to this film. (To avoid any possible confusion, it may be useful to repeat that any one student saw only one of the two films, so the results reported here are group effects, not individual reactions.) What are we to make of these results?

The fact that the frivolous images of *Blazing Saddles* were able to improve racial attitudes among prejudiced students is in line with the conclusions that we drew from Forbes's Alaska study. But these students' lack of responsiveness to a more serious film and the "boomerang effect" of *Blazing Saddles* on the less prejudiced students both call for explanations that go beyond the relatively simple framework in which we have been operating thus far. The authors of this study suggest that the prejudiced students' failure to respond positively to *Nothing but a Man* may have been a defensive reaction against the film's implicit indictment of people such as themselves, while the negative effect of *Blazing Saddles* on the initially less prejudiced students may have been an indirect consequence of that film's more general crudeness (Kindem & Teddlie, 1982). These explanations are both plausible, although the latter may be somewhat inconsistent with the rest of the study's data. However, regardless of what the underlying thought processes of these particular students may have been, this study serves to highlight a broader point— the fact that older viewers' responses to visual material about other races or cultures typically require a more complex explanation than do the responses of children.

This complexity can lead to outcomes that may appear paradoxical. There are several studies in which well-intentioned, ethnographically informed films or TV programs about other cultures not only failed to alter adults' stereotypical beliefs but sometimes actually strengthened them (Martinez, 1992; Shatzer, Korzenny, & Griffis-Korzenny, 1985; Shom, 1994). As such findings suggest, adult attitudes about people of other groups are undoubtedly much more intractable than are the views of children. Older viewers inevitably bring an extensive history of past experiences to bear on any particular encounter with a movie or other visual portrayal, and this history is bound to constrain the impact of that encounter. Furthermore, to put it bluntly, many adults often have too much of a stake in intergroup prejudice to allow themselves to be influenced by contradictory messages. Speaking specifically about racism, Chinua Achebe (1988) has speculated that "the West seems to suffer deep anxieties about the precariousness of its civilization and to have a need for constant reassurance by comparison with Africa" (p. 17). And, of course, this psychological process can also occur at a more individual level. A person with an insecure sense of self-worth can derive satisfaction by imagining that whole categories of other people are inherently inferior to him or her.

But Achebe also remarks that the "comforts" of racism or other forms of prejudice can be economic, not just psychological (p. 23), and here he may be touching on roots that go even deeper. As George Fredrickson (1988) has argued in a discussion of the origins of racism in America, negative stereotypes about people of African descent may have arisen during slavery as an attempt by slaveholders to justify the exploitation of fellow human beings (see Fredrickson, 1988, Chap. 14), and the subsequent history of such attitudes (not only toward blacks, but also toward other groups of people) can be seen at least in part as a series of rationalizations for economic and political discrimination. This is a crucial point. We may think of economic and political discrimination as the result of prejudice, but in historical terms, it is more appropriate to look at this relationship the other way around. Prejudicial characterizations of a particular group of people provide the semblance of an excuse when a different group comes to believe that it has something to gain by exploiting, excluding, expelling, or even annihilating those people. Indeed, this phenomenon can occur even when there are actually no racial or cultural differences between the two groups. In ancient Athens, slaveholders were able to convince themselves that their slaves were inherently inferior beings even though both the former and the latter were Greek (Finley, 1980). (Conversely, as Snowden, 1983, has demonstrated, racial prejudice was absent from ancient Greece.)

These considerations suggest that images by themselves will often be a weak instrument for addressing adult prejudice. Negative stereotypes that are anchored, consciously or not, in perceived self-interest cannot be countered very effectively by simply exposing people to positive images, unless the underlying perceptions of self-interest can also be reversed. And images may not be the best means of handling such a task. However, these skeptical conclusions should not lead us to overlook the significance of the positive evidence that we have reviewed in the preceding pages. As noted earlier, there have been some studies in which adults were found to respond favorably to visual depictions of victims of discrimination. Moreover, favorable results have been the norm in research with children. The children's studies should be especially pertinent to educators concerned about these matters. There is clearly much scope for the use of visual media in the educational system as a means of enhancing cross-cultural knowledge and understanding (Dambekains, 1994; Lankford, 1992, Chap. 11). Of course, it surely would be naive to suppose that positive lessons learned in childhood cannot be undone by later influences. But it just as surely would be irresponsible not to provide those positive lessons anyway.

PART 2

IMAGE AS EVIDENCE

VISUAL TRUTH, VISUAL LIES

◄o► In a TV commercial for a popular brand of laundry detergent, we see the following. A dapper-looking gentlemen with an air of impressive self-confidence holds up a napkin that seems to be terminally stained. Unperturbed, he plops the napkin into a pitcher of water and adds a measure of the detergent. He twirls the mixture around with a swizzle stick for a second or two, and then he takes the napkin out and holds it up for our inspection. Lo and behold: It is now immaculately, sparklingly clean.

Up to this point, our analysis of visual persuasion has focused on the nature and implications of iconicity. The little episode described above provides an introduction to a second characteristic property of most advertising images, their "indexicality." As defined by Charles S. Peirce, an index is a sign that has some physical connection to the object or event to which it refers (Peirce, 1991, pp. 239-240; see also Sebeok, 1991, Chap. 13). Fingerprints, footprints, weathervanes, and thermometers are standard examples of what Peirce had in mind here. Another example, as Peirce himself pointed out, is that of photography. Because they are produced by light rays reflected from the external world and recorded physically

129

on film or various electronic media, photographic images (including video) are indexical signs of the objects and events that are represented in them. (They are also, at the same time, iconic.) This physical connection to external reality has a crucial implication. By virtue of this connection, photographic images traditionally have been taken as proof that the scenes depicted in them really did occur as shown. In much the same way that a fingerprint or footprint testifies to the existence of the person who left it, a photograph can be seen as testifying to the reality of the situation it records. This aspect of photographic images plays a crucial role in ads such as the detergent commercial described above. As we look at the demonstration of the detergent's effect on the napkin, the fact that the image was produced photographically serves as an implicit assurance that the product really does do what it is shown to do in the ad. In other words, in ads like this, photography functions as evidence of an advertising claim. That function is what this chapter is about.

PHOTOGRAPHS VERSUS DRAWINGS

The potential value of photographs as evidence can be especially clear sometimes in ads that actually forsake photography and use drawings instead. Take the case of a picture that appeared in an ad for Komatsu, a manufacturer of construction equipment and industrial machinery (among other products) (see Figure 4.1). The basic point of the ad is that Komatsu's new excavator is so precise that it can be used to pour wine into a glass. The picture, a simple line drawing, demonstrates this feat, and it also shows a waiter looking on and recoiling with astonishment. The headline tells us, "Believe your eyes." Because of its simplicity and clarity, the picture conveys its basic message very efficiently. If a photograph had been used in place of the drawing, some of that efficiency might have been sacrificed. At the same time, however, precisely because a photograph has not been used, the ad has to rely on its verbal text to confirm that the picture represents a real situation. "What you see here is fact, not fiction," the body copy tells us. If the picture had been a photograph, that assurance would have been implicit in the image itself.

On the other hand, it also must be emphasized that there are many advertising situations in which photography can readily be dispensed

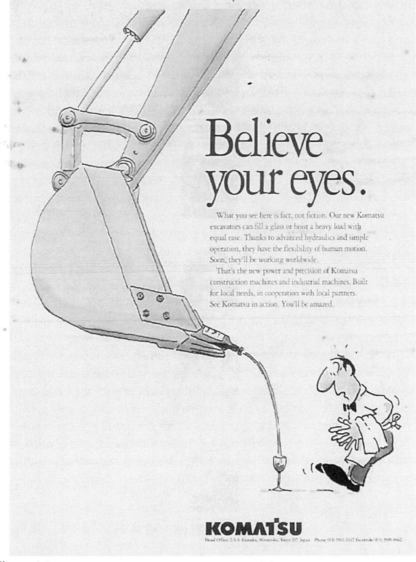

Figure 4.1.

with and the essential point of an ad's image can be conveyed quite adequately through a drawing. For instance, print ads for cars sometimes include handmade or computerized line diagrams of engines, suspension systems, or other features. As in our Komatsu example, such pictures are demonstrations of mechanical equipment. Ordinarily, however, the point of the diagrams is not to prove that a certain piece of equipment can perform some function or other but to explain how that equipment works. Consequently, the indexicality that a photograph would provide is not needed in such circumstances. Rather, it is iconicity that really matters, and line drawings therefore are perfectly adequate. Indeed, because they can simplify and distill the essential features of a complex object, diagrams can actually be more informative than photographs in ads of this sort.

Of course, line drawings and other handmade pictures can also be preferable to photographs for aesthetic reasons (Kimle & Fiore, 1992). An ad for Godiva Liqueur contains a painting of the Taj Mahal (see Figure 4.2). The elegance and romantic aura of the building are conveyed just as effectively by this picture as they would have been by a photograph. However, the picture adds to the aesthetic appeal of the ad in its own way. Its delicate brushstrokes and colors enhance the attractiveness of the scene, and its stylistic similarity to traditional Indian painting of the Mughal period (when the Taj Mahal was built) gives the knowledgeable viewer an extra source of pleasure. This type of stylistic reference to other art is also evident in an ad for Scoresby Scotch, which uses a comic book-like drawing of a man's face where other ads might have used a photograph (see Figure 4.3). The drawing's style is a parody of the pop-art paintings of Roy Lichtenstein, which are themselves parodies of comic books. So, for fans of pop art, this ad's picture offers a double attraction, and, because the picture is not intended as proof of anything, the fact that it is not a photograph does not matter.

PHOTOGRAPHIC PROOF

Commercial Advertising

With these qualifications in mind, let us now take a more detailed look at those circumstances in which ads do use pictures as evidence and, therefore, do need to rely on photographs rather than hand-made illustrations. As our detergent ad example suggests, commercial advertising

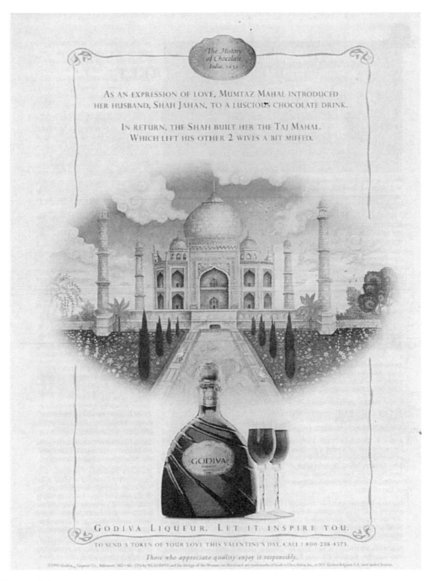

The History
of Chocolate
India, 1631

AS AN EXPRESSION OF LOVE, MUMTAZ MAHAL INTRODUCED
HER HUSBAND, SHAH JAHAN, TO A LUSCIOUS CHOCOLATE DRINK.

IN RETURN, THE SHAH BUILT HER THE TAJ MAHAL.
WHICH LEFT HIS OTHER 2 WIVES A BIT MIFFED.

GODIVA LIQUEUR. LET IT INSPIRE YOU.

TO SEND A TOKEN OF YOUR LOVE THIS VALENTINE'S DAY, CALL 1-800-238-4373.

Those who appreciate quality enjoy it responsibly.

Figure 4.2.

often relies on the implicit truth value of photography to get across the
point that a product is so effective, it has to be seen to be believed. The

Figure 4.3.

most typical example of this kind of thing is probably the comparison ad, in which we see side-by-side demonstrations of two different prod-

ucts (cleaning fluids, paper towels, kitchen appliances, etc.) or before-
and-after pictures of a product's consequences (weight loss, hair restoration,
muscle building, skin moisturizing, etc.). In all of these circumstances,
photography supplies crucial documentation, without which an ad can
lose much of its power to convince the viewer. For instance, if an ad for
a hair restoration drug used drawings instead of photographs, the ad
might still attract attention, but it would no longer have much value as
proof of the drug's effectiveness.

Aside from the specific case of comparison ads, commercial advertising can benefit from the indexicality of photography whenever a product's appeal is at least partly visual—a condition that covers a lot of
territory, including such things as makeup, jewelry, clothing, and household furnishings, as well as houses themselves, cars, and tourist resorts.
When such products or places are shown in ads, the use of photographs
implicitly reassures the prospective customer that what she or he is
seeing is a truthful representation of the real thing. Conversely, when an
advertiser in one of these categories deliberately chooses to employ
drawings instead of photographs, that often choice can be seen as a
significant statement in and of itself. A case in point is a current (Fall
1995) TV commercial for Saab that displays the product in the form of a
loosely drawn animated cartoon. As we saw earlier, line diagrams sometimes are used in car ads to illustrate the internal components. But here
we have a drawing of the car as a whole, and, in contrast to the typical
mechanical diagram, this picture is so sketchy that the make of the car is
scarcely identifiable. There is a good reason for this sketchiness, of
course. In the ad's print version (see Figure 4.4), the picture is accompanied by a simple slogan, "Peel off your inhibitions," which neatly encapsulates the message of the drawing's loose, free-form style. Clearly, this
style is meant as a visual analogue of the concept of freedom from
constraints. However, over and above this message (which is another
example of the type of meaning discussed in Chapter 2), the ad's lack of
a detailed photograph of the car can also be viewed as implying another
kind of statement, that is, that Saab's customers are sophisticated people
who do not care about appearances anyway. In other words, here the
significance of indexicality is demonstrated in reverse fashion: Where
looks do not matter, the indexical aspect of images can be dispensed with.

Figure 4.4.

Political Images

Turning from commercial advertising to the world of political ads and image-making, we encounter at least two major roles that indexicality is commonly called upon to play. The first of these involves ads in which members of the public express support for a politician or disapproval of her or his opponent. Ads of this sort have been a staple of political advertising since the earliest days of televised campaigns. They can take a variety of forms, ranging from person-in-the-street interviews to scenes of enthusiastic crowds cheering a candidate's speeches. For viewers who care what their fellow citizens think of a politician, these interviews or crowd scenes or other demonstrations of political sentiment can provide evidence on the state of public opinion. In such cases, therefore, the indexicality of the medium can serve as a guarantor of that evidence's authenticity.

Indexicality can also play an important role in a second kind of situation, when a candidate herself or himself is on the screen, in ads, debates, interviews, and so on. Even when the candidate's behavior is completely scripted and rehearsed, there are inevitably aspects of her or his appearance and demeanor that viewers can use to gain an intuitive understanding of the personality behind the stage persona. For this purpose, too, indexicality is indispensable. It is only because the politician's image is recorded photographically that it can provide the evidence for this probe into her or his authentic personality.

Social Issue Campaigns

Both in politics and in commercial ads, then, the indexical aspect of photography is often a principal factor influencing the viewer's response. However, it is probably in the area of social issue advertising and campaigns that indexicality performs its most critical functions. In the United States at least, the entire history of photography has been intimately associated with a variety of social movements that have used photographic evidence as rhetorical ammunition. Although the course of this history often extends beyond the confines of advertising in the traditional sense of the term, a review of some of its highlights provides a useful background for any examination of social issue advertising per se.

In the United States, the systematic use of photographic evidence for purposes of social advocacy can be traced back at least as far as the 1860s and 1870s, when environmentalist legislation led to the establishment of Yosemite as a state park (1864) and Yellowstone as the nation's first national park (1872). In the lobbying and publicity campaigns that preceded both of these actions, photographs were used extensively to convince legislators and the general public that the two areas in question were worth preserving as natural environments (Blodgett, 1993; Bossen, 1982). A major purpose of the photographs was to establish the fact that the two areas contained unusual natural features that merited protection. In the case of Yellowstone, in particular, photographs served as proof of the presence of certain rare and spectacular geothermal phenomena (geysers, boiling mudpots, steaming mineral pools, etc.) whose existence had been questioned by people who had known about them previously only through verbal accounts.

Although environmentalist photography originated as a means of publicizing the wonders of unspoiled nature, its subsequent history has been increasingly dedicated to documenting the damage done to nature by human beings (Bouse, 1991). This concern was present in many of the classic Dust Bowl photographs produced under government sponsorship during the Depression, and it was the major theme of two films, Pare Lorenz's *The Plow that Broke the Plains* (1936) and *The River* (1938), both of which were aimed at demonstrating the devastation caused by imprudent agricultural practices. More recently, environmentalists also have used video and photography to document threats to wildlife and endangered species. For example, in the late 1980s, the environmental activist Sam LaBudde took a job on a tuna-fishing boat and made a video that provided graphic evidence of the "incidental" slaughter of dolphins caught in tuna nets. The video included scenes of "dolphins crushed in the power block that hauls in the [nets]; dead dolphins by the hundreds being manhandled out of the mesh; a dolphin being filleted with a penknife by the [boat's] captain" (Brower, 1994, p. 120). LaBudde's video became part of a successful campaign to promote dolphin-safe methods of tuna fishing and to boycott tuna caught in other ways.

The basic strategy exemplified by LaBudde's video—the visual documentation of wrongdoing—has played a prominent part in other types of social issue campaigns as well. A similar strategy has been employed by animal rights activists who have stolen films of lab experiments to demonstrate the experimenters' mistreatment of animals. Documentation of immorality is also the intention of antiabortion videos that show the human features of aborted fetuses as support for the argument that abortion equals murder. Likewise, organizations concerned with child welfare or with the relief of poverty and famine have a long history of using visual documentation to arouse people's moral indignation at social injustice. As early as the 1870s, social reformers such as Jacob Riis, author of *How the Other Half Lives: Studies among the Tenements of New York* (1890), were producing photographs of slum life to illustrate lectures and treatises on the need for improved housing and social services.

One of the most distinguished figures to emerge out of this tradition was the photographer Lewis Hine, whose depictions of the awful working conditions of little children at the beginning of this century contributed to the passage of child labor legislation. Among many other accomplishments, Hine pioneered the use of before-and-after comparisons in social issue advertising. In a poster published in 1915, he showed two photographs of children, one at the top, the other at the bottom, separated by a picture of a factory (see Figure 4.5). The children in the upper photograph look happy and well cared for. The ones below look deprived, miserable, and unhealthy. The overall design of the poster makes it clear that the images are to be viewed as a sequence and that what we are witnessing at the bottom is the effect of factory work. The poster's punchy title spells this message out: "MAKING HUMAN JUNK."

For the most part, the types of social issue images that we have discussed thus far were deliberately produced for advocacy purposes. However, the history of social movements in the United States has also been influenced significantly by photographs and TV images that were originally created and exhibited as news. The most notable example of this process is surely the civil rights movement, whose impetus was enhanced tremendously by news photographers' documentation of the harsh police tactics that were used against it. Of particular importance were the memorable photographs from May 3, 1963, showing marchers in Birmingham, Alabama, being confronted by police dogs and hit with jets of water from specially equipped, high-intensity fire hoses. The day after these events, several of these photographs, including a picture of a dog lunging at a man's groin, were published in the *New York Times*, the *Washington Post*, and hundreds of other newspapers across the nation. That same day, President Kennedy announced publicly that the photographs made him sick, and a little more than a month later, he appeared on television to propose legislation that eventually would become part of the Civil Rights Act of 1964. In a retrospective assessment of the

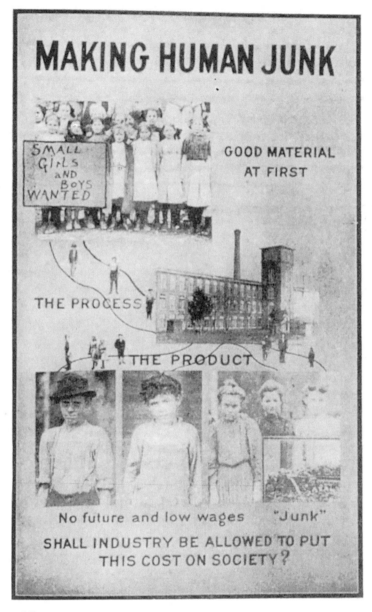

Figure 4.5.

significance of the Birmingham photographs, Senator Jacob Javits of New York declared that

> I know of nothing which has more keened the American people to the moral implications of the struggle called the struggle for civil rights, than the photographs which the American press and magazines have shown of actual events. . . . It is only because pictures backed up the words, no matter how authoritative, that [this injustice] has been credited. (quoted in Goldberg, 1991, p. 208)

By all accounts, this high valuation of the role of photography in the civil rights movement was shared by the movement's leaders. In a very informative history of these events, Vicki Goldberg cites a telling incident involving Martin Luther King, Jr. and a photographer who was taking pictures of a policeman beating a young marcher. The photographer became so enraged at the policeman's actions that he was about to stop recording the scene and try to intervene instead. But Dr. King reminded him of the importance of his pictures:

> Unless you record the injustice, the world won't know that the child got beaten. . . . I'm not being cold blooded about it, but it is so much more important for you to take a picture of us getting beaten up than for you to be another person joining in the fray. (quoted in Goldberg, 1991, pp. 209-210)

The civil rights movement and the other examples described above provide impressive evidence of the persuasive powers of photographic documentation. As Jacob Javits's statement points out, photographs come with an inherent guarantee of authenticity that is absent from words, "no matter how authoritative." And yet that guarantee of authenticity is not absolute. All it means—or, at least, all it *should* mean to the critical viewer—is that photographic media have the capacity to record visual appearances automatically, something that other modes of communication (including drawing and other kinds of handmade pictures) cannot do. But this automatic recording process is surrounded by a variety of human interventions, any one of which can have a substantial effect on a photograph's value as a truthful record of reality. In discussing these interventions, one can distinguish among the following five broad (and partially overlapping) categories.

VISUAL DECEPTION

First of all, the events that occur in front of the camera lens can be *staged*. If the viewer is misled into thinking that the resulting photograph (or film, video, etc.) is a record of unmanipulated reality, then that photograph—or, perhaps more accurately, the use of that photograph by an advertiser, politician, social activist, and so on—can be considered a lie. Second, after the photograph is produced, it can be *altered* by such traditional techniques as cutting and pasting or such newfangled ones as computer manipulation. If the viewer is not informed of the alteration and the photograph is presented as a veridical record of what was "seen" by the camera lens, then that photograph—or, once again, its presentation—becomes a visual fake or lie. Third, when photographic images are *edited* together in a sequence, their juxtaposition can be used to create a misleading impression about the relationship between the real-world events recorded in those images. Unlike staging or alteration, the presence of editing in itself is usually not concealed, but misleading editing can be considered a lie when it is shown without acknowledgment of the circumstances that have created the misleading impression (e.g., reversal of sequence, omission of a shot, etc.).

Fourth, at all stages of the photographic process—choosing and framing the shot, cropping the resulting image, editing images together, presenting the outcome to the viewer—the photograph's value as evidence about reality can be affected dramatically by the simple means of *selection*. By controlling what is shown to the viewer and what is left out, the person using the photograph as persuasive evidence can lead the viewer astray just as surely as through any of the more elaborate methods in our list. Finally, and even more simply, a photograph can mislead by being *mislabeled*. Of course, it might be argued that here the deception arises not from the image itself but from the words that go with it. However, it should be evident from what has been said above that a related argument can be made about the other four items on our list as well. It is the context in which an image is used, and not just the manipulation of the image itself, that determines whether it can be considered truthful or a lie. With this proviso explicitly before us, let us now take a closer look at each of these forms of visual fakery or deception. Because of the expanding role that computerized image-making is playing in advertising, the broader topic of image alteration will be discussed in a separate, concluding section by itself.

Staging

As far as unacknowledged staging in commercial advertising is concerned, it would be hard to come up with a more spectacular example than a 1990 TV commercial for the Volvo 240 station wagon. The commercial showed a "monster truck" running over a row of cars and crushing them all until it came to the Volvo, which remained intact. After this demonstration was investigated by the Texas Attorney General's Office, it was revealed that the Volvo used in the commercial had been specially reinforced with steel I-beams, that the supports of the other cars had been weakened, and that the monster truck rally had been staged. In response to these revelations, Volvo ran full-page ads in national newspapers apologizing for the ad. The advertising agency that had created the ad resigned from the Volvo account, from which it had been earning $40 million per year (Farhi, 1990; Horovitz, 1990).

This episode received extensive media coverage at the time, and it is still cited frequently as an illustration of misleading advertising (e.g., Davidson, 1995; Poff, 1995). However, it is a somewhat atypical illustration. The incidents of staging that have caused concern among critics of commercial advertising have usually been considerably less dramatic than this one. In the past, a typical target of criticism was the food and beverage industry's practice of substituting various photogenic but inedible substances, such as fake ice cream or fake beer foam, for products that do not look good on film or that are liable to do such inconvenient things as melt or lose their fizz. But such cut-and-dried examples have become less common as the levels of official and unofficial scrutiny of commercial advertising have increased. Nowadays, staging that misleads the viewer is more likely to do so by subtly blurring the boundaries between reality and fiction than through wholesale unacknowledged fakery. This tendency is most evident in the case of infomercials. By explicitly labeling themselves as commercial programs, infomercials avoid the charge of concealing their true nature from the viewer. However, by imitating talk shows and other genres of "reality" programming, they may be able to endow the events that occur in them with an aura of authenticity.

Confronted with the enthusiasm of an athletic woman demonstrating a new exercise machine, an erudite-looking man explaining the benefits of a new self-help program, and audiences cheerfully applauding these personalities, the viewer may lose sight of the point at which the script ends and these people's genuine behavior begins. Because what is most at issue here is not the actual fact of staging—which is openly acknowledged—but the degree to which it controls the nuances of people's expressions and responses, it is a much more complicated matter to pin a charge of deception on this kind of situation than on a case such as Volvo's monster truck rally, whose contrived character was never mentioned in the ad. As critics pointed out at the time, if the Volvo commercial had included a disclaimer or other acknowledgment of the staging, it would have escaped official censure, although in retrospect, one could argue that viewers might still have been unclear about the extent to which the car's resilience was due to the reinforcing I-beams.

The blurring of genre boundaries that occurs in infomercials has also had a long history in political advertising (Jamieson, 1992, pp. 147ff.). This history includes the Hollywood industry's use of faked "newsreels" of left-wing immigrants in an attempt to discredit socialist Upton Sinclair's 1934 campaign for governor of California (G. Mitchell, 1992); the staging of enthusiastic studio audience responses in the TV shows that formed a large part of Richard Nixon's 1968 presidential campaign (McGinnis, 1969); and the intercutting of staged and documentary images in Ronald Reagan's 1984 campaign advertising (Morreale, 1991). Today, this boundary-blurring form of advertising coincides with a more general trend toward the merging of informational, advertising, and entertainment/ fictional media (Griffin, 1992; Sandler & Secunda, 1993; Warlaumont, 1995). In addition to staged reenactments in crime dramas, tabloid news shows, and even regular news programs, there are also scripted programs that parody "spontaneous" talk shows—which, of course, is what infomercials do too, in their own way.

It has been argued that, as viewers become more aware of the presence of staging where it previously had not been employed, they may also become increasingly skeptical about the informational value of photography in general (Saltzman, 1989; Slattery & Tiedge, 1992). Because a similar argument also has been made repeatedly in connection with the computer manipulation of photographs, we will postpone consideration of this topic until we have discussed the alteration of images. For the moment, though, it must be emphasized that the blend-ing of documentary and fictional formats is not a new development in the visual media. In the area of social advocacy, for example, precedents for this phenomenon occur as far back as a century ago, in the photo-graphs of Jacob Riis. In a detailed examination of slides used by Riis to accompany his public lectures on the dangers of slum life, Maren Stange has noted that several images of criminal activity are actually posed, in some cases with real policemen playing the arresting officers (Stange, 1989, pp. 13-23). These posed pictures were interwoven with more conventional documentary material, and they were accompanied by storytelling that was meant to entertain as much as to instruct. So, although it may be true that new television genres have made the merging of reality and fiction more of an issue than it was before, attempts to assess the social impact of such mergers should not lose sight of the fact that they have a venerable ancestry in the history of American photography.

Editing

The manipulation of photographic images through editing has been debated extensively in discussions of news reports and documentaries, but its role in advertising has not received as much attention. As far as commercial advertising goes, a revealing demonstration of what editing can accomplish is contained in a video created by the Consumers Union to teach children about visual trickery in ads ("Buy me that," 1990). One of the ads analyzed in this video is for a game in which children throw a ball back and forth through the use of a stick with a cupped receptacle at one end (see Figures 4.6 through 4.9). In the ad, we see kids making miraculous diving catches with their sticks and instantaneously sending the ball flying on to the next player. In the real world, when a group of kids tried to use the sticks as shown in the commercial, not a single one was able to keep the ball from rolling out of the receptacle before she or he could toss it over to someone else. Reinspection of the ad reveals that the impression of seamless play is purely a result of editing. As soon as each kid makes contact with the ball there is a cut, and the next shot begins with the ball in action once again.

Under the heading of deceptive editing of "documentary" material, we might also want to consider a notorious political ad used in Richard

Figure 4.6, Figure 4.7, Figure 4.8, and Figure 4.9.

146

Nixon's 1968 presidential campaign. Aired only once, the ad juxtaposed images of Nixon's Democratic opponent, Hubert Humphrey, with scenes of warfare in Vietnam, protests in the streets of Chicago, and poverty in Appalachia. Because Humphrey was smiling in some of the shots, these juxtapositions created the impression that he was indifferent to the suffering and disturbances in the other images. "By adjoining a smiling Humphrey to helmeted soldiers crouched behind sand bags waiting to attack or be attacked in Vietnam, the ad implied that Humphrey, at least, was pleased by the U.S. presence in Vietnam, and, at most, joyous at the prospect of American deaths there" (Jamieson, 1984, p. 246).

Strictly speaking, this type of editing is not equivalent to our previous example, because here we can assume that the viewer must be aware, at some level of consciousness, that the juxtaposition is meant to be symbolic. In other words, on the face of it, this ad cannot be considered an attempt to create the illusion of seamless reality that was the object of the children's commercial. Nevertheless, it is likely that viewers' reactions to these two types of editing are actually very similar. Noel Carroll has pointed out that the kind of sequence found in the Nixon ad (a person's face followed by some other object) is probably modeled on an innate human tendency to look at other people's faces for signs of what they themselves are looking at and then to follow the path of their gaze to its object (Carroll, 1993, pp. 127-131). Consequently, even though we realize, with the analytical parts of our brains, that Humphrey is not really looking at the soldiers, our perceptual processes are preprogrammed to make an automatic connection between the two and to see Humphrey's expression as a reaction to the soldiers' plight. In that sense, this type of editing can be said to exploit our faith in the indexicality of photography just as effectively as the children's commercial does.

Selectivity

Aside from illustrating the powers of editing, our children's game example is also a clear instance of misleading selectivity. Out of the total amount of film that was taken when the commercial was shot, the edited version shows us only those segments in which the ball is in play and omits the inevitable aftermath of the ball rolling off the sticks. Selecting an unrepresentative image of a certain situation is the simplest method of using photography to create a misleading impression of reality. It may also be the most pervasive. In advertising, we encounter it whenever an ad focuses on the satisfied customer or unsatisfied voter or political success or social horror story that supports the ad's point, while leaving out all the cases that contradict that point. As Lang and Lang (1952) showed in one of the earliest systematic studies of viewers' responses to TV images, such selective representations take advantage of people's tendency to generalize implicitly from limited visual evidence, that is, to assume that what they are seeing on the screen (or in a printed photograph) is typical of the broader reality to which the image refers.

An especially dramatic demonstration of the potential effects of selective representation occurred during the Persian Gulf War. A prominent feature of news reports about the war was the repeated display of pictures of "smart bombs" being guided precisely onto their targets. These pictures came from military authorities, of course, and it seems fair to describe their release to the press as a public relations effort intended to generate favorable publicity for the military's new weapons systems and also, perhaps, to allay U.S. citizens' concerns about possible harm to Iraqi noncombatants. The pictures may have "created an illusion of remote, bloodless, pushbutton battle in which only military targets were assumed destroyed" (Walker, 1992, p. 84). However, subsequent reports indicate that, "of all bombs dropped on Iraq, only seven percent were so-called smart bombs, and of these at most 70 percent were thought to have hit their intended targets" (Lee & Solomon, 1990, p. xx). Furthermore, it appears that Iraq experienced substantial civilian casualties, especially in the city of Basra (Walker, 1992, pp. 87-88; see also Sifry & Cerf, 1991, p. 336n). In short, the selectiveness of the smart-bomb images may have misled viewers about one of the war's most serious consequences.

Unlike staging or the alteration of photographs, selective representation is a nonoptional, inevitable part of the photographic process. The photographer, cameraperson, or director must always make some selection from the unlimited variety of points of view and moments in time at which any particular situation could, in principle, be photographed. Consequently, establishing that one selection or another is misleading can often be a tricky matter. Whereas the mere presence of staging or alteration is sometimes enough to prove deception, the mere fact of selection never is. Rather, it must be shown that the selection is somehow unrepresentative of reality, and that can be complicated.

This problem is currently at the center of an acrimonious confrontation between environmentalists and their opponents (Bouse, 1995; Goshorn, 1995; see also Smith, 1992). As we noted earlier, environmentalists have traditionally used photographs of damaged landscapes as part of their efforts to promote the passage of protective legislation. The meaning of these photographs is now being contested by spokespersons for various economic activities (logging, ranching, mining, etc.) that might suffer adverse effects if such legislation were to go through. The simplest counterargument to some of the photographs is that they show only those areas of land that exhibit particularly severe damage and ignore other parts that may be undamaged or even flourishing. But critics of environmentalist photographs have also made more elaborate arguments, pointing out that the same stretch of land can look very different during the rainy season from the way it looks after a drought, or that seemingly damaged land can be shown to be flourishing in photographs taken a year or two after the ones used by the environmentalists. Furthermore, opponents of environmentalist efforts have also challenged the representativeness of historical photographs that environmentalists have used as evidence of the "natural" condition of the land. These arguments have included the contention that even pristine wilderness periodically suffers extensive damage from lightning strikes, avalanches, storms, and so on, so that historical images of dense vegetation or abundant trees may misrepresent the average conditions that would be observed in a certain area over a longer span of time. For our purposes, this controversy is of value primarily as a reminder that between visual truth and falsehood there sometimes can be a substantial gray area. Especially where selectivity is at issue, the boundaries separating representative images from their opposites are not always easy to establish.

Mislabeling

However, these words of caution should not be taken as an endorsement of complete relativism in these matters. Some visual deceptions are as blatant as can be. Consider the case of a political ad called "The Harbor" that was used by George Bush in his successful 1988 campaign for the presidency. Aimed at attacking Michael Dukakis's environmental policies during his tenure as governor of Massachusetts, the ad claimed that Boston Harbor was an environmental mess, it blamed Dukakis for this situation, and it ended with the ominous statement that now Dukakis was threatening to do for America what he had done for Massachusetts. These claims were made verbally in a voice-over spoken by an unseen announcer. The images accompanying this voice-over were mostly grainy close-ups of filthy-looking water, but there was also a shot of a danger sign indicating the presence of radioactive contamination in the area. More than any other aspects of the ad's visuals, this image was an alarming indictment of Dukakis. But it was subsequently revealed that there was a major discrepancy between the image's implied message (i.e., that Dukakis was responsible for radioactive contamination in the harbor) and the actual situation from which the image was taken in real life. In reality, the radiation warning sign was not in Boston Harbor at all. It was in the Boston Navy Yard, a facility that was under the jurisdiction of the federal government—that is, the same administrative entity in which Mr. Bush was at that very time serving as vice president. In other words, if there was anyone in this story with an official connection to the radiation sign, that person was not Mr. Dukakis but, arguably, Mr. Bush himself. So here we have an unambiguous instance of visual deception, as well as an example of mislabeling, which was the final item on our list of misleading practices. The ad's words, together with the images surrounding the radiation sign, lead us to assume that the sign is in Boston Harbor and is Michael Dukakis's responsibility. Neither of these is true. If the use of this image in this ad is not a visual lie, nothing is.

ALTERATION

Of all the forms of visual manipulation on our initial list of five, the one that appears to trouble critics the most is the alteration of images. Changing a photograph in such a way as to avoid detection seems to pose a direct challenge to our faith in photography as an automatic record of external reality. And yet convincing techniques for altering photographs have been part of photographic practice since the origins of the medium (Kobre, 1995). Early methods of alteration have been described in some detail by Jaubert (1989, pp. 9-14) in a grimly fascinating account of the role of altered photographs in the visual propaganda of political dictatorships. Among the various types of alteration discussed by Jaubert, perhaps the most striking is the visual obliteration of political figures who had fallen from grace or lost leadership struggles—for instance, the elimination of Leon Trotsky from a 1920 photograph of Lenin, following Trotsky's exile from Russia and murder under Stalin (pp. 30-31); the removal of Liu Shaoqui from a photograph of Mao Zedong, after Liu had been tortured and killed during the Chinese Cultural Revolution (p. 116); and the effacement, from a picture that included Fidel Castro, of a former associate who went into exile following Castro's support for the Soviet invasion of Czechoslovakia (p. 160).

Manipulation of Images by Computer

Media critics' concerns about the alteration of photographs have increased considerably since the early 1980s, when the communications industry began its wholesale transition to digital imaging technology, that is, the electronic encoding of photographs for purposes of storage, transmission, or computer-assisted manipulation (Prince, in press; Reaves, 1991, 1995a, 1995b). In addition to surveying the history of digital imaging technology and explaining its technical aspects, a book by William Mitchell (1992) provides a useful overview of applications of this technology that can raise questions of misinformation and visual falsehood. Mitchell groups these potentially problematic applications into three general categories: (a) *insertions*, exemplified by a *Newsday* cover photo in which a single fighter jet's image was pasted repeatedly into a scene, giving the impression of an entire formation of jets flying in unison (pp. 196, 200); (b) *effacements and elisions*, such as the deletion of a shoulder holster and pistol from a *Rolling Stone* cover photograph of the stars of *Miami Vice* (p. 202); and (c) *substitutions*, such as the grafting of Oprah Winfrey's head onto the body of Ann-Margret in a *TV Guide* cover image (p. 209) (for another example, see Figure 4.10). To these three categories, there surely should be added one more, encompassing the type of alteration that was made in *Time* magazine's June 27, 1994 cover photograph of O.J. Simpson. The darkening of Simpson's face in that photograph is an example of a very frequent digital retouching practice, which could be labeled a *change in physical appearance*.

When it comes to advertising, changes in physical appearance are actually among the most common applications of digital imaging. Espe-

Figure 4.10.

cially in fashion ads, computers are routinely used to accomplish such visual effects as making hair shinier and adding highlights; removing strands of hair that are falling in the wrong place; removing wrinkles, sun damage, pimples, and other skin blemishes; imparting an overall glow to the skin; whitening the whites of eyes and enlarging the pupils (for reasons mentioned in the introduction); reducing the size of hips and increasing the length of legs; and, of course, enhancing the apparent size of breasts. Furthermore, computers can be used to make grass greener, water bluer, and skies brighter; to add or remove flowers, trees, telephone lines, passing cars, or pedestrians; and to make selected parts of an image larger or smaller. All this and more can be done with greater precision and more convincingly than was typically the case with traditional, noncomputerized techniques of altering photographs. It is estimated that, currently (i.e., 1995), close to 90% of commercials employ some sort of digital effect, whereas 5 or 6 years ago, the corresponding figure was only 1 in 20 (Cooper, 1995, p. 29). Understandably, then, some observers of this trend and related developments in news and photojournalism have expressed apprehension about the diminishing credibility of all photographic media (Martin, 1991; Phelan, 1992; Ritchin, 1990; Wheeler & Gleason, 1995). In fact, a decade ago, when this story was just beginning, an article about computer imaging carried the following title: "Digital retouching: The end of photography as evidence of anything" (Brand, Kelly, & Kinney, 1985).

As we saw earlier, similar predictions have also been made in connection with the increasing use of staging in photographs that are supposedly based on reality. What are we to make of these predictions? Is it just media critics who are becoming more skeptical about the documentary value of photography, or is this growing skepticism likely to spread to the broader public? In thinking about this question, a crucial point to keep in mind is the fact that digital alteration in advertising often is deliberately designed to attract attention to itself. In contrast to the routine changes of physical appearance described above (which, of course, are typically meant to look "natural"), many ads that use other kinds of digital alterations are calculated to make the viewer notice the special effect.

A vivid demonstration of this point occurred in a series of ads featuring Paula Abdul that were put out by Coca-Cola a few years ago. Unfortunately, the Coca-Cola Company refused permission to reproduce images from the ads, but many readers may still remember what they looked like. The ads contained two of the techniques discussed by Mitchell: insertions and substitutions. Starting out with scenes from classic Hollywood movies (some of which had to be colorized, through the use of another digital procedure), the producers added the figure of

Paula Abdul, either by fitting her into the existing action or by having her take the place of someone else. As a result, in the final versions of these scenes, she appears to be dancing with Gene Kelly or interacting with other movie stars such as Cary Grant or Humphrey Bogart. Clearly, these alterations were meant to be noticed. In fact, surely that was the main point of these ads. Imagine a viewer who had somehow never seen any of the famous movie stars in the ads and failed to realize that the scenes were composites. To someone like that, the ads might be almost meaningless. So here we have an example of digital alteration that intentionally increases most viewers' awareness of the spectacular effects that can be achieved through this process. If increased awareness leads to greater skepticism (even for viewers who do not actually understand how the process works), it could be argued that the proliferation of this kind of ad presages a general loss of faith in the connection between photography and reality, and that this trend will not be confined to media critics.

Other ads have employed digital imaging techniques in even more obtrusive ways. In a commercial for Chanel No. 5, we see a person undergoing a smooth, incremental shape change and becoming someone else, as the image morphs between Marilyn Monroe (actually, a look-alike), who was reputedly a past user of the perfume, and Carole Bouquet, who is a current Chanel model. Confronted with this dazzling transformation, viewers may well realize that they are in the presence of a powerful new technique for altering images. It seems likely that such a realization may also come from the many TV commercials that feature eye-catching examples of computer animation. In images ranging from Budweiser's beer-guzzling ants to Timex's Statue of Liberty checking the watch on her wrist, TV viewers receive repeated demonstrations of the new technology's capacity to endow the most bizarre scenarios with the look of photographic reality. Furthermore, related visual effects are commonly highlighted in print ads as well. A dramatic two-page spread by Sun Microsystems gives us a minutely detailed view of a Tyrannosaurus Rex baring its teeth (see Figure 4.11). Because we know that this is not a living creature, the image's lifelike quality proclaims openly that we are in the presence of a medium with highly convincing powers of simulation. Indeed, the ad's text is an explicit discussion of computer imaging and of the uses of Sun workstations in this area.

Figure 4.11.

But less inspired manipulations may sometimes be equally effective in raising awareness of digital imaging. When Bob Dole announced his intention to run for president in 1996, a parody ad on the World Wide Web displayed a photograph of the former senator behind a podium containing a Dole pineapple sign. Although there is actually no business connection between Mr. Dole and his namesake company, the insertion of the company's logo in this image was hardly all that remarkable, either as political humor or as a visual gag, and many viewers may have overlooked the fact that the image was manipulated. Precisely for that reason, though, viewers who knew enough about politics to realize that the image was a fake may also have realized how easy it would have been for them to be duped as well, if not by this image then by some other application of the same technology.

These examples are all confined to forms of digital imaging that are actually being practiced on a large scale in today's advertising environment. The near future is sure to bring developments that will make this technology's presence even more widely felt. For instance, interactive ads increasingly will give viewers themselves the ability to manipulate images in order to previsualize the colors or styles or other features of various products, and virtual reality advertising will demonstrate even more effectively than today's animation the fact that photographic quality can be simulated. Under these circumstances, predictions about a widespread loss of faith in photography may seem especially compelling.

Viewers' Awareness of Computer Manipulation

But how much do people in general actually know about all this? To what extent is the broad public aware of the use of computers in advertising and elsewhere? In an attempt to address these questions, I and two collaborators, Alison Andrews and Jennifer Khoury, have recently completed a telephone survey of 100 Philadelphia residents. This sample, which was drawn through a random procedure from listed residential numbers, contained 45 men and 55 women, aged 18 and above. Forty-two of the respondents had not gone beyond high school in their education, whereas the educational level of the rest ranged from some college to graduate school. The survey questions dealt with three issues: awareness of the use of computers in image manipulation, perceptions regarding the frequency of visual deception, and opinions about the ethics and acceptability of computer manipulation.

Regarding their awareness of the use of computers for the alteration of images, the respondents were first asked about photography and film or video in general, and then asked specifically about advertising ("Do you know that some advertising images are altered by computer?"). Whereas 78 respondents indicated that they had a general awareness of computer alteration of photographic media, a smaller number, 58, responded positively to the specific question about advertising. These 58 were then asked if they had ever actually noticed the use of computer alteration while looking at an ad, and also whether they could give an example of an ad containing such an alteration. Twenty-one of the 58 responded affirmatively to the first question, and 18 gave examples, out of which 13 referred to specific ads (e.g., morphing faces in a Gillette ad, a moonwalking baby in an ad for Edy's Ice Cream, Coca-Cola's Paula Abdul ad, among others), while the remaining 5 were generic descriptions (e.g., "fixing facial flaws, removing scars, in any commercial"). Examples from areas outside of advertising had previously been given by 35 respondents in connection with the survey's initial questions about general awareness of computer alteration. These nonadvertising examples included movies (e.g., *Forrest Gump, Jurassic Park, Terminator 2*, etc.), still photos in magazines (e.g., *Time's* O.J. Simpson cover, airbrushing in *Playboy*, etc.), as well as 12 cases of personal experience with digital imaging, at photoshops or elsewhere.

After being questioned about awareness, all respondents were asked to indicate their perceptions of how often computer alteration is used in advertising, how often it is used to lie or mislead the viewer, and how often advertising images in general are used to lie or mislead the viewer in any way. The responses to these questions are given in Table 4.1 (in raw frequencies, with $N = 100$).

Finally, the respondents were also asked to state their opinions about the ethics and acceptability of computer alteration in advertising. These questions were posed in an either/or fashion, requiring respondents to indicate whether they considered this practice ethical or unethical, harmless or harmful, acceptable or unacceptable, and worthy of being allowed or prohibited. (Once again, the numbers in Table 4.2 correspond to raw frequencies, with $N = 100$.)

TABLE 4.1

	Computer alteration	Misleading alteration	Misleading advertising
Always	9	13	19
Often	39	30	32
Sometimes	19	29	27
Rarely	—	3	8
Never	1	18	—
Don't know	32	7	14

What do these figures add up to? To begin with, the high numbers of respondents indicating awareness of computer alteration suggest that some degree of familiarity with this practice is indeed becoming part of the general public's stock of knowledge, as one might have predicted from the obtrusiveness of the kinds of examples mentioned earlier, as well as the growing number of well-publicized movies featuring digital imaging effects. Moreover, it should be noted that, although general awareness of computer manipulation was somewhat higher among the more educated respondents than among their less educated counterparts, specific awareness of this technology's advertising applications was not related to level of education, and there were no significant education-related differences in the remaining data. In light of these apparently high levels of awareness, the respondents' other perceptions and opinions about computer-altered images could be seen as evidence of a substantial negative reaction to such images among the general public. Evidently, more than 40% of the respondents in this sample believe that computer alteration is not only frequently practiced but also frequently misleading, and comparable numbers of respondents consider it unethical and harmful (although fewer would actually prohibit it). All of this appears to be consistent with media critics' concerns that the ubiquity of computer-manipulated images will lead to an erosion of the public's trust in photographic media.

All the same, before we conclude that photography's role as evidence is about to evaporate, we would do well to take two additional points into account. First of all, there is a notable discrepancy between the number of respondents who said they were aware of computer alteration and the number who were actually able to provide a concrete example,

TABLE 4.2

	Ethical	Harmless	Acceptable	Allowed
Yes	24	23	38	36
No	42	40	32	29
Uncertain	34	37	30	35

either of an ad or some other type of altered image. This discrepancy suggests that, for the moment at least, many people's sense of this topic may be rather vague, and that the negative views expressed by some respondents may reflect a more generalized cynicism about the visual media (or perhaps a cynical *stance*), rather than a concrete reaction to specific information about the potential uses of digital imaging. This conclusion is supported by the high numbers of respondents who expressed the view that advertising is generally misleading, regardless of the use of computer alteration. So, perhaps people's inclinations to distrust actual images in actual ads (as opposed to the abstract notion of advertising imagery) may be less profound than some of the numbers above might indicate.

There is also a second reason for caution about any prediction of a general loss of faith in photography. Although media critics are correctly treating digital imaging as an epoch-making development, we must recall, once again, that photographs have always been subject to manipulation, and we should not assume that past generations of viewers were necessarily less aware of this possibility than people today may be. At the conclusion of the Civil War, photographs were introduced as evidence during the trial of the commander of the Andersonville prison camp, who was accused of barbaric treatment of Union prisoners. This event took place barely a quarter of a century after the birth of the medium; nevertheless, the prosecuting attorney felt that the authenticity of the images needed to be backed up by expert verbal testimony, which was provided by two medical doctors who certified that the photographs "were true and fair pictures" of the conditions in Andersonville (Goldberg, 1991, p. 24). Conversely, when films of Nazi death camps were shown to German prisoners of war at the end of World War II, many dismissed the scenes as fakes, and only one third out of 2,000 who were questioned conceded their reality (Fincher, 1995, p. 142).

These two episodes serve as striking illustrations of an important point, which has already been hinted at earlier in this discussion. Although photography's value as evidence originates in the technical nature of the medium (its ability to record appearances automatically), what ultimately determines any particular photograph's believability is the context of its use. No matter how genuine a photograph looks, we can always dismiss it as staged, unrepresentative, mislabeled, and so on if we do not trust the person who is using it as evidence. Conversely, even with full awareness of the possibility of manipulation, we are more likely to believe a photograph's evidence if we believe that the person who is using it would not resort to such tampering. So, although it may well be true that people are becoming more skeptical about photography as a reaction to digital imaging, in the final analysis, the future credibility of the medium will depend—as it always has—on the ethicality of the producers of images.

PART 3

IMAGE AS IMPLIED SELLING PROPOSITION

5

-◄o►-

EDITING
AND MONTAGE

-◄o►- A recent book on the advertising industry begins with a page-long list of slogans from successful car ads of years past. After reciting such lines as "Ford. Worth more when you buy it. Worth more when you sell it," or "Mercedes-Benz. Engineered like no other car in the world," the list concludes as follows: "Subaru . . . Subaru?" (Rothenberg, 1994, p. 3). The implication: The failure of Subaru's 1991-1992 advertising campaign, which is the book's central topic, is epitomized by the lack of a memorable tagline.

Later in the book, the author discusses the visual aspects of Subaru's ad campaign. However, the fact that he starts with the words (or rather their lack) is significant. People who analyze advertising often take their cue from the slogans, and this practice cannot be dismissed as simply a matter of verbal bias. Because of its capacity for the explicit expression of comparisons, causal relationships, and other syntactic constructions, verbal language is more efficient than are images at encapsulating the basic propositions and arguments on which advertising campaigns tend to be based. Of course, a TV commercial could effectively juxtapose an image of a Mercedes with pictures of poorly engineered clunkers. Nevertheless, if what is required is a direct, explicit statement of the ad's selling proposition, the Mercedes slogan quoted above says it all.

Yet making an explicit statement is typically not enough. It may be true that the main point of many ads is indeed reducible to an abstract claim or argument: "This car is engineered like no other"; "The president deserves to be reelected because his first-term policies produced economic growth"; "We should ban the use of CFCs to protect the ozone layer." Even in such situations, though, it seems self-evident that an ad's persuasiveness would be enhanced by including a concrete demonstration of the abstract claim (e.g., a picture of a well-engineered car), an appeal to the audience's emotions (e.g., pictures of happy children enjoying the fruits of economic prosperity), or simply some device for attracting attention (e.g., a dramatic shot of Antarctica, where the ozone layer has been forming occasional holes). In cases such as these, the iconic and indexical features of visual images can complement the syntactic explicitness of verbal language.

The Value of Indirectness

Images also come into their own in those circumstances in which the explicit statement of a selling proposition is either irrelevant to an ad's message or actually undesirable. In the history of U.S. television advertising, perhaps the most famous illustration of this possibility was the 1984 commercial used to launch the first Macintosh computer (see Figures 5.1-5.6). Set in a grim, futuristic architectural complex that could be a factory or perhaps a prison, this ad was based on a juxtaposition between two sets of images: on one hand, a troupe of dispirited-looking people with shaved heads and identical drab uniforms; on the other hand, a vigorous, athletic woman clad in a tight T-shirt and shorts. Through a bluish haze that accentuates their pallor and the robotic uniformity of their appearance, the people in the first set of images are shown assembling in front of a giant video screen, from which a menacing male face looks out at them and delivers a droning totalitarian incantation ("We are one people, with one will, one resolve, one cause," etc.). The images of the woman are intercut with this scene. She appears in a series of quick flashes, running straight at the viewer, her hands tightly grasping a long-handled hammer. As the man on the giant screen continues to harangue his audience, the woman charges into their midst,

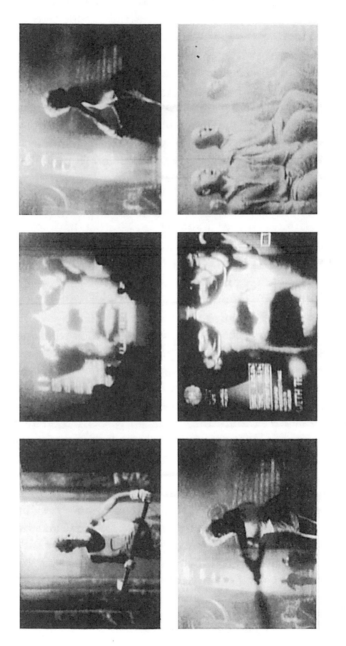

Figure 5.1, Figure 5.2, Figure 5.3, Figure 5.4, Figure 5.5, and Figure 5.6.

165

swings the hammer around, and hurls it straight at his mouth. In the ad's final shot, the white light of the exploding screen bathes the awestruck faces of the audience, while a supertitle makes the first and only reference to the product: "On January 24th, Apple Computer will introduce the Macintosh. And you'll see why 1984 won't be like '1984.'"

This ad was broadcast only once, during the 1984 SuperBowl, but its impact has been analyzed and discussed extensively. There is much evidence that the ad's viewers experienced considerable uncertainty about its meaning. Whereas the presence of a contrast of some sort may have been relatively easy to grasp, the exact nature of that contrast appears to have been more elusive. At the same time, however, there is general agreement that the ad was a tremendous success, generating intense interest in the Macintosh. To this day, it continues to win awards and is commonly referred to as one of the most effective TV commercials ever made (Voight, 1995). A recent TV program about advertising proclaimed it the greatest ad of all time. Evidently, then, in this one case at least, elusiveness of meaning was no impediment to success. Indeed, quite the opposite appears to have been true. By common consent, it was precisely this elusiveness that was largely responsible for the ad's extraordinary impact.

As critics pointed out at the time, the ad's lack of a straightforward message may have added to its appeal by enticing viewers to try to decipher the various allusions that are contained in its images. Moreover, the ad's elusiveness also generated extensive discussion by media commentators, thus creating even further interest in its interpretation. Viewers who recognized the reference to George Orwell's 1984 presumably would have made the connection to Big Brother eyeing the people from a video monitor. From this connection, these same viewers may have gone on to interpret the new Macintosh as an instrument of liberation from some form of tyranny, such as the rigid work styles demanded by other computer designs. A similar conclusion might have been reached even without the 1984 allusion by viewers who connected the ad's visual style to early-1980s sci-fi movies, which were known for their uniformly grim visions of the future as a totalitarian "dystopia." Significantly, the most prominent film in this genre was Blade Runner (1982), whose director, Ridley Scott, was also the creator of this ad.

There are a number of other elements that attentive viewers of the ad could have tried to weave into their interpretations. For example, the name "Macintosh" could have led some viewers to connect the woman's hammer to Scotland, where hammer-throwing is a traditional sport, whereas viewers inclined towards sexual symbolism could have been more impressed by the hammer's long handle than by its cultural roots. The mental effort of making such connections can engage a viewer's interest in an ad even when those connections are incidental to the ad's overall point. However, there is one additional feature of the Macintosh ad that arguably makes a crucial difference to the ad's message. This feature is the blue color in the images of the assembled masses and the face on the giant video screen. In the jargon of the business world, Big Blue is the name for IBM. So, for viewers who were able to make that association, either on their own or through the remarks of other viewers and media commentators, the ad's syntactic structure would have taken on yet another layer of meaning. If the woman in the ad represents the new Macintosh and the ad's factory- or prisonlike setting is IBM, then the implied overall message could be seen as a prediction that the flexible, dynamic Apple Computer is going to shatter the dominance of its rigidly bureaucratic rival.

This is a good example of a kind of message that an advertiser would probably not want to spell out explicitly. Although direct attacks on competitors are much more acceptable in U.S. advertising (both commercial and political) than in some other cultures, explicit criticism of another company's management style would probably be considered unseemly. It is certainly hard to imagine an advertiser calling a competitor totalitarian in so many words. Consequently, the relative obliqueness of the Macintosh ad's visual syntax can be considered doubly advantageous. On one hand, it enabled the ad to suggest a message that could not be expressed more openly; on the other hand, by stimulating viewers and media commentators to spend more time thinking and talking about the ad, the ad's obliqueness may have increased the likelihood that the audience would arrive at the implied message on its own—and that this message would make more of an impression.

"Cool" Media

The idea that an indirect message can be more involving and perhaps more persuasive than an explicit argument has been touched upon in a variety of ways by media theorists and practitioners. As far as visually oriented scholarship is concerned, the most widely publicized version of this idea has probably been Marshall McLuhan's (1964) conception of television as a "cool" medium. Exactly what McLuhan meant by the term "cool" was never entirely clear, but, roughly speaking, his basic notion seems to have been that low-definition stimuli engage the mind more fully than their high-definition counterparts and are therefore more effective at bringing about social transformation. One of his major reasons for claiming that television is a cool medium appears to have been the fact that the TV picture is relatively grainy and of low resolution, at least when compared to the sharper image of 35mm film.

But this aspect of McLuhan's theory is unconvincing. Although the relative graininess of the standard TV image may indeed lead the brain to do more work, there is little reason to believe that this particular type of mental filling-in has any effect on attitude change or emotional involvement. The low resolution of the TV image is essentially a technical matter, and the mental filling-in of that image basically is a routine perceptual process that the brain performs automatically, outside of the viewer's consciousness. This process should not be equated with what happens when our minds become engaged by the calculated suggestiveness of a visual scenario that holds something back from the audience. In the latter case, we respond to an invitation to complete a train of thought. In the former case, there is no such invitation. So, although McLuhan's broader point about the potential effects of incomplete information may be compatible with the concerns of this chapter, his specific application of that point to television is not particularly useful for present purposes.

Eisenstein and Montage

A more relevant set of ideas for thinking about the function of implicitness in visual media comes from the world of film scholarship. An especially influential source of such ideas is the work of Sergei M. Eisenstein, whose films and writings can be seen as a sustained exploration of the ways in which meaning can arise from the juxtaposition of visual images. As Stephen Prince (1990) has argued (in an essay titled "Are There Bolsheviks in Your Breakfast Cereal?"), many of the editing conventions currently found in television advertising are based on principles that were formulated by Eisenstein and his contemporaries in the early years of Soviet cinema. To be sure, the context in which these conventions function today is dramatically different from that of their original use (cf. Bordwell, 1993, p. 266). Indeed, Prince notes the ironic fact that visual devices that initially were developed as instruments of communist propaganda are now being deployed in the service of market economies and electoral politics. However, as Friedrich Hayek had pointed out more than 50 years ago, "neither propaganda in itself nor the techniques employed are peculiar to totalitarianism" (Hayek, 1944, p. 153).

Eisenstein was an intensely self-analytical director, and much of his theoretical writing draws on his own films as sources of examples. His views on the implicit meanings of visual syntax are put forth most compactly in an analysis of a famous sequence from his film *October* (1928). This film is a celebration of the events of October 1917, during which the Bolsheviks seized power in Russia. One of the preludes to those events was an attempted coup by a general who used as his rallying cry the traditional patriotic slogan, "For God and Country." In the film, Eisenstein uses this episode as an opportunity for antireligious propaganda. He begins by putting the slogan itself on the screen. This is followed by an image of a Christian church, apparently a direct reference to the first part of the slogan. But then a Hindu religious statue appears on the screen, and after that comes a statue of Buddha, and then a Muslim mosque, and images from a variety of other religions, until the sequence culminates with a Siberian ceremonial mask. In Eisenstein's own words, the sequence was described as a "succession of gods descended from a splendid baroque Christ through all kinds of divine images down to a wooden Chukshi idol" (Eisenstein, 1991, p. 117).

How did Eisenstein expect viewers to react to such a sequence? His general theory of visual composition and editing stressed the role of conflict in the creation of meaning. According to this theory, the juxtaposition or "montage" of two different images in an edited sequence or even within a single frame was supposed to stimulate the viewer's mind toward the creation of a new meaning, a synthesis of the meanings of the two conflicting images. In the specific case of the "God and Country" sequence, Eisenstein assumed that viewers would experience a growing sense of contradiction between their initial view of God and each succeeding image in the sequence. As he put it,

> Here a conflict arises between the concept "God" and its symbolization. Whereas idea and image are completely synonymous in the first Baroque image, they grow further apart with each subsequent image. . . . The gradual succession continues in a process of comparing each new image with its common designation and *unleashes a process that, in terms of its form, is identical to a process of logical deduction.* (Eisenstein, 1988, p. 180)

Up to this point, the consequences that Eisenstein is envisioning are roughly parallel to what has already been said earlier in this chapter about the role of visual syntax in stimulating mental activity. But then he adds one further, important claim:

> Everything here is already intellectually conceived, not just in terms of the resolution but also of the method of expressing ideas. . . . Whereas the conventional film directs and develops the *emotions*, here we have a hint of the possibility of likewise developing and directing the entire *thought process.* (Eisenstein, 1988, p. 180)

In other words, Eisenstein was not assuming that his viewers' mental grappling with the editing would lead to just any old conclusion. Rather, he took it for granted that viewers would reach the conclusion already designed for them by the filmmaker himself. Specifically, he assumed that the sequence would lead viewers "to draw anti-religious conclusions about what the divine as such really is" (Eisenstein, 1988, p. 180), and that the sequence therefore could be seen as "a unique and ironic way of debunking the image of God and thus the very concept of God" (Eisenstein, 1991, p. 117).

Nowadays, Eisenstein's assertion that he could control the end result of his viewers' interpretations may seem somewhat presumptuous and retrograde. Current scholarship in communication has tended to emphasize the notion that what the viewer makes of an image, or what the reader makes of a text, is out of the hands of the image's or text's creator. Furthermore, this notion would seem to be especially pertinent to the sequence from *October* and to visual syntax more generally, precisely because of the lack of explicitness to which the present discussion has drawn attention. All the same, it would be a mistake to dismiss Eisenstein's claim as mere wishful thinking on the part of an overly confident director. It may be true that individual viewers inevitably differ in their interpretations of the very same material, but this should not lead us to the extreme position of completely overlooking the creator's role in shaping those interpretations. In fact, the ability to intuit the viewer's perspective and to use that intuition as a means of affecting the viewer's response is surely a major—if not the primary—criterion of directorial competence. In the specific case of visual syntax, the lack of explicit means for expressing an argument may indeed lead viewers to take a more active role in the construction of meaning. Nevertheless, that fact should not blind us to the possibility that, in the hands of a skillful director, the conclusions at which the viewers arrive may be very substantially those that the director has invited them to draw.

Beyond reminding us that an active viewer is not necessarily an unpredictable viewer, Eisenstein's comments on *October* raise a further issue: What circumstances make a viewer active in the first place? The "God and Country" sequence from *October* is a good illustration of Eisenstein's contention that the viewer's search for meaning is stimulated by the experience of conflict, that is, of an unexpected juxtaposition. As Eisenstein's own analysis of the sequence indicates, the juxtaposition between the Christian image and the other cultures' religious objects was designed to appear paradoxical in the eyes of his largely Christian audience. However, there is also another way in which this sequence would have clashed with the expectations of Eisenstein's viewers. Occurring in the course of a narrative film, the sequence disrupts the forward flow of the narration. This disruption may in itself have enhanced viewers' mental involvement in the interpretation of this part of the film.

Unexpected Juxtapositions and Viewers' Mental Involvement

In the terminology of film scholarship, such rhetorical digressions from a movie's story line are referred to as "extradiegetic," or "outside the story," and there has been some discussion of the difference between extradiegetic arguments or comments, on one hand, and cases in which a director embeds a comment directly into the narrative, on the other. A simple example may help to make this distinction clear. In the final scene of Alfred Hitchcock's *North by Northwest* (1959), the newly married hero and heroine are getting into bed in the sleeping compartment of a speeding train. She helps him onto the bed, they embrace, and then there is a cut to the film's final shot, the train entering a tunnel, as the words "The End" appear on the screen. This cut, which uses visual syntax to suggest a crude analogy or metaphor, was subsequently parodied in *The Naked Gun 2½: The Smell of Fear* (1991). But there is a major difference between the parody and the original. In the parody, the sex scene takes place in an apartment house, and the shot of a train entering a tunnel is brought in out of nowhere, together with a variety of other sexual metaphors (e.g., a rocket blasting off, a dam bursting, exploding fireworks, etc.). So, in *Naked Gun*, as in *October*, the visual comment is extradiegetic. In *North by Northwest*, however, the train is part of the fictional world created by the story, and the sex/train juxtaposition entails a spatial shift within that world in addition to serving as a rhetorical device.

What difference does it make to viewers whether an analogy or other comment is made extradiegetically or is embedded in the narrative? In one of the most detailed examinations of these issues, Clifton (1983) has hypothesized that diegetically embedded comments may be less effective because they are more likely to be overlooked. For instance, in the specific case of the sex/train juxtaposition from *North by Northwest*, Clifton's argument would be that viewers could fail to notice the presence of an intended analogy and simply see the cut as a spatial transition. Such an interpretive option is not available to viewers of the *Naked Gun* sex scene.

How might Clifton's assumptions apply to advertising? Here, too, it is possible to make a distinction between comments or arguments that stand on their own and those that overlap with events inside the space and time of a story line. A relatively straightforward example of this distinction occurred in the presidential campaign videos used by the two major political parties in 1992. Although the overall strategies of the two videos differed considerably, both videos included short references to John F. Kennedy. In the Republican video, pictures of Kennedy were included in a series of images of major presidents of the past. These images were juxtaposed with shots of George Bush, suggesting that Bush was the embodiment of various notable qualities of his predecessors. In the Democratic video, JFK's appearance came in a scene recounting a brief meeting between him and Bill Clinton when Clinton was a young man. As in the Republican video, the juxtaposition between Clinton and Kennedy presumably was intended to suggest some analogy between the presidential aspirant and the former president. However, in the Democratic video, the juxtaposition between Clinton and JFK occurred as part of a story—that is, the formative experiences of Bill Clinton's life—whereas in the Republican case, the juxtaposition was more exclusively rhetorical.

Following Clifton's logic, we could say that the Democratic use of JFK's image was diegetic, and we could assume that the implied analogy between Bill Clinton and John Kennedy was probably less obvious to viewers than the Bush/JFK analogy in the Republican video. Note, however, that, strictly speaking, the latter juxtaposition does not fit Clifton's definition of an extradiegetic comment. For the most part, the Republican video was not structured as a narrative, so there was no story world from which the images of JFK could be seen as departures. It might be more appropriate, then, to label this example "nondiegetic." Indeed, in contrast to movies and fictional TV programs, the syntax of advertising is often entirely nondiegetic. Although TV commercials can and do tell stories—brief dramas in which the use of a product helps the consumer solve some problem or reach some goal—much advertising is constructed purely as an argument (e.g., a comparison between two products or candidates, or an analogy between the product or candidate and some desirable quality or admirable person) without any narrative story line.

Such purely nondiegetic ads may be contrasted with cases that contain both a narrative core and extradiegetic commentary, that is, a comparison or analogy or some other syntactic device that occurs in the context of a story and interrupts the flow of that story. As a case in point, one could consider the 1984 Reagan campaign video discussed in the introduction. In this video, the story of Ronald Reagan's swearing-in as president was interrupted by the interpolation of various scenes with no spatiotemporal connection to that event. Because these interpolations appeared in the midst of a narrative sequence, they fit Clifton's sense of extradiegetic commentary more closely than did the editing in George Bush's 1992 video.

According to Clifton's line of reasoning, we could conclude that both the extradiegetic and the nondiegetic forms of syntax are likely to be more effective than diegetically embedded commentary, because in neither of the former two cases can the presence of a rhetorical device be overlooked in favor of a purely spatiotemporal interpretation of the editing. Furthermore, because nondiegetic syntax is very common in advertising, it also could be argued that extradiegetic cases must be more obtrusive because they involve the disruption of expectations, whereas nondiegetic ads do not. However, these speculations must be tempered with some caution. There are at least two major considerations that complicate any attempt to take Clifton's ideas out of the context of fiction film and apply them to advertising. First of all, unlike the typical movie, most ads are designed to be seen repeatedly over a relatively short time span. Consequently, even if diegetically embedded arguments or propositions do go unnoticed initially, they could become more evident to viewers over time. Indeed, if it gives viewers a reason to keep watching an ad, such a gradual buildup of comprehension may actually work to the ad's advantage.

A second reason for caution in applying Clifton's assumptions to advertising has to do with the nature of advertising narratives. Because of the extreme brevity and lack of development of the incidents shown in TV commercials, the boundary between what is and what is not a story is not always as clear as in the case of feature-length movies. Accordingly, the distinction between extradiegetic and nondiegetic editing sometimes may be blurred. A recent luxury car ad provides a useful illustration of this possibility. The ad shows the driver of this car accelerating to pass another vehicle; at the ad's climax, as the pass is being completed, there is a brief flash of the image of a jet plane. This ad contains a number of the basic ingredients of conventional narratives. There is a central character with whom the viewer is invited to identify; this character is motivated to attain a certain goal; and the overall structure of the events in the ad follows a pattern of rising dramatic interest, reaching a peak just before the final resolution. In this context, the interpolated image of the jet is a fairly unambiguous example of an extradiegetic comment, suggesting an analogy between the speed of the car and the speed of the plane.

Imagine, however, what the ad would look like if we were to take out one or more of its narrative ingredients: for example, showing the car only from the outside, with no shots of the person driving it; or keeping the driver but removing the drama of the successfully executed pass. At some point, stripping away such aspects of the ad would leave us with an event that we could no longer think of as a story: a shot of a car driving down a road, with interpolated images of a jet plane. In fact, at that point, the ad would have become a standard example of nondiegetic syntax. Fitting either the original ad or the completely transformed version into our terminological system is not hard to do. But there are a number of points in between the two extremes that are much more ambiguous and problematic. Because an exact definition of what constitutes a story is notoriously difficult to come by, no further demarcation of the boundaries between extra- and nondiegetic syntax will be attempted here.

Because of the complications outlined above, Clifton's terminology and assumptions have to be loosened considerably to fit the conditions found in advertising. Nevertheless, the questions with which he is concerned are, if anything, even more crucial for advertising than they are for film. How is the syntax of visual commentary or argumentation woven into the broader tapestry of a visual image or sequence of images? How do viewers' expectations about this relationship affect their responses to visual comments? Clifton's distinction between diegetic and other forms of syntax provides one set of answers—admittedly very tentative ones—to these questions. A different, but related, set of answers comes from the work of Whittock (1990). Up to this point, our discussion of visual syntax has dealt exclusively with editing, in the sense of joining one shot to another. However, as Whittock points out, the kinds of syntactic relationships to which shot sequences give rise can also occur within a single image as a result of the juxtaposition between different elements of a visual composition or design.

Visual Juxtapositions Within a Single Image

Whittock illustrates this possibility with a brief scene from the beginning of John Ford's film *The Searchers* (1956). The film opens with a woman looking out at the desert landscape of Monument Valley, Utah. Out of the wilderness, the hero of the film (played by John Wayne) rides slowly toward the camera. He has no human companion, but his figure shares the frame with the towering form of an isolated, rugged butte (see Figure 5.7). Citing an earlier analysis by John F. Scott, Whittock observes that this juxtaposition between the rider and the landscape feature must have been intended as an analogy or metaphor. In other words, a type of visual comment that other directors might have handled through editing is here built into the composition of a single shot.

Figure 5.7.

Whittock's discussion of this scene is very much in line with notions about visual syntax that can be traced back to Eisenstein and other writers or artists of his time. The idea that meaning arises out of juxtaposition is traditionally associated with the term "montage," as used by Eisenstein and others. Today, this term is sometimes thought of as being equivalent to "editing," but in the sense in which it was employed by these earlier writers, it referred not only to sequences of images but also to the relationships among elements in the individual shots of a film or in a single still picture. This conception of montage was particularly influential among designers of political and commercial posters during World War II and in the two decades that preceded it (Teitelbaum, 1992). Since then, similar principles have become a staple of still-image adver- tising in print and in billboards (Barnicoat, 1972).

A magazine ad that is somewhat reminiscent of the opening shot from *The Searchers* has been used by Kodak to promote one of its high-definition films. The primary image in this ad is a present-day cowboy, who is shown in close-up (see Figure 5.8). He is wearing sunglasses and looking into the distance. In the lenses of his glasses, we see a reflection: a solitary, eroded crag, similar in shape to the butte in *The Searchers.* The primary purpose of this reflection is to demonstrate the extraordinarily fine detail that is obtainable with this particular type

Figure 5.8.

of Kodak film (Ektar 25), because the image in the reflection is actually shown to be a magnification made from a tiny 35mm original. However, as in the shot from the movie, the juxtaposition of the reflection with the main image also seems designed to suggest a symbolic connection between the man and the rugged Western landscape. But how likely are viewers to see such a connection?

In discussing the implied analogy in *The Searchers*, Whittock argues that the lack of a cut or other editing device separating the two elements of this analogy makes it relatively unobtrusive, and he assumes that first-time viewers may actually miss the analogy altogether. However, further exposure to the film should make the connection more evident: "After repeated viewings, the appropriateness of it, the link between rider and background, is likely to be more manifest. The metaphor's effect seeps in—it is not thrust upon one" (Whittock, 1990, p. 43). A similar argument could be made about the connection between the cowboy and the reflected landscape in the Kodak ad. Because the presence of the reflection can be attributed primarily to its value as a demonstration of the superior qualities of Kodak's film, viewers may initially be less aware of additional dimensions of meaning.

More generally, the syntax of this ad and of the scene from *The Searchers* could be said to follow a similar principle to the one we have already encountered in our discussion of diegetically embedded editing. In both types of circumstances, a rhetorical connection between two images or two elements of an image coexists with a spatial or temporal relationship. Therefore, the argument that was made before could be applied here too: If a certain juxtaposition can be interpreted "literally," as part of a simple shift in space or time, any additional rhetorical meanings may be less evident to viewers. And the same conclusion drawn before about this situation may also fit the present case: In a medium designed for repeated viewing, meanings that initially are opaque may actually be a desirable feature, because the possibility of uncovering such meanings could serve as an inducement for looking at an ad again.

The analogical or metaphorical linkage of a landscape or other type of background to the central figure of an ad (usually the product itself) is a common feature of advertising imagery. For example, the popular practice of showing a car on top of a hill or mountain, seen in ads for

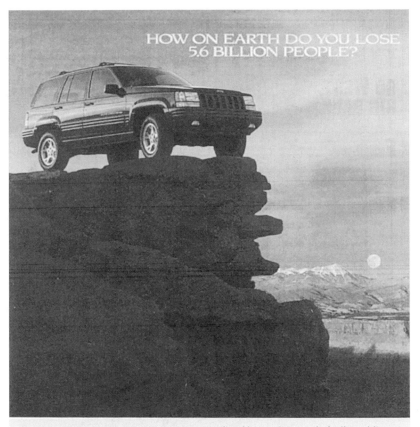

Figure 5.9.

Jeeps, Mazdas, and Toyotas, among others, not only demonstrates the car's superior off-road capabilities but also suggests that it is the "peak" of automotive excellence (see Figure 5.9). In ads of this sort, as in the Kodak ad, the central figure and the background occupy the same space. In all such cases, then, the additional, analogical aspects of the connection between the central object and the background may be less visible to viewers the first time around.

This kind of situation, the blending of a rhetorical comment and a spatial linkage, may be contrasted with cases in which two or more images are brought together solely for the purpose of suggesting an analogy or other conceptual relationship. A case in point is a print ad for Concord, a luxury watch (see Figure 5.10). Here, the product, shown in color, is juxtaposed with an elegant, black-and-white photograph of Monument Valley. This is the same landscape that we encountered in the opening scene from *The Searchers*. In the ad, however, the landscape and the watch are two separate images, linked to each other only through whatever abstract properties they have in common: timeless beauty, perhaps, or enduring value. In other words, this form of visual syntax precludes the option of a purely spatial interpretation. Accordingly, the conceptual links between images that are brought together in this fashion may be more immediately apparent to viewers.

Up to this point, our examination of visual propositions and arguments has been concerned with the ways in which they might be related to the more descriptive or narrative aspects of visual syntax. In the course of this discussion, we have come across a variety of implicit meanings that can arise when two or more images are brought together for rhetorical purposes. In many of the examples in this book, including the most recent ones, the apparent intent of the juxtaposition is to suggest an analogy of some sort, but analogy is by no means the only form of connection entailed in the rhetorical uses of visual syntax. The time has now come to attempt a more systematic account of the kinds of conceptual linkages that are most commonly encountered in the composition and editing of advertisements. Robert Goldman has argued that the "fundamental work accomplished within an advertising space is the connection and exchange of meanings between an object (a named product) and an image (another referent system)" (Goldman, 1992, p. 71). The juxtaposition between products and other images will indeed be the primary focus of the discussion that follows, although other kinds of

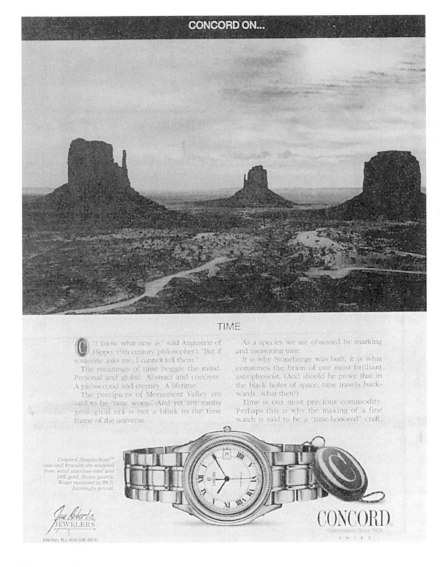

Figure 5.10.

syntactic relationships (e.g., between two components of a single image, as in our Kodak example) will also be addressed.

A TYPOLOGY OF
VISUAL PROPOSITIONS

What kinds of conceptual connections are typically created when advertising images are put next to each other in a sequence or in a single composition? The following four broad categories encompass a wide variety of more specific applications: (a) causal connections; (b) contrasts; (c) analogies; and (d) generalizations. Each of these items will be explained in detail shortly. First, however, it should be stressed that the four categories in this list are not mutually exclusive. Because of the considerable range of meanings that a single image can contain, there is typically more than one sense in which any one image can be connected to another, and advertisements often are deliberately designed to take advantage of such multiple linkages.

A paradigmatic illustration of this possibility occurs in a print ad for Haworth office furniture (see Figure 5.11). The ad is based on the juxtaposition of two images: on the left, a scene of traditional rural life in India, with a pair of Brahma bulls powering a water wheel; on the right, a modern, computerized office equipped by Haworth. The intended connections between these two images are spelled out in the caption: "Each is a proven, time-tested way to deliver power. However, only one is designed to keep sensitive electronic office equipment up and running long after the cows have come home." In short, here we have both an analogy and a contrast coexisting simultaneously in a single juxtaposition. It should be added, however, that the presence of such an unusually explicit verbal explanation of the visual juxtaposition diminishes this ad's relevance with regard to the more general purposes of our discussion, which is concerned primarily with cases in which the visual syntax operates more independently of words. With this observation in mind, let us now turn to an examination of the four categories listed above.

(a) Causality

A useful way of approaching this category is to consider a set of distinctions proposed by Leiss, Kline, and Jhally (1990) in an analysis of the basic formats of commercial advertising. They begin by defining what they call the "product-information format," in which the object or service being sold is the center of attention of the ad (pp. 240-243). They

Figure 5.11.

183

184 ◄◦► VISUAL PERSUASION

distinguish this form of advertising from those cases in which some other object or situation is juxtaposed with the product. In particular, they describe three kinds of things that may be connected to the product in this manner: people, lifestyles, and "images." The first of these three possibilities, which the authors label the "personalized format," links the product to its "typical" users or to models, celebrity endorsers, people who have been transformed by the product, and so on (pp. 246-258). In the "lifestyle format," the emphasis is more on the setting or social context of a product's use than on specific users (pp. 259-263). Finally, the "product-image format" creates a symbolic relationship between the product and "some more abstract and less pragmatic domain than mere utility" (p. 244)—for example, the nature scenes that are juxtaposed with a picture of the product in some cigarette ads (p. 245).

This list gives a fair representation of the various directions that visual syntax is likely to take when it seeks to link a product with someone or something else, and they all demonstrate the following basic point about such linkages. As a rule, whatever else may be happening in them, one element that they all have in common is that of causality. Juxtaposing a product with a celebrity endorser may be a means of certifying the product's value, but it is also likely to contain an implicit promise: If you use this product, you will be associated in other people's minds with some of the same qualities that this celebrity possesses. Showing a product with a typical user or with a lifestyle may serve the practical function of demonstrating how, when, and where the product should be used, but it is also a standard device for suggesting that purchase of the product will enable the customer to be seen as a certain kind of person open to particular forms of interactions with others. Linking a product with an abstract image is often intended as a visual analogy between product and image, but, just as often, it amounts to a claim that the product will lead to the kinds of satisfactions illustrated in the image. In short, most commercial advertising in which a product is juxtaposed with a positive visual portrayal can be seen as implying a causal link between the product and some outcome related to that portrayal.

Within this very broad category of causal syntax in commercial advertising, it may be possible to make a further distinction. For some of the kinds of causal claims made through visual images, we could reasonably ask the question, "Does this claim correspond to facts, or is it a lie?" In other cases, however, such attempts at accountability seem less appropriate. The dividing line between these two situations is not that easy to draw precisely, but the difference between them can be explored by considering two concrete instances. On one hand, think of a typical ad for perfume or cologne: a picture of the product juxtaposed with a romantic encounter between two glamorous people. On the other hand, imagine an ad for vitamin pills in which the product is shown with images of unspoiled nature or vigorous athletic activity. Someone who bought the perfume or cologne and yet experienced no change in her or his sex life might feel let down by the ad, and there may be many media critics and other people who think that such ads raise false hopes. Nevertheless, it is hard to imagine anyone attempting a strict test of veracity or falsehood with an ad of this sort. Would there have to be a poll of consumers to determine how many felt that the product had had the desired effect on their sex lives? Would standards have to be set regarding what should count as a sex-life effect and what should not? The absurdity of such speculations suggests that questions of factual accuracy are somehow inapplicable to an ad of this kind. In the case of the vitamin ad, however, if we were to discover that the vitamin in question has no medically ascertainable effect on health, we might have clear grounds for considering the ad deceptive. (Of course, this does not mean that the ad would necessarily be considered fraudulent in a legal context or that the writer supports legal sanctions against this form of advertising.)

If the contrast that has just been drawn is at all valid, we can go on to ask, What accounts for the difference between these two situations? A likely answer to this question comes from the traditional distinction between factual advertising claims and puffery. This distinction, which ordinarily is applied to the verbal content of ads, is based on the notion that there are certain kinds of statements, such as "Nobody doesn't like Sarah Lee," that no reasonable person expects to be literally true. Such puffery is therefore exempt from the scrutiny to which factual statements are subject. It could be argued that the use of sexual imagery in perfume ads, implying that the perfume will make the user sexually irresistible, is a form of exaggeration analogous to the kinds of verbal slogans mentioned above. If so, the difference between the perfume ad and the vitamin ad could be seen as a visual equivalent of the puffery-factual claim distinction.

These notions are admittedly speculative, but the underlying issues play an important role in commercial advertising, and similar questions could be asked about political advertising as well. We will return to these matters in a later section of this book. For the moment, it should be added that both political and social issue advertising often feature a form of casaul imagery that is quite rare in commercial ads, namely, imputations of blame rather than promises of benefits. The notorious pairing of Michael Dukakis and Willie Horton in attack ads deployed during the 1988 presidential campaign was a case in point (see Jamieson, 1992, Chap. 1). Note, however, that in this instance, the causal implication of this juxtaposition was also spelled out in words quite explicitly, because Dukakis was blamed openly for the parole program that allowed convicted murderer Horton to go out and commit another crime. In that sense, the visual syntax of these ads cannot be seen as a means of expressing an unspoken causal claim. However, it also might be appropriate to interpret the juxtaposition of Dukakis and Horton as an attempt to suggest—without referring to it verbally—some moral equivalence or similarity between the two. If this account of the ad's intentions is fair, then the ad as a whole could be considered a demonstration of the partial concealment of a visual analogy by an overlapping causal claim made both visually and in words. The ad is also another demonstration of the point made earlier about the possible coexistence of more than one type of connection between any one pair of images. As always, this point should be borne in mind as we move to the next item on our list of applications of visual syntax.

(b) Contrast

Juxtaposing two visual images to imply a contrast is not as ubiquitous an advertising device as cause-effect juxtaposition. Still, contrast does appear in several widely used formats of visual persuasion. In commercial advertising, visual contrast is a common feature of at least two kinds of situations, namely, product comparisons and before-and-after juxtapositions. Typically, both situations deploy images as proof of factual claims, as when a side-by-side comparison is used to demonstrate the relative stain-removing power of two laundry detergents, or photographs of the same person before and after dieting are shown as evidence of the effectiveness of a new weight-loss product. In cases such as these, the images ordinarily are accompanied by written text or spoken words that explicitly spell out how the visual syntax is to be interpreted.

Whether through voice-over narration or printed captions, the viewer is told how one image differs from another and what to look for in the juxtaposition between them: a difference in weight between the "before" picture and the "after," a contrast in color between the garment on the left and the one on the right, and so on. In other words, contrasts of this sort are designed to yield up their meaning directly, and the open-endedness of visual syntax is short-circuited by the ads' verbal content.

However, the use of contrast in ads is not always so straightforward a matter. We have already encountered one example of visual contrast with minimal verbal explanation in the 1984 Macintosh commercial that was examined at the beginning of this chapter. Another example occurs in a print ad for *U.S. News and World Report* (see Figure 5.12). This ad contains three hand-drawn pictures arranged in a row. The first panel is a portrait of Karl Marx. The second panel depicts Karl Marx perusing a copy of *U.S. News*. In the third panel we see Karl Marx transformed: His hair and beard are now neatly trimmed, and he is wearing wire-rim glasses, a tie, and red suspenders. The third panel also features a change in background color: In the first two panels, it was red; now it is green. Aside from the name of the magazine, the only other verbal text in the ad is a slogan, "News you can use."

This sequence of images can be seen as a combination of two of the four syntactic categories with which this discussion is concerned. On one hand, there is the juxtaposition between Panels 2 and 3, implying a relationship of cause and effect. On the other hand, there is the contrast between the image of Marx in the first two panels and his image in the third. What are we to make of this contrast? Taking our lead from the verbal slogan, we might conclude that the ad's main goal is to demonstrate just how useful the information in *U.S. News* can be. Even someone as hopelessly out of it as Karl Marx can learn the ways of today's world by reading this magazine. But this interpretation is certainly not the only way of looking at the ad's images. One alternative, which might occur to a viewer who was concerned about liberal bias in the news media, would be to see in the ad an implicit offer of a correction to that bias, that is, to see *U.S. News* as the implied antidote to other news organizations' antibusiness tendencies. Such a view of the ad might be less consonant with the verbal slogan than the first interpretation was, but it could be

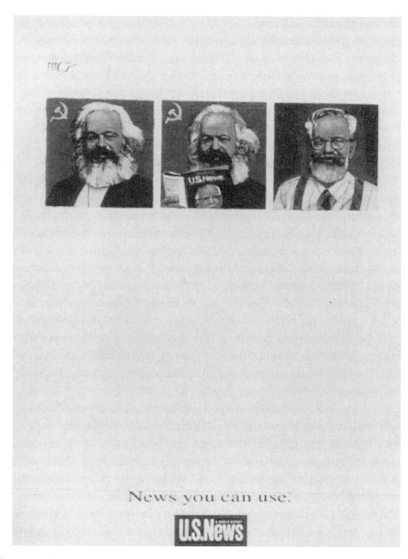

Figure 5.12.

argued that the first interpretation does not provide as good a fit with the political aspects of the ad's images. Of course, as always, these two interpretations should not be seen as mutually exclusive or, indeed, as excluding even further possibilities.

Unlike the kinds of contrast discussed earlier, then, the visual syntax of the *U.S. News* ad serves up a puzzle to the viewer, and the solution to this puzzle will depend to a certain extent on the viewer's own predispositions toward politics, business, and the media. The solution will also depend on the viewer's ability to recognize the drawing of Karl Marx in the first place. Because there is considerable evidence that pictures of historical figures are often unfamiliar to the general public (Messaris, 1994), perhaps this ability should not be taken for granted. The possibility that some viewers might not be able to identify the person in the pictures may seem to be a weakness of the ad. In fact, however, it could be argued that for this particular ad, such a possibility actually constitutes a strength. It seems likely that correct identification of Marx's picture would occur primarily among more educated viewers—to whom the ad was presumably addressed. The ad's images therefore could be seen as a puzzle that only a relatively select group of viewers is equipped to solve, and this characteristic could be considered an enhancement of the ad's overall appeal. Eliciting the interest and approval of a specific type of person is one of the principal goals of commercial advertising; giving viewers a sense that only people like them can discern a particular message may be an effective way of reaching that goal.

In addition to its functions in commercial advertising, there is at least one other area of visual persuasion in which visual contrast is a major feature. This is the area of environmentalist imagery. As noted in Chapter 4, visual media have been used for environmentalist advocacy for more than a century. For much of this period, the predominant category of environmentalist imagery was the pristine landscape, an idealized portrayal of scenery untouched by human activity. At least as early as the Depression, however, this positive image was joined by another, darker vision of damaged land. Eventually, these two strands of environmentalist imagery, the positive and the negative, came to be used in tandem, as montage sequences in a single movie or as two halves of a poster or print ad. Indeed, as Bouse (1991) has found, this kind of positive-negative contrast is now among the most characteristic visual strategies in a broad range of environmentalist media.

A typical positive-negative montage sequence occurs at the very beginning of a short video from the Wilderness Society. Titled *Ancient Forests*, this video was produced a few years ago at the height of public concern about logging in old-growth forests. The video starts out with a sequence of images from an intact forest: immense tree trunks rising into the sky; abundant ferns and mosses and other plant life; sunlight streaming through the dense forest canopy. Initially, these scenes are accompanied by soft nature sounds, but as the sequence progresses, these sounds are gradually replaced by a mechanical whine that begins indistinctly and eventually erupts into the full-throated roar of a chain saw. And then there is a cut to a new set of images: one sawed-off stump after another, until finally, we see a whole mountainside laid bare. This kind of juxtaposition, between mature forest and clearcut, is probably the most common form of positive-negative contrast in today's environmentalist imagery, but there are other forms as well. A striking example described by Bouse (1991) comes from a video about the problems of overcrowding and environmental degradation in some national parks. In a single camera shot taken at Yosemite, we begin with a view of an imposing cliff face, reminiscent of the pristine Yosemite landscapes of Ansel Adams; then, suddenly, the camera's perspective tilts down to the foot of the cliff, and the image is filled with a swarming mass of tourists.

It is instructive to examine the environmentalist uses of visual contrast in relation to the broader question of the difference between images and words as instruments of persuasion. Verbal denunciations of such environmental hazards as deforestation or tourist intrusions on wilderness are couched routinely in technical terms: species habitat depletion, ecosystemic impacts, and so on. This technical orientation makes it possible for environmentalists to present their arguments as the fruits of scientific wisdom. When representatives of the forest products industries bring up economic considerations, or when people in the tourism business talk about the public's need for recreation, environmentalists' verbal responses typically entail appeals to a broader, more objective view of the very same principles: economics, public health, or what have you. But the terms of the debate seem to shift significantly when one turns to the visual aspects of environmentalist rhetoric. As the examples we have just examined suggest, in the visual imagery of environmentalism, the primary appeal appears to be not to science but, rather, to aesthetic considerations. Although the soundtrack may refer to technical matters or abstract values, the immediate impression that the viewer is likely to derive from the visual sequences is this: Clearcuts are bad because they're ugly, and tourism is bad because crowds are unpleasant. These are messages that an environmentalist advocate might be reluctant to put into words. They seem too vulnerable to dismissal on grounds of superficiality or elitism. But because of the open-ended, implicit nature of meaning in visual syntax, equivalent messages can be expressed with much greater impunity through images. If we grant the possibility that visceral, not very reflective, not very scientific responses to the images may be highly effective for some viewers—perhaps even more effective than the more objective verbal arguments—then what we have here is one more demonstration of the power that stems from visual images' lack of an explicit syntax.

(c) Analogy

We have already come across several examples of this category of visual syntax earlier in this chapter. In the history of cinema, analogical juxtaposition or montage is among the clearest precursors of the syntactic devices that are now found in visual advertising. If there is a single scene that can be considered the origin of this tradition, that scene is the one from Eisenstein's *Strike* (1925), in which a massacre of striking workers by government troops is intercut with shots of animals being butchered in a slaughterhouse. This extradiegetic use of analogical cross-cutting for rhetorical purposes made a big impression on Eisenstein's contemporaries, and he had any number of imitators, not only in Moscow but also in Hollywood, where Charlie Chaplin's notorious comparison between factory workers and sheep (*Modern Times*, 1936) was one of many direct copies of Soviet-style editing. Eventually, though, extradiegetic analogies became a rarity in fictional movies. As film critic Andre Bazin (1967) argued, the interruption of a movie's story line by the insertion of an extraneous image may have been incompatible with Hollywood cinema's increasing tendency toward unobtrusive narration. Consequently, when such an interruption is encountered in more recent movies (e.g., the *Naked Gun* sex scene discussed earlier) it is almost invariably a deliberate parody.

In contrast to its eclipse in movies, extradiegetic analogy has become one of the standard techniques of visual persuasion in both commercial and political advertising. For instance, in the single category of automotive ads, one can encounter analogies to lions (Toyota), tigers (Exxon), cheetahs (BMW), military aircraft (Dodge, Honda, Jaguar, etc.), and Fabergé eggs (Lincoln) (see Figure 5.13). It may be worth noting that

Figure 5.13.

analogical editing is also common in music videos, such as Madonna's "Take a Bow," in which a sex scene is intercut with a bullfight. Here, as in the case of the car/animal juxtapositions listed above, the enduring influence of Eisensteinian montage principles seems especially clear (Prince, 1990).

Why should advertisers want to display their products in conjunction with images of lions, tigers, and the like? A major reason, of course, is that the juxtaposed image may have the power to affect viewers more strongly than can a picture of the product itself. To people surrounded by cars and images of cars, a lion or a tiger is likely to be a more arresting spectacle. However, there is more to it than that. As far as the fundamental characteristics of visual syntax are concerned, the principal function of analogical juxtaposition is its capacity to act as a partial substitute for adjectives and adverbs—two types of meaning that images cannot express directly. If the creator of an ad wants to make the point that a certain car is powerful, the verbal text can convey this message explicitly, through such words as "dynamic," "breathtaking," "supercharged," or, indeed, "powerful." When it comes to the ad's pictorial content, though, this aspect of verbal syntax, the adjective-noun relationship, has no direct visual counterpart. One alternative, then, is simply to show an image of the car accelerating rapidly and trust the viewer to make the appropriate inference. Another alternative—which will seem particularly attractive to the advertiser if the car's acceleration does not appear that impressive on film—is to resort to analogical juxtaposition. Showing the car next to some other object or entity that also possesses power increases the likelihood that the viewer will get the point, not so much because of the doubling of powerful objects as because the juxtaposition should lead the viewer to intuit what it is that they have in common.

Whereas the basic function of analogical juxtaposition may be to act as a stand-in for adjectives or adverbs, as far as its structure is concerned it is more reminiscent of the verbal simile. Both simile and analogical juxtaposition bring together two different entities to make a comparison between them: "This car is as powerful as a tiger, as fast as a jet plane, etc." The fundamental difference between the verbal figure of speech and the visual construction is that the basis of the comparison—power, speed, or whatever—can be stated explicitly through words but must always remain implicit in the case of the images. There is also another important difference between words and images in this area: Ordinarily, a verbal simile indicates explicitly which of the two entities being compared is the starting point of the comparison (e.g., the car) and which is being brought in as an analogue (a tiger, a jet plane, etc.). Images, on the other hand, have no explicit means of making this distinction, and there are circumstances in which it actually can become meaningless.

As an example, the Madonna sex/bullfight sequence mentioned earlier can be seen as a comment about sex, but it probably can also be seen as a comment about the kind of thrill that some people get from watching men engage in violent sports. In other words, the sequence is both about the violent aspects of sex and about the sexual aspects of violence. Of course, in the case of advertising, such a bidirectionality is much less likely to occur because the viewer's automatic assumption will be that the starting point or target of the comparison is the product itself. This assumption is the basis of a print ad for Toshiba copiers, in which the product is shown next to a picture of Old Faithful (see Figure 5.14). In the absence of any caption, the viewer presumably would see the ad as a routine example of analogical syntax: The copier is as reliable as Old Faithful. But the caption reverses the direction of the comparison, implying that it is the copier and not Old Faithful that sets the standard for reliability. This clever play on the viewer's expectations is made possible by the fact that, in principle, the visual juxtaposition can indeed be read both ways.

In taxonomies of verbal figures of speech, similes traditionally have been distinguished from metaphors, although the latter term also can be used more inclusively to encompass both figures. Whereas similes maintain a separation between the two entities that are being compared, metaphors involve the substitution of one entity for another. Accordingly, the Exxon slogan "Put a tiger in your tank" is a metaphor, which can be turned into a simile by separating the tiger from the gasoline: "Exxon is as powerful as a tiger" or "With Exxon in your gas tank, your car will be as powerful as a tiger." If analogical juxtaposition is partially equivalent to a simile, is there some aspect of visual syntax that is equivalent to the simile-metaphor distinction?

A print ad for Saab, which we discussed in a different context in Chapter 1, provides a suggestive answer to this question. This ad is based on two kinds of similarities between a person and a car: a visual similarity and a conceptual one. Visually, as many observers have noted, the fronts of all cars bear some resemblance to human faces (headlights = eyes, front grille = mouth, etc.). The conceptual similarity is specific to this particular car. Presumably, the ad's basic point is that this car is made

Figure 5.14.

so intelligently that it functions as if it were an extension of the driver's body. If the ad had been designed according to conventional principles of analogical juxtaposition—that is, as a visual simile—the car and the man's face would appear separately from each other. In fact, however, in the ad as it actually is, the car replaces the top of the man's head, blending smoothly with the rest of his features. By virtue of this substitution, the ad may be considered a visual equivalent of a metaphor as described above. This particular type of visual metaphor, in which one object actually blends into another, was formerly confined primarily to print ads, perhaps for technical reasons. But the advent of computerized morphing has made it much easier to do this kind of thing in video too. Nowadays, the car and the tiger in Exxon's TV commercials trade shapes smoothly.

Although montage-style juxtaposition may be the most distinctive type of analogical syntax, the use of analogy in visual advertising is also capable of taking other, less obtrusive forms. Consider the case of a print ad whose task is to draw attention to the elegant styling of a car. A traditional montage approach to this task might result in an ad featuring two images side by side: on one hand, the car; on the other, some other embodiment of elegance. In fact, such a design was actually used a number of years ago in an Oldsmobile ad in which the car was juxtaposed with a pair of ice skaters striking a classic pose. But what if the ad's creators decide on a less symbolic representation, featuring a picture of the car against a more realistic background, parked in a driveway, for instance, or pulling up in front of a restaurant? The chances are that even in such circumstances, the ad will contain features designed to serve as analogues—albeit less obvious ones—of the qualities that the viewer is intended to discern in the product itself. The architectural style of any buildings shown in the background; the clothing of any people shown in or with the car; even such seemingly peripheral features as the font employed in the ad's verbal text are all likely to be chosen for their ability to echo the car's elegance. In this sense, then, it could be said that analogy is bound to be a basic organizing principle of any well-designed ad.

(d) Generalization

As an introduction to the final item in our list of categories of visual syntax, let us examine a pair of print ads for Johnny Walker whisky (see Figures 5.15 and 5.16). The overall messages of the two ads overlap

Figure 5.15, and Figure 5.16.

197

somewhat, and there is a common theme: People everywhere enjoy Johnny Walker. But the ads differ radically from each other in the way in which this theme is expressed. One of the ads takes what might be called a literal approach, actually showing a picture of the entire earth as seen from space. In the other ad, however, the idea of Johnny Walker's universality is conveyed by stringing together a number of landmarks from specific places around the globe: London's Big Ben, Paris's Eiffel Tower, a Kyoto temple, and so forth. It is this concatenation of individual images that interests us at this point. What we have here is the expression of a generalization—"everywhere on earth," "in all parts of the world," and so on—through the presentation of several concrete examples of what the generalization is about. This syntactic device is popular in both print and television advertising. One of the forms it takes in TV commercials is the so-called vignette ad, in which quick flashes of various people or activities or lifestyles are woven together to create a generalized portrait of "the Pepsi generation" or the kind of person who uses Microsoft computer software.

Why use a number of images to imply a generalization, instead of conveying it in a single picture or verbal slogan? Sheer quantity is not necessarily an advantage. For many viewers, the Johnny Walker earth-from-space image may be more compelling than the series of landmarks in the other ad. However, the landmark collage does suggest certain shades of meaning that are absent from the picture of the globe. The cities represented by these landmarks—London, Paris, Kyoto, and so on—are mostly places with an aura of sophistication, cosmopolitanism, and glamor. It is very easy to imagine a different collection of cities that would be equally international and yet would have none of these added qualities. Moreover, such qualities as cosmopolitanism or sophistication are somewhat more abstract and elusive than the basic notion that a certain product is enjoyed everywhere. An ad could attempt to convey these more elusive qualities in a single image—a smartly dressed couple sipping Johnny Walker in a Parisian cafe, let us say—but for every concrete manifestation of an abstraction, there is the risk that viewers may miss the specific connotations that the image has been designed to convey. To some viewers, a Parisian cafe by itself may signify old-world culture or traditional cuisine more than cosmopolitanism or sophistication or glamor. Creating a collage of multiple individual examples—not only Paris but also London and other cities—may increase the chances that the viewer will form the desired aggregate impression of the intended meaning by intuitively grasping what it is that the various images have in common.

There is considerable similarity between the kind of image sequence with which we are concerned here and Eisenstein's "God and Country" sequence from *October*, discussed earlier in this chapter. Both situations entail the accumulation of individual instances for the purpose of implying a generalization. But the sequence from *October* has an additional, complicating factor. The various religious images that were intended as demonstrations of the "primitive" origins of all religion were counterposed collectively to the single image of Christianity. In analytical terms, therefore, the entire sequence could be seen as a combination of two different syntactic relationships: on one hand, the stringing together of individual manifestations of a more general point; on the other hand, the application of this generalization to one further, special instance.

Variations on this kind of two-part structure are employed widely in present-day advertising. In an environmentalist ad produced for the Advertising Council, this structure was adapted to the parameters of the printed page. The ad features two rows of four images each (see Figure 5.17). The first six (read from left to right and top to bottom) are photographs of the eyes of various animals. The final image is a photograph of a human baby's eye. The caption reads, "Sooner or later, you'll come across an endangered species you care about." But this is a good example of a situation in which the caption is not simply a verbal translation of the visual message. In fact, the visual message can be read as an argument against the assumption expressed in the words. The point of the images is presumably that we should care about the rest of nature as lovingly as we care for a human child—and, conversely, that if the rest of nature suffers, human children eventually will suffer too. Despite the fact that this ad uses a print format whereas Eisenstein worked in film, the essential principle on which the ad is based is very close to the formula Eisenstein created in *October*. The most important difference between the two is that the ad's "target" image, that is, the human child, shows up at the end of the sequence, whereas *October*'s image of Christianity comes at the very beginning. But in each case, the particular arrangement of the images emerges from the specific requirements of the context, and it surely would be fruitless to try to formulate a general rule for choosing one over the other.

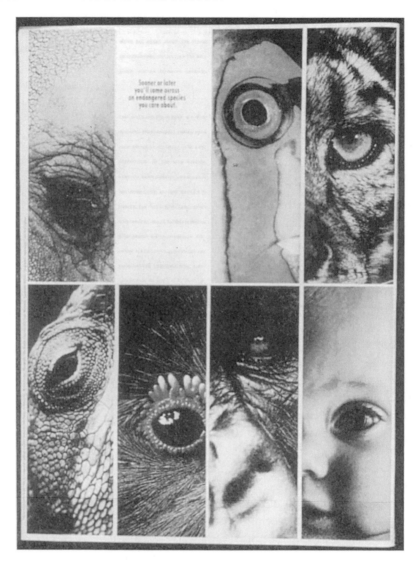

Figure 5.17.

All the same, it does seem to be true that the standard practice in contemporary advertising is to position the "target" image at the end of sequences that use this overall two-part structure. Sequences of this sort have become especially common in political ads, such as a 30-second TV spot used by Angus King, an Independent, in his 1994 campaign for Governor of Maine. King was running against the incumbent governor, and the aim of this particular ad was to associate King with progress and change. The ad consisted of four pairs of images shown in sequence. Each pair was accompanied on the soundtrack by the words, "This is change [Image #1]. This is not [Image #2]." The entire sequence went as follows:

- an astronaut in a space suit ("change")
- a mummy wrapped in gauze ("not")
- a Boeing 747 taking off ("change")
- a man peddling an old-fashioned flying machine ("not")
- a computer-graphics display ("change")
- an old-time telephone switchboard ("not")
- Angus King, casually dressed, with supporters ("change")
- the incumbent, in business suit, in front of lectern ("not")

The ad's concluding lines were "Angus King. This change will do us good."

This ad provides a clear and straightforward illustration of the possibility of combining two different forms of visual syntax in a single, interlocking design. Each pair of images contains a contrast, whereas the overall sequencing of the pairs generalizes this contrast and extends it to the final pair, the pictures of King and his opponent. The intent of the visual generalization is also expressed in words: change versus not change. Note, however, that there is a subtle difference between what the words are saying and what the images seem to be about. The pictures of the mummy, the flying machine, and the switchboard are not just examples of lack of change; in comparison to the way things are today, in the 1990s, these pictures are actually emblems of extreme obsolescence, of a remote past, even of death (in the case of the mummy). Likewise, the pictures that represent change do so not by showing us the future but by portraying the dynamic technologies of the present. The implication that emerges from these two contrasting streams of images is that Angus King is in touch with what is happening in today's world, whereas his opponent is out of it, stuck in the past. Compared to the ad's verbal soundtrack, which doesn't specify what change is being offered, this visual message seems more compelling. Indeed, one might ask whether there was any need here for words in the first place. If the verbal message is less effective than the visual one, what, if anything, do the words contribute? A likely answer is that they make it easier for the viewer to get a sense of the ad's overall structure. The soundtrack's repetition of the same verbal formula four times in a row makes it obvious immediately that the accompanying images also should be interpreted as a sequence of four pairs, whereas without the soundtrack, the clustering into pairs might have been somewhat less self-evident.

The relationship between images and words in the Angus King ad touches on a more general point about what can be done with images in advertising. Because of the lack of explicitness of visual syntax, and the consequent demands that are placed on the viewer's interpretive faculties, there is a limit to the syntactic complexity that images can be expected to convey reliably by themselves. Although exceptional instances of elaborate and precedent-defying syntax certainly do occur, most advertising, whether in print or on television, tends not to stray very far from the four basic syntactic categories that we have reviewed here. Indeed, the Angus King spot, with its combination of syntactic relationships—a contrast, a generalization, and the addition of a "target" item to the latter—represents a relatively high degree of structural intricacy for an ad.

As this ad demonstrates, one way of attaining complexity in visual syntax is to repeat or combine items from our list of four syntactic categories. In turn, it could be argued that these four categories are themselves the products of a more elementary set of structural links. More specifically, it seems that the four categories can be derived from two underlying syntactic operations: on one hand, causal connection; on the other, comparison. The first of these two operations corresponds to the first item in our list of four syntactic categories. All three of the remaining categories arguably are the result of an underlying comparison. If the intention of the comparison is positive (i.e., if the point is to draw attention to a similarity between two things), then the outcome is an analogy. If the intention of the comparison is negative (i.e., if it is aimed at indicating a dissimilarity), the outcome is a contrast. If a comparison is positive and repeated, the outcome is a generalization.

In the abstract, then, the visual syntax of advertising may be described in terms of a relatively small number of basic categories and underlying operations. In practice, however, these categories and operations inevitably entail nuances of meaning that can complicate the picture considerably. Think of the difference between two print ads that were both featured in a single campaign for *U.S. News and World Report*: on one hand, the Karl Marx ad discussed earlier; on the other hand, an ad that used a similar three-panel format and was based on Emmanuel Leutze's familiar painting of George Washington crossing the Delaware. In the first panel, we see a left-to-right reversal of the scene from the painting, with Washington headed in the wrong direction. In the second panel, he is still heading in the wrong direction, but he is reading a copy of *U.S. News*. The final panel, post-*U.S. News*, shows the scene as Leutze depicted it, with Washington now proceeding correctly. Both of these ads are examples of before-and-after contrast, but beyond this commonality, there is substantial disparity in the implications of their syntactic structure. The progression of the panels in the Marx ad, from communism to capitalism, invites the viewer to relate this particular before-and-after contrast to the broader sweep of recent history and to see *U.S. News* as an intellectual force in that history. Such far-reaching implications are less readily discernible in the structure of the Washington ad, which, despite its historical content, is essentially just a sight gag, because the change in Washington's direction of travel—neither an actual historical event nor, in any obvious sense, a metaphor—seems meaningful only in terms of Leutze's painting. In short, even two ads produced from a common template can differ markedly in their syntactic connotations. From the viewer's perspective, then, interpreting an ad's syntax is not just a matter of registering the presence of such abstract categories as contrast, analogy, and so on. These categories should be thought of as frameworks for further interpretation, not as the interpretive process's final goal.

VIEWERS' INTERPRETATIONS
OF VISUAL SYNTAX

What do viewers make of visual syntax? Do they have an intuitive sense of the various syntactic devices we have examined so far? Do they have a conscious understanding of these devices—an understanding that they could communicate to others? How are these interpretational skills affected by experience with visual media? Up to this point, our discussion of visual syntax has been based mainly on theory rather than empirical evidence. It is time to turn to some data.

A reasonable starting point is the following question: Is there any evidence that viewers actually do make the kinds of syntactic connections that the creators of ads want them to make? This question has been addressed directly in an experiment by Mitchell and Olson (1981). The experiment was based on four versions of a print ad for an imaginary brand of tissues. The first version contained a picture of the product but no other image. Instead, there was verbal text declaring that the tissues were soft. In each of the other three versions, the picture of the product was juxtaposed with an image, but there was no text. The three juxtaposed images were a kitten, a sunset, and an abstract painting, respectively. Each of the four versions of the ad was shown to a separate group of viewers; the viewers were then asked to rate various aspects of the product and the ad. For our purposes, the key finding is this: Both the verbal text and the image of the kitten produced higher ratings of the tissues' softness than did the other two images. Moreover, the softness rating for the kitten image was even higher than the one for the text.

What do these results tell us? In our earlier discussion of four major categories of visual syntax, it was noted that visual communication does not have an explicit equivalent of adjectives or adverbs, and that a common way of making up for this lack in advertising is to employ a visual analogy. That appears to have been the effective function of the tissue-kitten juxtaposition for the viewers in this study. In other words, this juxtaposition evidently was taken as an analogy. What this study shows, then, is that at least this one form of visual syntax is capable of getting the point across as well as—or even better than—a verbal statement.

As a demonstration of the ability of a visual juxtaposition to convey a claim about a product, Mitchell and Olson's experiment could be considered the definitive study of viewers' potential comprehension of visual syntax. Still, because the viewers' exposure to the ads was controlled by the experimenter, their interpretations may not have been entirely representative of what happens during the more casual, routine perusal of magazine ads or TV commercials. It would be useful to have supplementary data reflecting people's responses to ads encountered in their everyday viewing of visual media. In an attempt to measure such responses, Zuckerman (1990) studied high school students' ratings of ads that had appeared previously in magazines that these students were known to read.

Zuckerman's study was conducted with a group of high school seniors enrolled in a multisection introductory psychology course. Some time before the main part of the study, a preliminary survey was used to collect data on the students' magazine reading habits. Guided by these data, Zuckerman put together a sample of magazine ads that most of the students were likely to have come across during the preceding months. Her major goal in the construction of this sample was to come up with ads in which a visual juxtaposition adds something distinctive to the meaning of a product. A prototypical example of what she was after is the case of Marlboro cigarettes. Before the appearance of Marlboro's Western ads in the 1950s, filtered cigarettes were considered a woman's product, at a time when there were considerably fewer female smokers than male. The introduction of the Marlboro man was an attempt to impart a new, masculine image to filters. So, if we were to find that people do indeed think of Marlboros as being masculine, we could conclude with some confidence that this finding must have been due to the advertising, rather than to any inherent attributes of the product itself. This line of reasoning served as the template for Zuckerman's study design and the selection of her sample ads.

As in the Marlboro example, all of the ads in Zuckerman's sample entailed a juxtaposition between the product and some other image that could be seen as adding a distinctive quality to the product's meaning. In terms of our category scheme for visual syntax, these juxtapositions all would be characterized as some combination of analogy and causality. For instance, Marlboro advertising can be seen as implying either similarity (just as the cowboy is masculine, so are the cigarettes) or a cause-effect connection (smoking Marlboros makes you masculine) or, indeed, both of these at the same time. In a further attempt to investigate whether viewers' perceptions of the products were due to the juxtaposed images rather than whatever qualities the products might have had inherently, Zuckerman's sample included pairs of ads for similar products but with different images. In the case of cigarettes, for example, a Marlboro ad was paired with an ad for Benson & Hedges, whose ad campaign at the time featured images of wealthy, cosmopolitan-looking people in urban settings. If it can be assumed that there is nothing in these two brands of cigarettes themselves that makes them either urban or rural, an examination of viewers' perceptions of each of the two brands becomes a reasonable basis on which to assess the contribution that the respective images may have made to those perceptions.

After the complete sample of ads had been assembled, Zuckerman used the ads to create two sets of slides: on one hand, pictures of the products by themselves, extracted from the rest of the ads (a pack of Marlboros, a pack of Benson & Hedges, etc.); on the other hand, the associated images by themselves (cowboys on horseback, people in evening wear preparing an elegant meal, etc.). The high school class in which the study was conducted was divided into two smaller groups, and each subgroup was shown one of the two sets of slides. Both subgroups were asked to rate each slide on a set of 5-point, bipolar adjective scales (e.g., urban-rural, masculine-feminine). The same scales (a total of 23) were used for all the slides, although of course not all of the scales were equally relevant in every case.

The results of this procedure can be summarized compactly as follows. There was a strong tendency for the ratings of the products to match the ratings of their associated images; there was also a corresponding tendency for the ratings of each pair of products to diverge from one another. So, whereas the pack of Marlboros and the cowboys received ratings of 1.67 and 1.15, respectively, on the masculine-feminine scale, the corresponding ratings for the pack of Benson & Hedges and its associated image (which included a woman) were 3.82 and 3.35. Similarly, on the urban-rural scale, the numbers for Marlboro were 3.39 (product) and 4.41 (image), whereas Benson & Hedges received 1.82 (product) and 1.97 (image). In interpreting these results, it should be borne in mind that the ratings of the products were produced by a different subgroup of viewers from the ones who rated the images. In other words, the convergence in these two sets of figures cannot be the result of viewers' deliberately adjusting the numbers to make them match. Zuckerman assumes that the product ratings that she obtained in the study reflect perceptions that were formed before the study, in the course of the viewers' prior exposures to the same advertising campaigns that she included in her sample. Because the product ratings (by one subgroup of viewers) matched the ratings of the associated imagery (by the other subgroup), she concludes that those earlier perceptions of the products must have been shaped by the juxtaposed images that had appeared with them originally and that she was now testing separately.

In short, the findings support the conclusion that the visual syntax in these advertising campaigns had worked as intended.

Can Viewers Articulate Their Awareness of Visual Syntax?

Zuckerman's study was a rare attempt to investigate product perceptions that were presumably formed through exposure to the visual syntax of real advertisements, encountered in natural circumstances. As such, this study complements the more common approach represented by Mitchell and Olson, whose experiment employed ads that were created specifically for that occasion and that viewers had never seen before. What neither of these studies tells us, though, is how aware the viewers were of the visual devices to which they were reacting. Did they have an explicit understanding of the visual syntax in the ads, or were their responses the result of a more unconscious mental process? A major reason for scholarly interest in this topic is the likelihood that explicit awareness of visual syntax, or any other persuasive device, may make viewers more discriminating in their responses to advertising.

Among scholars as well as advertising practitioners, it is commonly assumed that viewers often do not have such an awareness. Rossiter and Percy (1983) have suggested that the "mere association of a product with a positively evaluated stimulus such as an attractive picture . . . may be sufficient to alter attitude toward the product without any 'rational' belief change preceding the effect" (p. 112). Likewise, people in the advertising industry itself routinely refer to the belief that juxtaposed imagery can impart meaning to a product through unconscious association, along the lines of so-called Pavlovian conditioning (i.e., the phenomenon investigated in the classic psychological experiment involving a dog, a bowl of food, and the ringing of a bell). This assumption is expressed succinctly in the title of an article by Stout (1984): "Pavlov founded advertising because he showed that imagery could be transferred."

In an attempt to investigate viewers' ability to articulate an understanding of visual syntax, Karen Nielsen and I conducted a study based on two ads, one commercial and the other political (Messaris & Nielsen, 1989). The political ad was an extract from the 1984 Reagan campaign video described in the introduction. As noted at the time, this video's editing structure, a back-and-forth juxtaposition between Ronald Reagan's 1981 inauguration and early morning scenes of Americans going to work, could be taken either as an analogy (Reagan = man of the people) or as a causal link (Reagan has put people back to work). The other ad used in the study was a TV commercial for Smucker's fruit preserves, in which the product was juxtaposed with scenes of traditional life on the farm, suggesting an equivalence in wholesomeness between the former and the latter. These ads were shown to viewers of two different educational levels (high school or below vs. college or above) as well as a group of TV professionals employed in production. Only one of the two ads was shown to each viewer.

After each screening, the viewers were interviewed individually regarding their interpretations of the ads. The ultimate goal of these interviews was to establish whether the viewers had made any explicit, nonnarrative connections between the two sets of images featured in each ad (e.g., "Smucker's jelly is wholesome just like the pictures—typical middle-American pictures"; "It's an attempt to relate Ronald Reagan with down-home American values"). The numbers of viewers who did make such connections varied considerably depending on educational level and professional experience. Among the TV professionals, the numbers in question were: 100% for the Smucker's ad, 87% for the Reagan video. The corresponding figures were 100% and 59% among the college-educated viewers versus 50% and 22% among their less educated counterparts.

A Nonverbal Assessment of Viewers' Awareness

These findings appear to support the assumption that substantial numbers of viewers—especially people with relatively lower levels of education—may not have an explicit understanding of the analogical or cause-and-effect implications of visual syntax. But a major objection can readily be raised against this conclusion. Because of the study's reliance on viewers' own verbal explanations of their interpretations, it is entirely conceivable that the data may reflect facility with language rather than what actually went on in the viewers' minds. The less educated viewers may have understood the purpose of the ads' visual syntax but lacked an appropriate vocabulary for expressing that understanding. Although every effort was made to adjust for this possibility in the analysis of the interview transcripts, it clearly would be very helpful to have an alternative, less verbal means of assessing people's awareness of visual structure.

I have made a tentative move in that direction using a traditional nonverbal technique for the investigation of people's cognitive frameworks (e.g., see Carroll & Casagrande, 1958; Meyers, 1984). The technique's central feature is a classification task. As adapted for present purposes, this task employs magazine ads and involves the following procedure. Initially, viewers are shown a single "target ad" by itself. Then they are shown two more ads, side by side with the target ad. One of the two new ads is similar to the target ad in terms of visual syntax. The other new ad has a different visual structure, but the content of its image(s) is similar to the content of the target ad. For example, one combination we have tested begins with an ad for Oneida silverware in which an image of the product is juxtaposed with a picture of a puppy in a store window (see Figure 5.18). This juxtaposition was apparently intended as an analogy, a fact that is hinted at in the accompanying slogan: "Some things you decide with your heart." The implication is that one should yield to the attractions of Oneida silverware just as one gives in to the appeal of a cute puppy. Following this target ad, we show viewers a BMW ad and an ad for Program flea-control tablets (see Figures 5.19 and 5.20). In the BMW ad, the image of the car is juxtaposed with a picture of a cheetah. As in the case of the target ad, this is an analogical construction (both BMW and the cheetah are characterized by superior swiftness and beauty), but the content of the associated image is different. The Program ad simply shows a cute dog receiving the product. Here the content is virtually identical to that of the target ad, but there is no analogical syntax.

The viewer's task in all of this is to match the target ad with one of the two other ads. Each viewer is instructed to choose whichever of the two other ads seems to be—in her or his own judgment—closest to the target ad in its strategy. It is left up to the individual viewer to decide what constitutes each ad's strategy, and there are no other instructions (and, of course, no reference to the distinctions explained above). The methodological assumption behind this kind of procedure, as it has been used in previous research, is that the viewer's choice reveals which of the two alternative classificatory criteria (in our case, content vs. syntax)

Figure 5.18, Figure 5.19, and Figure 5.20.

is most salient to him or her. Because there is always a possibility that viewers might choose at random or use criteria that were not envisioned by the researcher, some versions of this procedure also call for a verbal explanation of each choice. However, regardless of whether such verbal explanations are included, research employing this procedure typically entails a series of several matching tasks, not just one or two. If a certain type of response (e.g., matching by content rather than syntax) is repeated across several different combinations of ads (or other kinds of stimuli), the need for verbal explanations is diminished, and it becomes more feasible to confine the data to purely nonverbal responses.

As a first step in developing a nonverbal method for the assessment of viewers' awareness of visual syntax, this procedure was tried out in an introductory undergraduate course in visual communication. The testing was done at the beginning of the semester to avoid any influence of the course's content on the outcome. On the other hand, substantial numbers of students had had other courses or practical experience in visual media. It became possible, therefore, to study whether these previous experiences would make any difference in the students' responses. As it happened, the results contained no evidence of such a difference. The responses to the matching tasks exhibited a pronounced pattern that remained the same for both the more experienced and the less experienced students. Regardless of their background knowledge about visual media, the majority of the students—between 70% and 80% for each specific combination of ads—matched the ads according to visual syntax rather than content. This trend occurred across a wide range of matching tasks, but there were two notable exceptions that shared a common characteristic. Whereas all the other matching tasks used ads with two-part or simple repetitive structures, in both of the exceptional cases, the ads' visual structures entailed a three-part interplay among as many separate images. For example, there was a target ad in which a bottle of perfume is juxtaposed with a kissing couple—a standard convention—but also with a fluttering swan—not so standard (see Figure 5.21). Although viewers had the option of matching this to another three-part ad, featuring a bottle of nutritional supplements, a body-builder, and a charging bull (see Figure 5.22), 82% chose the alternative option, a fashion ad with a model whose looks and pose were similar to those of the kissing-couple woman (see Figure 5.23).

Figure 5.21, Figure 5.22, and Figure 5.23.

The relatively low numbers for the three-part ads do not necessarily mean that the students were completely unaware of these ads' structures. A viewer could have some level of understanding of an ad's visual syntax and yet still consider the actual content of the images to be the more important aspect of the ad's strategy. Consequently, although these results do suggest that simple visual structures are more salient than complex ones in the eyes of viewers, it would be inappropriate to treat the numbers quoted above as estimates of absolute levels of awareness. The relationship between awareness and type of visual syntax certainly needs to be explored further with a more extensive sample of advertisements. Further research is also needed on the relationship between awareness and viewers' background experiences. The fact that performance on the matching tasks was not affected by previous media experience suggests the possibility that our earlier findings with the Reagan and Smucker's ads may indeed be artifacts of the verbal nature of the tests employed in that study. However, to be able to make such a judgment more confidently, we would have to have data from a broader range of educational levels and types of media experience.

Does Awareness Lead to Critical Viewing?

As noted above, a major reason for being concerned about viewers' explicit awareness of visual syntax is the possibility that awareness may lead to a more skeptical or critical attitude toward potentially misleading uses of visual media. This is a widely held assumption, but not all advertising critics subscribe to it. It has been challenged most memorably in Kiku Adatto's (1993) analysis of the 1988 presidential campaign. Adatto observed that much of the news and editorial commentary about that campaign dealt with advertising and other aspects of campaign imagery, as opposed to the candidates' positions on substantive issues. And yet this heightened news media attention to political image-making did not seem to be accompanied by a more critical attitude on the part of the public at large. Indeed, it is tempting to conclude that some viewers may have ended up appraising the campaigns on the basis of the quality of their images rather than the practical consequences of the candidates' statements.

A similar conclusion emerges from a study by Enoh Ebong (1989). As part of an investigation of viewers' responses to political imagery, Ebong tested a type of visual juxtaposition that is a staple feature of politicians' self-presentations in TV ads, posters, and campaign literature. This type of syntax involves the juxtaposition between a politician and an image representing the kinds of values that he or she supports. In Ebong's study, these images included shots of rural landscapes (support for agriculture and/or environmentalism); soldiers and military equipment (defense); family members; and flags (patriotism). Viewers were shown still pictures incorporating these various juxtapositions. For the most part, the pictures were taken from the printed campaign literature of politicians running for the U.S. Senate in states outside the middle-Atlantic region in which the study was conducted.

Viewers' responses to these pictures were elicited through individual interviews. In some of these responses, explicit comments on the juxtapositions did go hand in hand with a skeptical attitude—just as many media critics would have predicted or hoped. For instance, one viewer made the following remarks about a formal portrait of a politician surrounded by his family:

> He is trying to emphasize family traditions and family values. He could be either Republican or Democrat, they both do this. I almost wouldn't vote for this individual based on this photograph. It's a cheap shot. Everybody runs and gets their family and their kids around them, and I think it provides no information about them. (quoted in Ebong, 1989, p. 136)

Incidentally, the person who made these comments was a 42-year-old man with a college education. Ebong's sample included a broad spectrum of ages and educational levels, and it was mainly among the more educated viewers that such sentiments were expressed. However, for reasons we have already discussed, this aspect of her findings—which was derived purely from verbal responses—should be treated with caution.

The scorn that is evident in the statement quoted above was echoed in other viewers' responses to the various juxtapositions in the pictures. A politician standing in front of a flag was criticized for being "so wrapped up in the damn flag" (Ebong, 1989, p. 124); a politician sporting a tie and jacket while seated in a military vehicle (in the style of Michael Dukakis) was lambasted for being "so out of place that he may be bordering on hypocrisy" (p. 133); and a politician kneeling in front of a water trough during a visit to a farm was dismissed as follows: "He doesn't look like he's at one with his surroundings at all. In fact, it even looks like it was superimposed, or it could have been" (p. 128).

But these reactions were by no means typical. On the contrary, among viewers who dealt explicitly with the visual juxtapositions in their comments, the more frequent response appears to have been approval, not rejection. For example, whereas the viewer in our most recent quotation saw the picture of the politician visiting a farm as a possible fake, other viewers discussed the very same juxtaposition in wholly positive terms—even while acknowledging its contrived quality. In the following pair of interview excerpts, the first speaker is a young woman who did not go beyond high school in her education, whereas the second speaker is a young, college-educated man. The first speaker has just been asked by the interviewer if the farm-visiting politician was successful in putting across his message to her:

Definitely. [Interviewer: Why?] Well, he's actually out there where the help is being needed. Of course, I guess that's the picture he's trying to come across with, that there is help needed in this area, the farmland of America or whatever. And he has his tie off as if he's ready to get down to work to help the farmers or whomever he's here to visit for that day. [Interviewer: Do you like the way he's portrayed in the photograph?] Definitely. It would come across as a picture that would state the message that he's trying to give—which is for the working values and the working people of America, the actual farm people I guess. Your neighbors. I definitely think he portrays that. (Ebong, 1989, pp. 128-129)

In the other photograph [a politician standing in front of a flag], you recognize and pin-point him immediately as someone who's running for Congress, running for a voted office. This one [the farm visit], you get the image that his concern is the water and the farm, not that he's a politician. And his picture is not going to lead you to believe that he's running for office or that he wants your vote. And so it's going to stick in your mind, and he makes you think that he's more sincere in his interests because it's almost a less effective device for remembering that he wants your vote. [Interviewer: So that goes to the back of your mind, and what you see more is what he's interested in . . . is that what you're saying?] Right. Because he didn't go for the pot shot that will remind you that he's running for office. He went for some meaning behind it that runs the risk of not letting you remember he's running for office, and that in itself says something. (Ebong, 1989, p. 129)

In both of these quotations, an explicit appraisal of the picture's structure leads to a positive reception of the message rather than greater resistance toward it. The first viewer says she likes the picture because it success-fully links the politician to the values he wants to invoke, whereas the second viewer praises the picture for eschewing an obvious political message in favor of what seems a more sincere approach. These re-sponses are consistent with the implications of Adatto's analysis of the news media's preoccupation with political image-making instead of substantive issues. To the extent that the broad public is affected by that preoccupation, ordinary viewers may also adopt the habit of evaluating politicians largely in terms of their success or failure as image crafters.

At the same time, though, regardless of the validity of this inference, the quotations we have just examined also underscore a broader point, namely, that it is unreasonable to assume an automatic, mechanical connection between awareness of image-making conventions and rejec-tion of those conventions. Although a committed skeptic might argue that all image-making should be rejected unless it is backed up by hard facts (e.g., some evidence that a politician actually has helped farmers or improved agriculture), such an attitude would seem to be more of a matter of personal bias than a product of strict logic. Not surprisingly, then, Ebong's study shows that awareness of image-making conventions does not necessarily lead viewers to adopt this attitude.

This aspect of Ebong's findings has been supported further in sub-sequent research conducted by Tatlow (1992). Ebong's data on viewers' critical responses were by-products of a broader investigation of how people interpret political advertising. In Tatlow's study, on the other hand, critical viewing was the central and systematic concern. At the heart of Tatlow's research was an attempt to devise a test of viewers' responses to potentially misleading visual syntax. This situation is best illustrated through an example that Tatlow ended up using in her study: a TV commercial for the Mitsubishi Eclipse. As we have already seen, automobile advertising is often based on analogical montage, and that was the case in this ad. The ad juxtaposes the Eclipse with an award-winning race car, the 3000GT. The cars are both red, and they are both shown speeding around the same race track. On the soundtrack, a voice-over announcer makes the point that the 3000GT has won awards, while the tune "Dueling Banjos" is heard in the background. Because of the visual juxtaposition of the two cars and the rapid pace of the ad,

Tatlow assumed that an uncritical viewer might mistakenly come away from the ad thinking that the Eclipse had won awards too. This assumption became the rationale for Tatlow's test of viewer's responses to the ad. Viewers were asked, "Which of the following claims is made in the Mitsubishi commercial?" and they were given three basic choices: "The 3000GT has won awards," "The Eclipse will win awards," and "The Eclipse has won awards," as well as various combinations of the above. Only the first of these choices was considered correct.

Reasoning along similar lines, Tatlow constructed a "critical viewing instrument" consisting of a total of 20 questions based on 14 different commercials as well as six video clips excerpted from news programs. The study was conducted with college students drawn from two courses, one on film history, the other on introductory physics. The students in the film history course, which was offered by the university's Radio-Television-Film Department, had extensive backgrounds in media study (as measured by Tatlow's survey), whereas the other students' experiences with this topic of study were far more limited. Tatlow's central hypothesis was that the film history students, who had more explicit knowledge about montage and other visual conventions, would score higher than the other students on her critical viewing instrument. However, the study also tested a secondary hypothesis. All students were given a version of the Cornell Critical Thinking Test, which measures a person's ability to use logical reasoning skills to draw inferences from given facts. On the basis of the students' scores from this procedure, Tatlow tested the hypothesis that critical viewing would be enhanced by general critical thinking ability, independently of specific media experience.

The results of the study produced no support for the first of these two hypotheses. The expected relationship between media-study background and critical viewing did not materialize. On the other hand, there was some weak evidence in favor of the second hypothesis, although this part of the study was complicated by problems in the administration of the Cornell Test. In other words, these findings suggest that the way to become a critical viewer is to be a critical thinker in the first place. Of course, this does not mean that knowledge about visual media is completely irrelevant to critical viewing. Interest in media is common among college students today, and it is likely that the students in the physics class may have had some exposure to visual terms and concepts. However, what seems clear from this study is that the extra knowledge gained through specific media courses does not increase one's tendency to be a critical viewer.

What are the implications of these findings for those of us—students as well as teachers—who believe that a visual education can lead to a more critical viewing public? Are our efforts pointless, and should we therefore throw up our hands in despair? The answer to this question depends on how we envision the proper contents of a visual curriculum. The teaching of visual media is characterized by a dichotomy between two fairly divergent approaches: on one hand, detailed attention to formal variables (types of camera shots, lighting, etc.) without much discussion of broader social implications; on the other hand, high-level social critique without a concomitant attention to the formal qualities through which media exert their power. Judging from Tatlow's findings as well as the other considerations we have examined here, we would have to conclude that formal mastery alone is insufficient to generate a critical attitude, whereas the kind of social criticism commonly practiced in media courses may be too abstract to make an impact on students' handling of specific instances of visual manipulation or deception. Between these two extremes, however, there is surely considerable scope for blending criticism with detailed formal study.

CHAPTER

6

◄O►

SHOWING
THE UNSPOKEN

◄O► Because of the lack of explicitness of visual syntax, arguments made through images often need to be supported by words (Meyers, 1994, Chap. 10). Even relatively simple visual juxtapositions can be hard to make sense of without a verbal explanation. Consider the case of a thought-provoking print ad produced by the Humane Society of the United States (see Figure 6.1). The ad contains two images, one above the other: on top, a photograph of a pair of puppies; below, a photograph of a pair of baby foxes. Both pictures engage our attention as well as our affections. But how much of the intended meaning of the ad would we be able to figure out if the pictures had been presented by themselves, without any captions or other text? The similarity in the animals' appearance and in the composition of the two photographs does suggest that some kind of analogy is intended. Beyond that, though, what?

The point of the ad is actually to argue against the wearing of furs, and this argument is expressed with considerable economy in two pairs of captions. Each of the pictures is labeled "Canine." This reinforces the visual analogy. But the picture of the puppies is introduced with the

You wouldn't wear these.

Canine.

Canine.

Why would you wear these?

They're cute, fluffy little bundles of love—we take them into our homes and our hearts, and we make them part of our families.

Or at least we do that for the puppies in the top picture. The young foxes are from the same canine family, but they'll be caught in traps, or forced to live in confinement and then electro-

cuted just for people to wear on their backs. It doesn't make sense, does it?

For more information, contact The Humane Society of the United States.

The Humane Society of the United States
2100 L Street, NW, Washington, DC 20037

Figure 6.1.

words, "You wouldn't wear these," whereas the picture of the baby foxes is followed by a different caption: "Why would you wear these?" So, in addition to the analogy, the ad invites us to think of the images in terms of a contrast: Whereas human beings take dogs into their homes and treat them as part of their families, they kill foxes just to produce an item of luxury apparel. These thoughts are elaborated at greater length in additional text below the images and captions, although this text is probably not as essential for the viewer as the main captions are. In fact, the two contrasting captions by themselves are arguably all that is really needed to get across the basic antifur point of the visual juxtaposition. Without those captions, however, it seems doubtful that any viewer would be able to discern that message.

The relationship between advertising images and text has been examined by Kaplan (1990) in a study of communication-technology print ads. Kaplan was interested in what he calls "visual metaphor," a category that overlaps considerably with analogical juxtaposition, as described here. He found that 24% of the visual metaphors in a sample of ads drawn from general interest magazines needed the accompanying text in order to be understood (p. 44). So, at least when it comes to general interest magazines, it appears that a substantial number of analogical ads cannot function adequately without text. On the other hand, however, as we have already seen, there is another type of ad (not examined by Kaplan) in which a full textual explanation of the visual syntax might actually be counterproductive. In this type of ad, the meaning of the images is best left implicit, as it was, for instance, in the famous 1984 Macintosh-launch commercial discussed in Chapter 5. By evoking IBM in its images while avoiding any direct verbal mention of that company, the Macintosh commercial was able to suggest a message that might have been considered too abrasive or confrontational if it had been put into words.

Ads of this sort, which show us the unspoken, will be our main subject in the pages that follow. To begin with, it is worth emphasizing that these ads need not avoid words altogether. Although the Macintosh commercial had no narration and only a single concluding panel of rather cryptic text, an ad's visual message can remain partly or wholly implicit even when there is extensive verbal commentary ostensibly telling us how to interpret the images. This possibility is illustrated in a striking environmentalist ad from ECO, the Earth Communications Office. This entire TV ad is composed of alternating visual images and panels of text. In the following shot-by-shot transcription, the text is presented in upper case throughout, as it appears in the ad itself:

- THE POWER OF ONE.
- NOT SO LONG AGO, A LITTLE GIRL IN ALABAMA WANTED TO GO TO THE SAME SCHOOL AS EVERYONE ELSE.
- *black-and-white film clip:* African-American child being escorted into school building by law enforcement officers
- AND A GENTLE MAN FROM INDIA WANTED TO RAISE CONSCIOUS-NESS WITHOUT RAISING HIS VOICE.
- *black-and-white film clip:* Mohandas Ghandi, raising a finger to his lips
- IN EAST GERMANY, A MAN WANTED TO BREAK FREE.
- *black-and-white film clip:* man jumping over barbed wire
- AND A WOMAN TRAVELED THE WORLD, GIVING HOPE TO THOSE WHO HAVE NONE.
- *black-and-white film clip:* Mother Teresa greeting a group of women
- THIS IS THE POWER OF ONE.
- *black-and-white film clip:* Chinese student confronting tank
- TO PROTECT YOUR HOME IN THE AMAZON.
- *color film clip:* man in jungle clearing, blocking path of bulldozer
- TO PREVENT POACHING OF THE AFRICAN MOUNTAIN GORILLA.
- *color film clip:* tight close-up of gorilla's face
- *color film clip:* Diane Fossey studying gorilla
- TO RESCUE HARP SEALS IN FINLAND.
- *color film clip:* man running with baby seal in his arms
- OR TO CARE FOR THE ENVIRONMENT IN OUR OWN BACK YARD.
- *color film clip:* lake; woods; mountains; clouds racing across the sky
- THE POWER OF ONE IS TO DO SOMETHING.
- ANYTHING.

These images are accompanied by music, and there is no verbal narration on the soundtrack, but the panels of text provide an unusually detailed, point-by-point explication of how each image should be interpreted and what they all add up to. As summarized in the last two lines of text, the ad's apparent goal is to encourage people to take individual action for good causes, whatever those causes might be. Viewed in this light, the ostensible aim of the images is to demonstrate some of the many ways in which even a single individual can make a big difference in the world. So, on the face of it, the relationship between the ad's words and images seems quite straightforward: The images supply the concrete examples that make the verbal argument more compelling. However, a closer look at the images suggests that there may also be some more complicated things going on here.

To begin with, the fact that half of those images have to do with environmental issues does not mesh entirely with the text's concluding statement about the value of doing "anything." And this tension between the ad's overall structure and its stated conclusion leads to the following questions: If this is a piece of environmentalist advocacy—as the preponderance of environmentalist images would suggest—why show the other images at all? Are they there simply as additional, graphic evidence of "the power of one," or do they serve any extra purpose? One way of addressing these questions is to view them against the backdrop of recent developments in U.S. environmentalism. For several years, environmentalists in the United States have been coming under increasing attack for allegedly being concerned only with the welfare of "white middle-class elitists" (Braile, 1994, p. 13) and ignoring the environmental problems afflicting nonwhites and the poor. Mainstream environmental organizations have responded to this criticism by seeking to become more inclusive—both within the United States and internationally—and also by devoting more attention to broader political issues. Both of these tendencies are evident in the images used in the ad. Although the series of images begins and ends in the United States, in between it takes us to Africa, Asia, Europe, and South America. And, as we have already noted, half of the images deal with political matters that go beyond the concerns of traditional environmentalism.

In other words, the arrangement of the ad's images appears to have at least two separate levels of meaning. On one level, it serves as a visual counterpart to the ad's explicit verbal message about the value of individual effort. On another level, though, it can be seen as containing an implicit message of a different kind: that mainstream environmentalists do care about social injustice and that their concerns are not exclusively focused on matters affecting privileged whites. These themes are expressed most pointedly in the ad's central transition between the Chinese student stopping a tank and the young man confronting a bulldozer in the Amazon—a juxtaposition implying through purely visual means that there is an affinity or equivalence between environmentalist goals and the political struggles of oppressed people everywhere. So, part of the aim of the ad may be to respond to criticism of traditional mainstream environmentalism. And yet by doing so primarily through the images, while making a somewhat different point at the explicit verbal level, the ad avoids the appearance of being overly defensive, which could undermine its credibility.

Using images to counter criticism may also increase acceptance of the message by viewers who would react more skeptically to an equivalent verbal statement. Judith Williamson (1978) has argued that, by virtue of its implicitness, visual syntax can make the connection between two unrelated entities (e.g., a product and an image, or, as in this ad, one social movement and another) appear "natural," something that viewers take for granted without questioning it too deeply. The most fundamental connection put forth in the ad is between two categories of social activism: on one hand, environmentalism (protecting rainforests, gorillas, baby seals, and pristine wilderness); on the other hand, movements for political freedom and social equality (civil rights, anticolonialist, anticommunist, antipoverty). For some viewers, a direct statement that there is indeed some equivalence or affinity between these two categories might be problematic. Expressing this idea less obtrusively, through visual implication instead of verbal declaration, may be a way of lowering such viewers' resistance.

The use of visual syntax to lessen the obtrusiveness of controversial claims is a convention with a long history in U.S. advertising. In his examination of advertising practices during the 1920s and 1930s, Roland Marchand (1985) describes the early stages of this history:

> The potential superiority of the "visual statement" became evident in cases where the advertiser's message would have sounded exaggerated or presumptuous if put into words, or where the advertiser sought to play upon such "inappropriate" emotions as religious awe or a thirst for power. For instance, a copywriter might well have hesitated to advertise a product as just the thing for the man who lusted after power over others. But an illustration with a man standing in a commanding position, perhaps overlooking an impressive urban vista, might convey the same message. . . . No advertiser would have dared to present his product under the headline "God endorses." But a well-placed, radiant beam of light from a mysterious heavenly source might create a virtual halo around the advertised object without provoking the reader into outrage at the advertiser's presumption. (pp. 236-237)

Marchand also notes that some advertisers quite consciously thought of the benefits of images in these terms. This point is reflected clearly in the following statement by Earnest Calkins, an agency president: "A picture . . . can say things that no advertiser could say in words and retain his self-respect" (quoted in Marchand, 1985, p. 236).

Nowadays, examples of visual claims that would be unacceptable in verbal form can be found in most kinds of advertising. But there are two major areas of commercial advertising in which such uses of visual syntax have become standard practice. These two areas correspond to two different types of images that print ads and TV commercials commonly link to products: (a) images of social status; and (b) images of sex and romance. In all likelihood, these are also the image categories most frequently encountered in the visual syntax of commercial advertising.

IMAGES OF SOCIAL STATUS

A 1993 Hyundai commercial shows two glamorous, smartly dressed women waiting for valet parking outside a posh restaurant. Flashy cars pull up in front of them, and the women make highly suggestive remarks about the male drivers: "He must be overcompensating for a, uh, shortcoming?" "Now *he* obviously has feelings of inadequacy." And then a Hyundai Elantra appears, and out of it steps a handsome he-man. The women are suitably impressed: "I wonder what *he's* got under the hood." The ad concludes with this tag line: "Solid, well-built, and long-lasting. Actually, we're talking about the car."

This ad demonstrates a number of characteristics of commercial advertising in the United States: its often blatant sexuality; its increasingly frequent depictions of assertively sexual women; and its growing tendency to portray sex ironically and with self-mocking references to the advertising of the past (e.g., in this case, the old advertising clichés about cars as phallic symbols and means of attracting women). In short, American advertising is not noticeably reticent about sex. So what does this commercial have to do with our main topic, the use of images to convey messages that an advertiser may not want to state explicitly? As the advertising critic Leslie Savan has observed, there actually is a topic that this ad treats very gingerly, but that topic is not sex. It is social status. "All of Hyundai's feminist-toned genital jousting is really a fig leaf to cover something much more intimate: class shame. . . . Everything in this ad is geared to help potential customers overcome the embarrassment of buying a Hyundai. At $7149, Hyundai's Excel is still the lowest-priced new car in the U.S." (Savan, 1994, pp. 229-230). Savan also quotes Hyundai's marketing director, who says that Hyundais are seen "as cars bought by people who can't afford anything else" (p. 230). Accordingly, although the ad's dialogue never refers directly to this issue, the visual contrast between the Hyundai man and the sexually challenged luxury car drivers can be seen as an implicit attempt not just to mitigate Hyundai's low status but to reverse it.

In this particular ad, the reason for avoiding explicit references to social status is no mystery. It is perfectly understandable that an advertiser would not want to make an open acknowledgment of potential weakness or vulnerability. But what about the reverse situation, namely, advertisements for products with high-status appeal? On grounds of simple logic, one might expect that such ads would not shy away from direct verbal statements about social status. One might expect, for instance, the kind of verbal copy that we find in a print ad for Jaguar, an unambiguously upscale automobile (see Figure 6.2). The ad contains a picture of the car and, in the background, a high school. The text explains the circumstances: It invites the viewer to imagine how former classmates will react when he or she drives up for a class reunion in a Jaguar. For many Americans, high school reunions are intimately associated with status consciousness; it is taken for granted that participants will use the occasion for the mutual appraisal of one another's career achievements. The ad is therefore as good an example as one could hope to find of a direct reference to social status. And this reference is made largely through words.

As it happens, however, this ad is an atypical specimen. When we look at other ads for luxury products—whether cars, clothes, or gadgets—we find that explicit mentions of status appeal are the exception, not the rule. This does not mean that social status is entirely absent from these ads. But its presence is signaled indirectly, through more elliptical language, and—crucially—through images. We will examine such ads in more detail shortly. Before we do so, though, it will be useful to explore

Figure 6.2.

the reasons for this reticence. To a great extent, social status is a covert, implicit entity in American advertising. Why should this be?

Reasons for Ads'
Reticence About Social Status

One possible answer is that status concerns are incompatible with the American belief in social equality and a classless society. This answer may seem obvious, and there may be some truth to it, but, at the same time, it has to be treated with some caution. It may well be the case that Americans are more likely than people of other nationalities to proclaim an indifference to social status. However, as far as the actual consequences of social status are concerned—how much of a difference it makes to the way in which one is treated by other people; how much of a motive it is in one's own aspirations—any assumption that the United States is less status-bound than other societies is probably illusory. Indeed, in certain respects, the opposite may be true. Income inequality in the United States is currently greater than in any other large industrialized nation (Brown et al., 1995, p. 144), and some of the things that income has always bought are deference, privilege, and priority—in brief, the rewards of status. So, although American ads' indirectness about status may well be due partly to a clashing faith in equality or classlessness, it would be a mistake to make the further assumption that a faith in equality actually means that status does not matter. It is precisely because it does matter, and matters a lot, that advertisers are reluctant to refer to it openly in words.

So, faith in classlessness is most likely not the best explanation for advertising's reticent handling of social status. As is often remarked, when Americans profess a faith in equality, it is not really a classless society (i.e., equality of outcome) that they are talking about. What they have in mind instead, and what many do indeed believe in, is equality of opportunity, both as an ideal and as an actual condition of life in the United States. And this belief has very substantial consequences for the way in which people think about social status, because, in a society in which it is assumed that people can write their own destinies, those who end up in the lower rungs of the status hierarchy carry a bigger burden of failure than they would in a more rigid, inflexible system. Thus, paradoxically, Americans' faith in equality of opportunity may have made the topic of social status more uncomfortable and anxiety-provoking in the United States than it is in less mobile societies. And it is this unease, in turn, that seems to be reflected in advertising's avoidance of explicit verbal invocations of social status.

Art as a Sign of Status

Having considered the reasons for advertising's indirectness about social status, let us now look at how that indirectness is accomplished through visual syntax. Leaving the world of expensive automobiles behind, we turn to other kinds of goods and services. A print ad for Pulsar watches displays the product beneath a copy of a famous Renaissance painting, Sandro Botticelli's "La Primavera" (see Figure 6.3). In a fashion ad, a man wearing a Pierre Cardin outfit is shown with a woman by his side in front of a statue by Alexander Calder. An ad for American Express portrays an elegantly dressed group of theatergoers sitting next to a huge Gold Card. Ads for Parker pens picture the product side by side with a jazz musician and a ballerina. Whatever text there is in these ads refers to matters other than social status. Yet no knowledgeable viewer will miss the visual syntax's upscale connotations.

All of these ads are examples of analogical juxtaposition between a product and some form of art. As one commentator has put it, "Advertisers frequently include works of art among the props being photographed—they serve as tokens of high culture, superlative skill, supreme value (the product being advertised is supposed to acquire these qualities by association or contiguity)" (Walker, 1983, p. 58). Speaking specifically about advertisements that reproduce paintings, John Berger (1972) has similarly noted that "art is a sign of affluence; it belongs to the good life; it is part of the furnishings which the world gives to the rich and the beautiful" (p. 135). The use of art to connote superior status has a long history in commercial advertising (see Dyer, 1982, p. 35) and an even longer history in the iconography of Anglo-American culture. In a study of the development of genteel culture in the United States, Richard Bushman (1992) has documented the use of such status-conferring props as musical instruments in family portraits dating from at least as early as the 18th century.

Partly because of this long history, the association between art and high status in advertising is so strong that one might easily take it for granted. In fact, however, this association is somewhat more complex

FROM THE GLORIES OF THE GOLDEN AGE.

The Renaissance The defining moment in European history when the creative genius of Man found perfect expression in Art and Science alike.

The Renaissance The inspiration of the Pulsar Collection.

Timepieces that incorporate the most modern technology and the high aesthetics of the Golden Age.

PULSAR
Inspired by the past for the future.

Available at Goldsmiths, F Hinds, John Lewis, H Samuel and leading independent jewellers nationwide

Figure 6.3.

than it may first appear to be. Although it is true that some works of art and the tickets to some kinds of artistic performances can be very expensive, sheer expense is not the principal mechanism through which the images in this genre of advertising make their point. To get a better handle on why it is that these images can act as signs of status, we need to take a broader look at how social status is communicated in the United States and similar societies.

Conspicuous Consumption and Conspicuous Leisure

The most influential, and still definitive, treatment of this topic is Thorstein Veblen's (1953) *The Theory of the Leisure Class*, originally published in 1899. At the heart of Veblen's theory is a distinction between two different ways in which people communicate what their place is in the status hierarchy. Veblen's label for the first of these, conspicuous consumption, has passed into general usage. In thinking about this concept nowadays, people are likely to visualize ostentatiously expensive purchases made primarily for status display. It is commonly assumed that the United States has just gone through a whole period, the decade of the 1980s, in which upwardly mobile consumers were fixated on status-driven expenditures, whereas the current decade has seen a turning away from such concerns (see Rothenberg, 1994, p. 29). In the words of an ad agency chief executive, "The notion of a consumer buying things based on sheer status has gone away" (quoted in M. Wells, 1995, p. 4B). But this conception of conspicuous consumption as a merely transitory preoccupation, an activity that people cast off when times get tougher, is an oversimplification of the concept. At all times and at all social levels, people living in a society in which status is determined by money are expected to signal that status through the way in which their money is spent. So, even during periods of forced frugality, publicly visible expenditures are bound to retain an element of status display. In this sense, conspicuous consumption is a persistent feature of many areas of consumer activity, not an occasional goal that people pursue through the purchase of individual status-display items.

Despite its ubiquity, though, conspicuous consumption is arguably the less important of the two major categories in Veblen's theoretical scheme. Veblen recognized that the raw level of expenditure is not always the most salient indicator of social status. Instead, he drew attention to a second aspect of status communication that he labeled "conspicuous leisure." In contrast to conspicuous consumption, this term has never even come close to being a household word, but Veblen's estimation of its significance is reflected in the title of his book. The basic idea behind the somewhat tangled concept of conspicuous leisure can be described as follows. To the extent that social status depends on how much money one possesses, one's ability to forgo money-making activity can serve as an indicator of status. A crude illustration of this idea is the stereotype of the wealthy professional who takes off from work in the middle of the week to play golf. But Veblen's conception of conspicuous leisure extends considerably beyond this relatively simple situation. As an index of social position, leisure is most effective not when it is dissipated fruitlessly but when it serves as the opportunity for personal cultivation and refinement. The reason for this is simple: Cultivation and refinement persist after the leisure time has been expended; therefore, their value as social markers is more permanent. Accordingly, it is to these aftereffects of leisure, which could be termed "secondary" indicators of status, that Veblen ultimately points us.

As these remarks suggest, Veblen's theory would imply that it is conspicuous leisure rather than conspicuous consumption that best accounts for the use of art as a status signifier in advertising. The typical role of art in such circumstances is not to represent costliness—which, after all, could be symbolized equally well by other means—but to suggest that the consumer is a person of discriminating taste and, therefore, of high status (cf. Bourdieu, 1984). Consequently, art itself is often represented indirectly in luxury product advertising, implying that the viewer possesses the superior connoisseurship needed to decipher such a representation. Thus, whereas the Pulsar ad mentioned previously gave us a straightforward reproduction of a Renaissance painting, an ad for Rolex Cellini watches contains a present-day photograph, a portrait of a woman wearing a watch, posed and lit in the style of a Renaissance portrait (see Figure 6.4). Similarly, several ads have featured illustrations of women modelled after the central figure in Botticelli's "Birth of Venus" (see Figure 6.5). And, in a more jocular vein, an ad for Saga Mink coats shows us a fashionably clad model toting a package in the shape of a painting; through a rip in the wrapping, we get a glimpse of the face of the Mona Lisa (see Figure 6.6).

Of course, art (together with music, ballet, etc.) is not the only way in which conspicuous leisure manifests itself in advertising. Any object or situation that is linked to the world of superior sophistication and taste

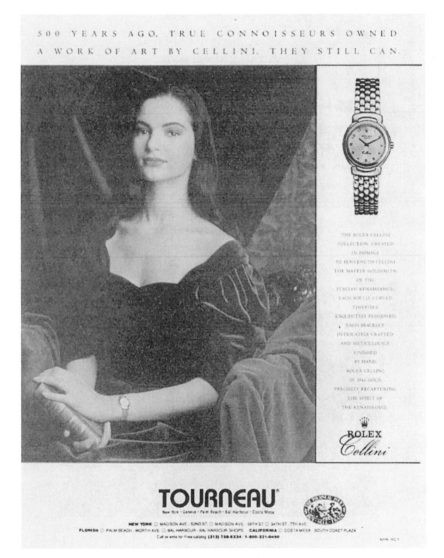

Figure 6.4.

Secret of the Sea is the precious cream with an oceanful of moisture.

And now Secret of the Sea is a collection of lipcolors that kiss your thirsty lips with moisture...nailenamels so rich they can only do you good.

Twelve divine shades of Secret of the Sea lipcolor and nailenamel. You may want them all.

There are two ways to be a goddess. One is to be born that way.

The other is to know the Secret of the Sea.

Secret of the Sea
by Dorothy Gray

Figure 6.5.

can, in turn, serve as a link between that world and the advertised product. Foreign travel, or simply images of foreign locations, can serve as such a link when the location in question is the site of significant

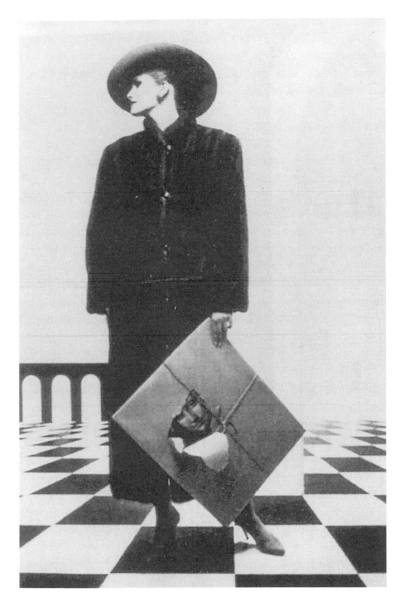

Figure 6.6.

cultural, historical, or archeological interest. And, paralleling the tendency toward indirectness in upscale ads' portrayals of art, there may be a move toward the increasingly unfamiliar in ads featuring foreign locales. Paris, Venice, and other European cities are still common venues for the advertising of high fashion and other luxury products. But the inevitable reorientation toward such places as Samarkand or Ulan Bator has already appeared on the horizon.

Viewers' Responses to Art in Ads

How do viewers respond to images of art or other signifiers of refinement and sophistication in advertising? The efficacy of such images in conveying a sense of premium quality has been demonstrated most impressively in the ongoing campaign for Absolut Vodka. Since the mid-1980s, the campaign has been commissioning artists to produce original paintings or other illustrations for Absolut's print ads. The first ads in this series were by such celebrity artists as Andy Warhol and Keith Haring, but more recently, the series has encompassed the work of less well-known figures as well. This inclusion of emerging talent is presumably significant in itself, because it associates Absolut with the cutting edge of high culture. Although the original-art ads are only one part of Absolut's overall campaign, it is commonly agreed that their contribution to that campaign has been highly effective (Ind, 1993, p. 20). Predictably, the strategy of commissioning original works of art has been adopted by other advertisers too. For instance, in ads for Bombay Sapphire Gin (distributed by the same company that originally handled Absolut), the product is juxtaposed with various artists' stylized versions of martini glasses (see Figure 6.7).

Viewers' responses to artistic themes in print ads have been investigated more systematically in research by Crames (1990). The specific focus of her study was on surrealism. Anyone who is familiar with the history of 20th-century art is likely to have noticed the pervasive influence of surrealism on luxury product advertising (Homer & Kahle, 1986). As a relatively esoteric art movement, surrealism has elite appeal, and its characteristic combination of highly realistic style and reality-defying content is a particularly effective way of attracting the spectator's eye (for reasons discussed in Chapter 1). Furthermore, surrealistic imagery in advertising is often modeled deliberately on the work of the major surrealist painters, especially René Magritte, and this aspect of the ads

THE BOMBAY SAPPHIRE MARTINI. AS ARRANGED BY ULLA DARNI.

Figure 6.7.

enhances their elite connotations even further because it affirms the connoisseurship of viewers who are able to make the connection.

Crames showed a variety of surrealistic ads, together with nonsurrealistic ads for similar products, to two groups of viewers (age range: 23-47). These groups were chosen according to the Claritas Corporation's marketing breakdown of the U.S. population into some 40 distinctive socioeconomic and lifestyle clusters (described in Weiss, 1988, and subsequently updated). Crames's viewers were drawn from one of the top clusters ("Money & Brains," which ranked second in this scheme) and a less affluent one ("Shotguns & Pickups," which ranked 24th). Viewers were interviewed individually about their perceptions of each ad, and they were also asked to rate the ads on quantitative scales. As Crames had expected, the surrealistic ads tended to get higher ratings on scales dealing with status and cultivation (e.g., "superior-inferior," "cultured-common," etc.). There was also a tendency for the "Money & Brains" group to like these ads more than did the "Shotguns & Pickups" group. Crames attributes this tendency in part to the fact that "Money & Brains" viewers appeared to be more aware of the artistic echoes in the surrealistic ads.

This difference in awareness of surrealism's artistic antecedents emerged most sharply in connection with an ad for Grand Marnier Liqueur. In general, Grand Marnier's long-running (but recently reformulated) series of print ads can be considered canonical examples of the use of surrealism in advertising. The ads all featured standard surrealist devices (objects suspended in mid-air, impossible transformations or combinations of objects, etc.), and many ads contained variations on themes by Magritte. For instance, in an ad labeled "A Grand Portrait," we see a large, framed picture of an orange hanging on a wall (see Figure 6.8); in front of the wall, floating above the floor with no visible support, a bottle of Grand Marnier and a liqueur glass cast their shadows on the wall and on the orange; but the shadows that fall on the orange conform to its spherical shape—even though it is supposed to be a picture and, therefore, flat. This deliberate interpenetration of picture and reality is typical of Magritte, and the same goes for the levitating objects. Furthermore, the picture-within-a-picture of an orange (a key Grand Marnier Liqueur ingredient, incorporated in all the ads) is a direct parody of a Magritte painting of an apple ("The Listening Chamber," 1953). In Crames's study, connections to Surrealism were mentioned explicitly by 12 of the 31 "Money & Brains" viewers, and four of these referred

A GRAND PORTRAIT.

Figure 6.8.

specifically to Magritte. None of the "Shotguns & Pickups" viewers made any comments of this sort.

Going beyond the overall differences between surrealistic and non-surrealistic ads, Crames's findings also hint at a further distinction within the former category. Among the "Shotguns & Pickups" group, there appeared to be a preference for those surrealistic images that could be explained according to some underlying logic. For the "Money & Brains" group, however, the images that seemed to hold the greatest appeal were the instances of "pure" surrealism, devoid of any logical underpinning. This distinction can be illustrated through a comparison between two print ads for high-quality watches. (These ads were not included in Crames's study, but they provide a convenient demonstration of her basic point.) An ad for Tag Heuer features a dramatic, bird's-eye view of a horse and rider vaulting over the gap between two skyscrapers (see Figure 6.9). The rider is clad in show-jumping attire, the tops of the buildings are covered with grass, and there is a bar over the edge of the building from which the jump has originated. A caption spells out the following message: "SUCCESS. IT'S A MIND GAME." In an ad for Lassale, by Seiko, we are confronted with a characteristically Magrittean violation of the picture-reality distinction: Out of a picture frame floating above a surreal geometric landscape, a man's arm reaches into that landscape toward a pair of watches also suspended in mid-air (in a manner somewhat reminiscent of a painting by Salvador Dali) (see Figure 6.10). Both of these ads are highly successful evocations of the dreamlike lack of logic that is often associated with surrealism. But the Tag Heuer ad can also be seen in a different light. Taking our cue from the caption, we could interpret the yawning chasm beneath the horse and rider as a metaphorical representation of the mental fears that must be overcome on the road to success. So, whereas the Seiko ad can be described as a case of "pure" surrealism, the Tag Heuer ad's metaphorical aspects provide a logical underpinning for its mind-bending imagery. The different reactions of Crames's two groups to these two forms of surrealism suggest that, whereas wealthier people may have learned to appreciate surrealistic violations of real-world expectations for their own sake, the broader public is probably more comfortable with such violations when they can be explained in some fashion.

Crames's findings on surrealism provide support for our more general assumptions about the role of art as a status signifier in advertising, but one should not leap to the conclusion that the connection between art and status is automatic. A useful note of caution about this connection comes from a study by Rodriguez-Ema (1994). This study tested college students' responses to a sample of ads containing relatively well-known works of art. For any one product, half of the viewers saw the ad with

Figure 6.9.

the art in it, whereas the other half saw an alternative version without art. For instance, there were two versions of a print ad for Denim Generation jeans. Both versions were two-page spreads. In the version with art, the left-hand page contains a picture of the jeans and, beneath

Figure 6.10.

it, a line of text: "You would be perfectly happy without these jeans." This sentence is continued on the next page: "But you'd be naked."

Above those words is a picture of Michelangelo's "David." The nonart version of the ad follows a similar format. The left-hand page has the same picture of the jeans and the same words as before. On the right-hand page, the text now reads, "But you'd be buck naked," and the image above it is of an elk.

As this example makes clear, this pair of ads was part of a single overall campaign, and the same was true of many of the other pairs in Rodriguez-Ema's study. In other words, the ads containing art were not attempts to create a different, more upscale image for their products in comparison with the nonart ads. As one might expect, then, the results of this study did not reveal any notable differences in ratings between the two types of ads. Art may be an efficient indicator of social status in the appropriate circumstances, but its meanings obviously encompass much more than that, and those additional meanings can be tapped by advertising just as surely as the status connotations are.

IMAGES OF SEX AND ROMANCE

For several months during 1994 and 1995, people driving past Philadelphia's 30th Street Railroad Station were confronted by a huge billboard bearing an advertisement for WDRE, a local alternative-rock station (see Figure 6.11). This ad was composed of two black-and-white images. On the left was a somewhat anachronistic, 1950s- or 1960s-style picture of a clean-cut young man and woman embracing. This image was labeled, "Life as you know it." On the right, against a black background, was a picture of a pair of handcuffs, one closed, the other open. The label on this image was, simply, "WDRE." An informal written survey in a graduate course on visual communication revealed two major patterns in the interpretation of this combination of images. Out of a total of 23 students in the class, 12 saw the ad as an implicit promise of freedom from the confines of conventional existence: "This picture is trying to say—that WDRE uncuffs you, sets you free—lets you get away from the binding relationships and commitments that you face each day." "Life as you know it is analogic to wearing handcuffs (being tied down or restrained). WDRE represents an alternative—the opposite of the first image—& therefore freedom. (May be alternative rock.)" "A quiet, sub-

Figure 6.11.

urban, married life is like handcuffs. WDRE releases you, giving you back your freedom."

In all of these statements, the handcuffs are interpreted as a symbol of freedom, presumably because of the fact that one of them is open. However, for eight of the remaining students, the meaning of the hand-cuffs was markedly different. In the eyes of these eight students, the ad was not just about escape from convention. It was also about "alternative" sexual practices and, specifically, S&M: "WDRE claims to broadcast 'alternative' or 'underground' music. The left image suggests boring, conventional way of showing attraction b/w 2 people. The right image shows a symbol of 'alternative' ways to have sex—S&M." "Everyday life is vanilla and Ozzie & Harriet, along with most music. We are like the S&M of life & music (i.e., on the 'edge' like punk was)." "Life As You Know it is—60s blasé relationship stuff. Whereas w/WDRE is suggest-ing that on WDRE it is some sort of S&M sex stuff—something more daring & outrageous than the normal, boring stuff." (Three students' interpretations fit neither of the two patterns described above; for exam-ple: "I've never understood this ad. It's been bugging me every time I've come home from NY via 30th St. Station.")

It appears highly unlikely that the "alternative," S&M-oriented interpretations of the ad were simply aberrations, unintended and unforeseen by the billboard's designers. Although the students who offered these interpretations were in the minority, their numbers account for a substantial proportion of the total. Furthermore, whereas 6 of the 12 students who saw the ad in terms of freedom indicated that they had no prior familiarity with WDRE, the corresponding number for the "alternative" group was only one out of eight. It seems reasonable to conclude, then, that the S&M theme was introduced into the ad by its creators as an implicit, unspoken statement aimed at viewers in the know. In that sense, the billboard is a relatively straightforward example of the use of visual syntax to convey a sexual message that is absent from the ad's verbal text.

But it would be an error to see this ad as a typical representation of the treatment of sex in U.S. advertising. As already noted, sex per se is not necessarily handled indirectly, either in ads or in the broader media culture of the United States. The open verbal discussion of sexual gratification that has become a staple of advice columns, talk shows, novels, and so on is also found in certain kinds of advertisements. Take the case of a print ad for Herrera men's cologne. A small image at the top of the page shows two women in elegant evening wear having a tête-à-tête in a ladies' room. Most of the ad is taken up by text, detailing their bantering conversation. They are sisters, they are at a party, and one of them is urging the other to marry the man with whom she has come. After a series of high-style quips, they finally get around to the main point of the ad. "Well, does he wear a really sexy cologne when you're making love?" asks sister Charlotte. "I suppose you have a recommendation," says Lisa. Charlotte recommends Herrera for Men—"the one that comes in the box with dots"—and the dialogue concludes with the following exchange. Lisa: "You think he'll like it?" Charlotte: "Oh. I think he will. But I'm sure you will."

This is an unusually wordy ad, but its unabashed proclamation of a link between the product and sexual pleasure is not particularly noteworthy as far as cologne or perfume advertising is concerned. Except to extreme puritans or cultural naifs, the idea that these products are worn to increase sexual attractiveness is hardly controversial. Consequently, in advertising for these products, images are not a substitute for some hidden, unarticulated message. When such ads lack words, their absence is not a matter of suppression but of the avoidance of redundancy. And what is true of fragrances is also true of makeup, jewelry, some kinds of clothes, certain grooming products, and any other product or service whose function is to enhance the user's sexuality. Sexual attractiveness is rarely the sole object of such products, but, on the other hand, it is rarely a negligible aspect of their appeal. In all such cases, American advertising is relatively open in its treatment of sexuality.

If sex in itself is not something that advertisers need to be wary of, when does it become a subject for covert presentation? There are at least three types of situations in which this is the case: first, when sex is being used metaphorically and what the ad is really promising is something else; second, when the link between the product and sex is frowned upon; and, third, when the type of sex is socially unacceptable.

Sex as Metaphor

We have already encountered an example of the first of these categories, namely, the WDRE billboard. That billboard was a genuine case of a visual message that could not be expressed verbally. Imagine, for instance, a different version of the ad, in which the images were accompanied by an explicit verbal slogan: "WDRE: For those who are into the S&M lifestyle, or just want to know more about it." The reason such a verbal version is improbable is not just that people might resent the open mention of S&M. More fundamentally, the problem with the slogan is that sex is not really what the ad is about in the first place. The original ad's reference to S&M is metaphorical and is yet one more example of a process that is becoming increasingly widespread in American popular culture. In a society in which the limits of sexual expression are increasingly being pushed outward, people who want to use sex as a badge of sophistication or rebelliousness must increasingly have recourse to the more outré varieties of sexual activity. In particular, the use of S&M as a means of appearing hip and iconoclastic has by now become almost an established convention in music videos, movies, and, of course, advertising. Because these uses of S&M imagery are ultimately about something else—thumbing one's nose at convention—an ad that explicitly promised an actual S&M experience would be beside the point.

While kinky sex is one popular variety of sexual metaphor in American visual culture, a more common form of metaphorical sex occurs in food ads. Consider the case of a TV commercial for Skippy Reduced-Fat Peanut Butter. The commercial opens with a shot of two tubby men drawing in their paunches as an attractive woman walks by. On the soundtrack, a throaty-voiced female announcer says, "Fat! For years, people have tried to hide it. Stuff it"—cut to shot of man helping woman squeeze into evening gown—"Even burn it"—shot of women on exercise machines—"Well, we have a new idea. We cut it." On the screen appears a tight close-up of a knife digging into peanut butter, followed by a shot of the product. The announcer points out that the new Skippy has 25% less fat than the regular variety and is "sooo creamy. You can spread it"—shot of peanut butter being spread on a slice of bread—"devour it"—shot of kid gulping down bread and peanut butter—"and just love it"—shot of man feeding woman. After another shot of the product, during which the announcer says, "Cut the fat; don't cut out the Skippy," the commercial concludes with a continuation of the previous scene of the man and woman. She takes some peanut butter on her finger and sticks it into the man's mouth. He licks off the peanut butter. The announcer says, "Wow!"

The verbal content of this commercial gives us one reason for the common association between food and sex in advertising. Reduced-fat foods (or other kinds of reduced-calorie products) can help people lose weight and, presumably, become more attractive. This type of food-sex connection is found in ads for such things as diet sodas (e.g., the Diet Coke ad in which female office workers ogle a shirtless, Diet-Coke-guzzling construction worker), breakfast cereals (e.g., a Kelloggs's Special-K ad featuring a young woman striking sexy poses in front of a mirror), and low-fat yogurt (e.g., an ad in which a couple eating yogurt in an elevator scandalizes an older woman waiting outside because they are making loud moaning sounds of pleasure).

To the extent that these ads are about the relationship between reduced-calorie foods and a sexier appearance, their use of sexual imagery is not metaphorical, nor is it something that has to be expressed indirectly. The verbal soundtrack in the Skippy commercial makes no bones about the fact that the product can help people avoid the embarrassment of being unattractively overweight. But there is another kind of connection between food and sex in this ad, and even more so in the yogurt commercial. Through the licking of the finger and the moaning sounds, both ads suggest that the experience of eating the product is somehow equivalent to sex. This is the metaphorical part of the food-sex connection, and this kind of meaning cannot be expressed explicitly through words (e.g., "you will have an orgasm when you eat our yogurt"), because literal sex and orgasms are not what these ads are really selling.

Why should certain foods seek to associate themselves metaphorically with sexual pleasure? A psychoanalytically inclined observer might point out that this kind of association is also a feature of some people's actual experiences of sexuality. For instance, a national survey of people's sexual habits revealed that several respondents fantasized about (or, in some cases, allegedly practiced) such acts as licking whipped cream off a sexual partner or having intercourse in a tub full of Jell-o (Patterson & Kim, 1991, pp. 79, 82). But, these connections aside, the use of sex as a metaphor for the pleasures of food may also have something to do with the way humans respond to images of these two kinds of experiences. Human beings are biologically programmed to have a strong emotional response to the visual appearance of sex. But the same is not true for food—or, at least, for the kinds of processed, "artificial" foods featured in most advertisements.

In any event, whatever the reason(s) may be, the metaphorical use of sex as a means of promoting the sensual delights of food is so pervasive that some advertisers have begun to treat it as a joke. This is the case in a TV commercial for Foster's lager. The commercial begins with a man and woman in bed, feeding each other ice cream. The action heats up, the camera moves in for tighter close-ups, and the man pulls off his shirt. But they have reached the bottom of the ice-cream container. "More," the woman purrs. The man gets up, goes to the kitchen. He looks into the freezer compartment of the refrigerator, and we see another tub of ice cream. But then the camera travels to the shelves below, and a can of Foster's lager comes into view. Cut to the woman in the bedroom, waiting impatiently. Suddenly, from another part of the house, we hear the sound of a TV sports announcer. Seething with frustration, the woman turns to the viewer: "Don't you just hate it when that happens?"

Questionable Sex-Product Links

Moving beyond sex as metaphor, let us now examine a second category of ad in which visual syntax is used to convey an unspoken sexual message. In this kind of ad, the link between the product and sex is disparaged or condemned by public opinion. Cars, liquor, and cigarettes are among the most prominent examples of products in this category. As the Hyundai commercial that we examined earlier makes clear, the idea that cars can be used by men to attract women has become an object of open ridicule. This does not mean that sexual associations have necessarily disappeared from men's (and women's?) thoughts about cars, but it does mean that such associations are unlikely to be advertised explicitly and with a straight face. Indeed, the Hyundai commercial's mocking attitude toward the car-sex connection is not an entirely new development, although self-parody is, of course, increasingly prevalent in advertising as a whole. As early as 1968, we find an ad for Dodge Charger, one of the archetypal "muscle cars" of that period, making a joke about automotive sex appeal. The ad shows a sexy woman posing invitingly next to the car and looking directly at the viewer. Under this picture is the following declaration:

> Mother warned me . . . that there would be men like you driving cars like that. Do you really think you can get to me with that long, low, tough machine you just rolled up in? Ha! If you think a girl with real values is impressed by your air conditioning and stereo . . . a 440 Magnum, whatever that is . . . well—it takes more than cushy bucket seats to make me flip. Charger R/T SE. Sounds like alphabet soup. Frankly, I'm attracted to you because you have a very intelligent face. My name's Julia.

It goes without saying that the real purpose of these lines is to reassure men about the efficacy of automotive seduction. At the same time, though, these lines are also a direct acknowledgment of the scornful attitude with which the putative car-sex connection is regarded by people with "real values." Because of this attitude, advertising that aims to put forth such a connection unironically is likely to do so purely through images, without any related text. A print ad displays a pickup truck surrounded by young, swimsuit-clad men and women. To viewers inclined to see a sexual implication in this juxtaposition, the image probably makes its point just as surely as the Dodge Charger ad did. But the absence of any corresponding verbal statement shields that implication from the kind of ridicule that was parodied in the Hyundai commercial. After all, the men and women in the ad could be "just friends."

Although the association between cars and sex has traditionally been thought of as a defining element of the American psyche, in the history of advertising, that association has not been nearly so strong as the one between sex and liquor. Aside from perfume, probably no product has been connected with sexually or romantically oriented advertising as consistently as some forms of alcoholic beverages have. The logic behind this connection is spelled out with exceptional clarity and directness in a 15-year-old print ad for Courvoisier Cognac. Above an image of two brandy snifters positioned side by side, the ad gives us the following verbal comment: "Sometimes, romance needs a little nudge" (see Figure 6.12). This one-liner says it all. In fact, in retrospect, it may have appeared to the advertiser that that line said too much. Even when that ad was made, the notion that liquor is an appropriate sexual lubricant was widely frowned upon, and in the years since then, that notion has come under increasing attack, particularly on college campuses and also in connection with advertising directed at low-income neighborhoods and ethnic minorities (Scott et al., 1992).

For these reasons, the frankness of the Courvoisier ad's language is very much the exception in liquor advertising. Even at the time when that ad appeared, Courvoisier ads were much more likely to exclude sex from the verbal text, confining any sexual connotations to the images, and this tendency has continued since then. A 1994 ad juxtaposes the Courvoisier label with a picture of a man and a woman framed by the outline of a brandy glass (see Figure 6.13). She has a glass in her hands, while his has been put aside. She is curled up on his lap, with her shoes off and her short dress barely concealing the tops of her thighs. One of her legs is stretched out across the center of the image. But the sensual tone of this display is absent from the ad's brief verbal text, which simply says, "WHAT MAKES A MOMENT A MEMORY." A similar strategy— sexually/romantically suggestive imagery, no-sex text—can be found in other current or recent ads that continue the traditional association between liquor and sex. An ad for Crown Royal whisky juxtaposes the product with a romantic, nighttime view of a couple having a drink on

Figure 6.12.

a balcony overlooking a city; the tag line reads, "Taste royalty. Crown Royal."

More generally, however, American advertisers may (temporarily, at least) be distancing themselves from the sex-liquor theme. Although sexual or romantic imagery has certainly not disappeared from U.S. liquor ads, nowadays its presence is often treated with the same kind of self-deprecating irony that has also insinuated itself into car ads. So, an ad for Domaine Ste. Michelle Champagne Brut gives us the traditional juxtaposition between a bottle of the product and a kissing couple (with a glass of champagne in the woman's hand), but the caption treats this association as a joke: "During the holidays, one's thoughts turn naturally

Figure 6.13.

to porous, fast-draining soil" (see Figure 6.14). (The ad's body copy contains an extensive discussion of the superior soil at the producer's vineyards.) Less coyly, an advertising poster for Steele Reserve Beer features the following headline: "RESEARCH SAYS SEX SELLS BEER." Underneath these words is a photograph of two copulating rhinos.

Unlike either cars or liquor, most brands of cigarettes tend to use sex only as a secondary feature of their appeal. This tendency is related to broader trends in cigarette advertising. Having to contend with an increasingly hostile social environment, cigarette ads today appear to be centrally preoccupied with counteracting society's negative attitudes toward smoking. A principal weapon in these campaigns is visual syntax. In billboards and magazine ads, packages of cigarettes or, in some

Figure 6.14.

cases, just the brand names by themselves are juxtaposed with images of vigorous outdoor activities and pure, unspoiled environments. For instance, a picture of the Grand Teton mountain range, which has been featured in any number of environmentalist photographs, was used as the centerpiece of an ad for Richland cigarettes, and another view of the Tetons appeared in an ad for Skoal chewing tobacco.

With such visual juxtapositions between cigarettes and images of purity or well-being, the ads implicitly address the major source of public concern about smoking: its bad effects on health. In parallel with this goal, however, much cigarette advertising is also aimed at reversing another facet of society's negative view of smoking, namely, the perception that it is unattractive and antisocial. This is where romantic or sexual imagery enters the picture. The same ads that show unspoiled outdoor locations often include a lone couple in the scene, and the ads featuring vigorous activity commonly show a woman horsing around with a man. The romantic element in these compositions is usually underplayed, but that is in keeping with their presumable objective, which is not really to prove that cigarettes have aphrodisiac powers but, more simply, just to show that they are not a turn-off. Accordingly, an ad for Kool depicts the brand name embedded in a waterfall, while the tiny figures of a man and woman make their way through the surrounding landscape. In an ad for Parliament Lights, a scantily clad couple is shown looking out on a calm sea and cloudless sky from a perch on top of an immaculately white building. A Newport ad shows us a woman vaulting over the spray of an open fire hydrant, with a male companion egging her on. This ad also contains a slogan, "Alive with pleasure!" These words reinforce the theme of health and vigor, but their relationship to the picture's sexual content is tangential at best. Because neither of the other two ads contains any textual reference to the themes with which we are concerned (Parliament's only slogan is "The Perfect Recess," and Kool has no slogan at all), all three ads are good illustrations of the use of visual syntax to convey completely unspoken controversial messages.

In our earlier discussion of the Newport ad (Chapter 2), it was noted that the erupting fire hydrant is probably a deliberate joke, one more example of the current tendency of advertising to absorb criticism and recycle it in the form of parody. As Ewen (1991) and others have noted, the same is probably true of much of the sexual innuendo in various ads featuring the notorious "Old Joe" Camel. But whereas self-parody may have served to defuse attacks on some other areas of advertising, critics' animosity against cigarette ads has been exacerbated by Joe Camel and has led to a partial withdrawal of the character. A primary reason for this Camel hatred has been the perception that the ads' combination of a cartoon character with images of sexually charged nightlife serves as a lure for adolescents and even children. And this brings us to our third major category of visually mediated, unspoken sexual messages. In ads for cars, liquor, and cigarettes, indirect treatment of sex stems from negative social attitudes toward the sexual associations of these specific products. Our final category, on the other hand, encompasses ads that face social disapproval because of the type of sexuality they deal with, regardless of product. In particular, there are two areas of sexuality whose expression in advertising is especially controversial: adolescent sex and homosexuality.

Controversial Sexuality

Most contemporary societies invest a substantial amount of energy in the control of adolescent sexual activity. To a considerable extent, this phenomenon appears to be a simple result of parents' and other caretakers' concerns about sexually transmitted diseases or unwanted pregnancies. However, other motivations also could be involved. When former U.S. Surgeon General Joycelyn Elders made a passing remark to the effect that sex education courses should perhaps teach adolescents about masturbation, the vehemently negative public reaction suggested that there may be some adults who find the idea of young people's sexuality per se deeply disturbing. Because of these attitudes, mass media representations of teenage sexuality are always vulnerable to attack, especially if the topic is portrayed in a titillating manner, as one might expect it to be in commercial advertising.

The brief, abortive 1995 campaign for Calvin Klein jeans provided a telling demonstration of this point. The print version of the campaign entailed individual portraits of young people in provocative poses: a female touching her breasts, a male lounging on the floor in his underpants, and two of the models, one female, one male, wearing jeans that were hiked up at the crotch, revealing a flash of white underwear beneath (see Figure 6.15). This was hardly the first time that sexually suggestive imagery had appeared in advertising by Calvin Klein, whose previous campaigns had included not just a man in underpants but also complete nudity, both male and female. However, the apparent youth of the

Figure 6.15.

models in these new images immediately became the focus of complaints, some of which came from the advertising industry's trade publications. Writing in *Adweek*, advertising critic Barbara Lippert had this to say about the two models with the hiked-up, underwear-revealing jeans:

> She, with her pink nail polish, pink lips and blonde hair parted in the middle, represents a wholesome young Cybill Sheperd Breck girl type, except that while the face refers to *Seventeen* magazine, the pose down under is pure *Penthouse*. I guess that's supposed to be typical jailbait fantasy stuff. . . . The guy in the white panties (OK, briefs) is another case. His face, with its ring of curls, is so angelic, his blue socks and sneakers so poignantly boyish, that it seems the photographer picked him up in the park by offering him free ice cream and a ride in his car. Very NAMBLA. (Lippert, 1995a, p. 34)

These comments are typical of the criticism directed at the ads. In effect, the images were accused of bordering on pornography. Interestingly, as the references to "jailbait fantasy" and "NAMBLA" (North American Man-Boy Love Association) suggest, Lippert's criticism also seems to have been premised on the assumption that the implied viewer was a male adult. Although this assumption was based mainly on the TV versions of the ads (see Lippert, 1995b), Lippert is an experienced interpreter of advertising, and her remarks on this point cannot be dismissed lightly. All the same, it is worth remembering that the target market for jeans—and, consequently, the target audience for jeans ads—includes a substantial proportion of teenagers. It might have been instructive to hear critics' responses to that aspect of the ads.

The Calvin Klein campaign was withdrawn quickly, but other ads featuring a jeans-sex association have not faced similar difficulties, despite the fact that most jeans ads are addressed at least partly to adolescents and that many contain adolescent-oriented themes. The likely reason for this difference is illustrated most pointedly by a British TV commercial for Levi's jeans that was part of a hugely successful, long-running series (not to be confused with Levi's current U.S. campaign). The setting is a cafe in a sun-baked landscape somewhere in the American Southwest. In comes an old man in overalls that hang loosely from his desiccated torso. He walks up to the counter, which is tended by a beautiful young woman. Suddenly the view shifts to the side, where a staircase to an upper floor is marked with a "Rooms to Let" sign. Down the stairs comes a ruggedly handsome young man. His shirt is open, and he is in his underpants. The old man looks at him in shock. The young woman looks at him longingly. He walks behind the counter, opens the refrigerator, takes out his jeans, and slowly slides into them, as the old man and two other old people look on with troubled expressions. Then he strides past them and out the door. With the young woman gazing after him, he mounts his motorcycle and drives off into the distance.

This ad's negative image of old people (a type of portrayal that has become increasingly common in teenage-oriented advertising) imbues it with a markedly adolescent sensibility. However, the two young people in it look to be somewhat past their teens, and a song on the soundtrack explicitly mentions the age of 21. So, while effectively linking jeans, sex, and an adolescent undertone, the ad bypasses the problems it might have faced if its young protagonists actually had been adolescents. This type of strategy appears to be a common way of handling sexual content in advertising for products directed at young people. The combination of adolescent themes or markers with postadolescent models may be the key to attracting teenage viewers without stepping over the boundary that Calvin Klein's ads seem to have violated.

Of course, the fact that a sexy ad uses adult models is still no guarantee that adult public opinion will approve its dissemination to a young audience. Even if the ad is judged entirely acceptable by adult standards, its placement in media specifically aimed at teenagers can obviously be problematic. A current print ad for Tabu perfume shows a female painter swept up in an embrace by her nude male model (see Figure 6.16). Her clothed body shields much of his from our view, and, in any case, neither nudity as such nor the connection between perfume and sex can be considered controversial in the context of contemporary U.S. advertising. Nevertheless, while the ad was accepted for publication in magazines with an adult readership, it was turned down by *Seventeen* and *Sassy*, whose readers are primarily teenage girls.

The presence of a naked man in the Tabu ad also raises another issue, which leads to our final topic in this discussion of visual syntax and sexual imagery. As we have already noted (see Chapter 1), male nudity is becoming more frequent in commercial advertising. Naked men have appeared with naked women (e.g., in a fragrance ad by Calvin Klein); with clothed women (as in the Tabu ad or a fashion ad by Versace); and all alone (e.g., a Joop! cologne ad) (see Figure 6.17). To some extent, this trend is surely a reaction against the frequent criticism that advertising people have received for their past tendency to sexualize women more than men. The trend toward male nudity also may reflect a growing female audience for sexualized images of men. At the same time, though, some of these images of naked men may be intended at least in part for a gay audience.

It is commonly accepted among marketing and advertising professionals that gay and lesbian consumers offer particularly promising opportunities for marketers (see Turow, in press). The reasoning behind this assumption has been summarized as follows:

> The gay and lesbian market is an untapped goldmine. Because gays are highly educated and usually have no dependents, they have high levels of disposable income. Geographic concentration and a strong word-of-mouth network make them easy to reach. And because these consumers are disenfranchised from mainstream society, they are open to overtures from marketers. (Kahan & Mulryan, 1995, p. 40)

A number of marketers are indeed making such overtures. For example, the Miller Brewing Co. created an ad in honor of Gay and Lesbian Pride Month (June) of 1995. The ad ran in several gay and lesbian publications and featured a large close-up of a peacock feather with the slogan "Celebrate Pride" above the Miller logo. There is considerable evidence that such ads are effective ("Target market," 1995). However, they also face the possibility of negative reactions from people who are hostile to gays and lesbians. Furthermore, this possibility surely increases for ads that have a sexual or romantic theme and appear in general-audience publications—neither of which was true of the Miller ad.

The specter of these problems is reflected in advertising that suggests gay or lesbian sexuality but also permits a heterosexual interpretation. According to Danae Clark (1995),

> In fashion magazines such as *Elle* and *Mirabella,* and in mail-order catalogs such as *Tweeds, J.Crew* and *Victoria's Secret,* advertisers (whether knowingly or not) are capitalizing upon a dual market strategy that packages gender ambiguity and speaks, at least indirectly, to the lesbian consumer market. (p. 145)

Figure 6.16.

This ambiguity may be a matter of clothing, body posture, or other aspects of physical appearance, but it may also involve physical contact between two women. A Guess ad shows a pair of models nestling against each other and holding hands. This pose could be taken as a depiction of a lesbian relationship, but it could conceivably also be seen as a friendly cuddle between heterosexuals. When it comes to men's images, on the other hand, sexual ambiguity in advertising is more often signaled by appearance only, because physical contact between men (other than aggressive contact) is more tightly circumscribed by public standards. Even when a man is portrayed with others, gay sexuality is typically implied not through his interaction with them but through various subtle cues of clothing, grooming, pose, and so on that may not carry connotations of homosexuality for viewers who are not gay themselves (Stabiner, 1982).

Figure 6.17.

Of course, all advertising conventions are in constant flux, and this is particularly true of the conventions with which we are concerned here. Although unambiguous depictions of sexual/romantic interactions between women or between men are generally confined to ads in lesbian and gay publications, some noteworthy examples have begun to appear in other venues as well. In a Tanqueray gin ad that ran in *Rolling Stone* and elsewhere, Mr Jenkins (a continuing character in Tanqueray advertising) is shown in a gay bar, seated across from a man in drag who raises a glass in a toast to him (see Figure 6.18). The ad's body copy reads as follows: "Surprised to find a glamour girl in a gay bar, Mr. Jenkins sends her a T&T . . . though he admits she *is* rather burly for a glamour girl." A Diesel jeans ad in the August 1995 issue of *Premiere* (a movie magazine) goes a step further (see Figure 6.19). This two-page spread, in black-and-white, depicts what appears to be a World War II victory celebration for a submarine returning to the United States. In the background, we see a wildly enthusiastic crowd welcoming the sub and its crew as they prepare to disembark. In the foreground, two male sailors embrace and kiss each other on the lips. Not surprisingly, *Premiere* received letters of protest when this ad was published. As Larry Gross has pointed out, hostility toward gays and lesbians is one of the few forms of social prejudice that many people still feel free to express openly (Gross, 1995, pp. 63-64). Nevertheless, as the United States and other progressive societies become increasingly accepting of differences in sexual orientation, perhaps the gay and lesbian presence in advertising will become less controversial, and the need for ambiguity and elusiveness in this area will eventually decline.

Figure 6.18.

Figure 6.19.

Epilogue
Ethics of Visual Persuasion

◄o► Outside of business schools and advertising departments, academic authors who write about advertising often take a dim view of their subject. Commercial advertising, in particular, is often seen as a malignant cultural force, a creator and perpetuator of values and lifestyles that many critics deplore. It should be evident from what I have written up to this point that I do not share such extreme views about advertising as a social institution. Individual ads can be reprehensible, of course, when they make false claims (e.g., fraudulent weight-loss pills), sell harmful products (e.g., tobacco), promote immoral causes (e.g., a gay-baiting politician), or employ unfair persuasive techniques (e.g., subliminal advertising). But all of these potential problems have to do with specific ads, products, and methods. It is one thing to criticize ads on such grounds and quite another to condemn advertising as a whole.

Critics who take the latter approach are usually voicing a more fundamental dissatisfaction with consumer culture and the market economy, and although some of this dissatisfaction may be understandable, it seems to me that it is often motivated by an unrealistic view of the alternatives. However, this is not the place for a debate about political philosophy, nor do I intend to present here a general discussion of visual ethics, a topic that I have analyzed in some detail elsewhere (Messaris, 1990). Rather, it seems appropriate to conclude with a brief comment about the ethical ramifications of the specific visual devices discussed in this book. I have dealt with three broad characteristics of visual images that I consider crucial ingredients of the process of visual persuasion: iconicity, indexicality, and the absence of an explicit propositional syntax. In the context of an ad, each of these characteristics can be used either ethically or unethically.

ICONICITY

As we have seen, the iconicity of images makes it possible for ads to elicit our attention and emotions by simulating various significant features of our real-world visual experiences. By virtue of their iconicity, visual ads are able to erect before our eyes a mirror world, with whose inhabitants we are invited to identify or to imagine that we are interacting. These acts of identification and imaginary interaction have real-world consequences. Some of the most revealing analyses of advertising have described the ways in which viewers use the characters they see in ads as reference points for their own evolving identities (Barthel, 1988; Ewen, 1988; Ewen & Ewen, 1982). For example, Carol Moog (1990) recalls how, as a young girl, she studied the posture of a woman in a refrigerator commercial to learn how to carry herself as an adult (p. 13). Together with fictional movies and TV programs, ads are a major source of images that young people can use to previsualize their places in the world of sexual and status relationships. It can be argued that advertisers have an ethical responsibility to take these circumstances into account in fashioning the images that they place before the public.

What might constitute a violation of this ethical responsibility? Critics of advertising images often focus on the discrepancy between the vision of life offered in ads and the needs or abilities of real people. Drawing on her practice as a psychotherapist, Moog (1990) cites the story of a young lawyer who expressed dissatisfaction with her life because she had not lived up to her potential as a member of "the Pepsi generation"—that is, "beautiful, sexy, happy young people . . . a generation that didn't slog through law school, work twelve-hour days, or break up with fiancés" (p. 15). Moog presents this vignette as a reminder of the fact that "advertisers are not in the business of making people feel better about themselves, they're in the *selling* business" (p. 16). As this statement implies, commercial advertising often does create a vision of a fantasy world that may become a source of dissatisfaction in people's real lives, and this is especially true of ads that use sex or status as part of their appeal. Some people may find this practice objectionable in and of itself, although in my view it would be rather fatuous, as well as somewhat puritanical, to suggest that advertisers should stop purveying the images of "beautiful, sexy, happy young people" that led to Moog's client's distress. However, there is a related trend in advertising that does seem to me to raise especially troublesome ethical issues.

In recent years, ads aimed at young people have increasingly sought to appeal to an adolescent sense of frustration and resentment at the constricting demands of adult society. There may be a lingering element of this type of sentiment in the dissatisfaction expressed by Moog's client, but the kind of advertising to which I am referring is quite different from the old, Pepsi-generation style of happy, carefree images. Instead, these more recent ads, for products such as athletic shoes, off-road vehicles, or video games, often make a point of displaying abrasive, belligerent behavior and physical recklessness (cf. Lull, 1995, pp. 73-81). A defender of such ads might argue that they are simply being honest. Adolescents often have good reason to chafe at the standards imposed on them by older people and to recoil from the vision of the future that many of them face. The aggression and recklessness depicted in some of these ads are no doubt authentic expressions of how many young people feel. To put a happy face on those feelings could be considered hypocritical. Nevertheless, with due respect for such views, I would argue that the type of resentment exploited in these ads is unproductive at best, counterproductive at worst. Dissatisfaction that leads to impulsiveness and disregard for other people gains nothing from being expressed openly. In that sense, I would say that the ethics of this genre of advertising are certainly questionable.

This is not to say, however, that advertising aimed at young people should necessarily revert to the untroubled imagery of earlier times. It should be possible to portray and address youth honestly without pandering to the irresponsible tendencies that are sometimes associated with adolescence. For instance, despite the criticism that has recently been directed at the advertising of Calvin Klein, it seems to me that there are many Calvin Klein ads that manage to strike this balance quite effectively. In particular, the print ads for cK one fragrance have generated record-breaking sales while presenting a view of youthful sexuality that is remarkably unglamorized (compared to most other ads) and, furthermore, notably inclusive both racially and in terms of sexual orientation (see Figure C.1). This inclusiveness deserves special mention. The cK one ads are among the few examples of mass-produced imagery in which the mingling of people from different backgrounds appears relatively natural, rather than an artificial (albeit well-meaning) concoction of the media.

But, again, this comment should not be interpreted as a blanket endorsement of unvarnished naturalism in all of advertising. In a recent discussion of the portrayal of blacks and whites in the mass media, DeMott (1995) has argued that movies and ads present a phony picture of harmony between the races that serves to obscure the unpleasant truth about race relations in the United States. I do not find this argument persuasive. For one thing, information about racial friction is abundantly available elsewhere in the media. More importantly, though, I think it is a mistake to assume that people always look at advertising images expecting to see the way things really are in society. Almost by definition, the portrayals of the good life presented in ads carry with them the implicit understanding that they are idealizations, not documentary reports (cf. Schudson, 1984). What people look for in such ads is a vision of the way things ought to be. Furthermore, when an ad is produced by a large corporation, people are likely to see this vision as an indicator of socially approved values—even though it also may be understood tacitly that those values do not correspond very closely to current social reality. From this perspective, the kinds of advertisements that DeMott criticizes—depictions of people from different racial and ethnic backgrounds living together in harmony and prosperity—are actually highly desirable. For example, an American Express Gold Card ad (attacked by DeMott) shows elegantly dressed blacks and whites occupying adjacent box seats in an opulent-looking theater or concert hall, while an ad for Chubb Insurance portrays two suburban families, one black, one white, posing together in a setting of obvious wealth (see Figures C.2 and C.3). Such ads should be praised, not subjected to carping objections. In my view, they are models of the responsible use of advertising's iconic powers.

Figure C.1.

INDEXICALITY

We have already discussed the misuses of indexicality at some length in Chapter 4, which also contained an overview of uses of photographic

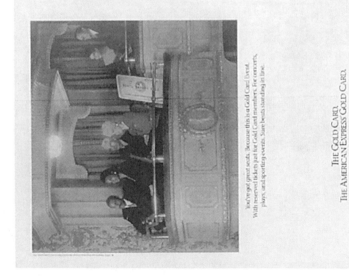

Figure C.2 and Figure C.3.

evidence in support of major social causes. There is no need to recapitulate either of these accounts here. However, I do want to emphasize a point that was implicit in much of what I had to say in that chapter. Although I think it is important to try, as I did, to spell out the formal characteristics of misleading or fraudulent images, I would insist that the ethicality of photographic evidence can never be determined solely on formal grounds. Let me give two examples to illustrate this contention.

The first example has to do with staging and concerns an ad that we have already discussed in Chapter 4: the 1990 Volvo TV commercial in which a monster truck flattens other cars but fails to squash a Volvo 240. Although the scene shown in that commercial turned out to have been staged, it appears that there was a factual basis for the staging. According to a Volvo spokesperson, the idea for the commercial had come from a 1988 incident at a Vermont monster truck rally in which a Volvo actually had withstood a monster truck's weight. The spokesperson also noted that Volvos had proven their resilience in tests conducted after the commercial was aired. Why then was it necessary to reinforce the car with I-beams for the commercial itself? The explanation suggested by this spokesperson was that the commercial's repeated takes might have subjected the car to more stress than it would have experienced in a single monster-truck encounter (see Savan, 1994, p. 100).

These facts and arguments provide a reasonable explanation of the thinking that may have gone into the creation of the commercial. Do they also justify the staging? Critics of this episode have typically considered the staging unacceptable, regardless of the circumstances. Leslie Savan (1994), who provided the details that I have just cited concerning the Volvo spokesperson's explanation, argues that even adding a "dramatization" tag to the commercial would not have been sufficient to exculpate its creators (p. 100). I suspect that most people would agree with this assessment, and, although I feel that the spokesperson's argument does go a long way toward providing an acceptable justification, if I had to make a yes-no choice, I too would say that the staging was inappropriate.

But now consider a second incident that raises similar questions. In describing this incident, I feel compelled, for ethical reasons of my own, to alter the particulars so as not to reveal the identity of the organization and the specific individuals involved in it. However, the basic situation that I am going to describe is modeled on an actual event that happened some years ago. Let's say an antiracist organization has proof that a certain politician has met with, and embraced, a well-known racist. The embrace has been filmed, but the organization is not able to gain access to the film. So instead, it creates a composite photograph of the two men embracing, and it uses this photograph in an ad designed to warn voters about the politician's racist sympathies. The photograph is not labeled a composite, nor does the text of the ad, in which the politician's embrace of the racist is described, refer explicitly to the photograph in any other way. What are we to make of this situation?

For purists, the judgment is undoubtedly easy. Because the ad's context can reasonably be seen as implying that the photograph is an undoctored document of the embrace referred to in the ad's verbal text, by strictly formal standards the use of this photograph can be considered a straightforward case of misleading alteration. Nevertheless, my own view of the ad is much more ambivalent. As in the case of the Volvo commercial, it seems to me that our judgment of this ad needs to take into account what difference the visual manipulation makes to the viewer's understanding of the ad's factual content. In the Volvo case, as we have seen, it could be argued that the basic facts about the Volvo 240's structural strength were conveyed accurately in the commercial, even though the incident used to demonstrate those facts was staged. In the case of the antiracist ad, this kind of argument can be made with much greater force. There is no question that the embrace between the politician and the racist did occur, and that it was recorded on film. So what the viewer is being misled about in the ad is not the ad's fundamental contention, but rather the evidentiary value of the photograph used to prove (implicitly) that contention. Should this count as deception?

If pressed, I would have to say yes, but I would add that this particular kind of deception—or perhaps just this one incident—seems to me to be relatively benign. My own personal experience with this ad may be relevant here. When I first encountered the ad, I already knew about the politician's embrace of the racist, and I had seen the film on which the composite photograph was based. So, when I realized—after repeated scrutiny—that the photograph was, in fact, a composite, I experienced no feelings of having been deceived in any important way. Admittedly, my lack of moral outrage was also due to my underlying faith in the organization that produced the ad, as well as my support for its cause, and perhaps these factors have clouded my overall judgment of this particular case. But my more general point here is that such factors inevitably play some role in our assessments of the ethical implications of visual practices. Perhaps the two examples I have given here do not warrant making that role more than a bit part. Perhaps there is no situation in which that role should be a principal one. Nevertheless, I suspect that there is also no situation in which that role is entirely absent.

LACK OF PROPOSITIONAL SYNTAX

Because picture-based communication does not have an explicit syntax for expressing causal claims, analogies, and other kinds of propositions, arguments made through sequences of images can be said, *in principle*, to be more open to the perceiver's own interpretation than are verbal arguments. In practice, of course, experienced creators of ads and other forms of visual persuasion are able to employ the tacit conventions of the medium in such a way as to elicit relatively uniform and consistent responses from their viewers. Nevertheless, the implicit quality of pictorial syntax and argumentation endows visual persuasion with a type of deniability that verbal persuasion cannot claim. In Chapter 6, we discussed various ways in which this deniability can make it possible for advertisers to express ideas that they might be less willing to put into words. In some cases, reluctance to spell things out verbally is a response to societal inhibitions. In other cases, however, this reluctance arguably stems from the fact that the advertiser's claims are fraudulent and might be more vulnerable to counterargument or even legal action if they were made in the more explicit syntax of words. Rather than repeating the examples discussed in Chapter 6, let me give one more, concluding illustration of this possibility.

Some time ago, one of the tabloid TV news programs did an exposé on the topic of nutritional supplements for body builders. According to the program, these substances are no better at inducing muscle growth than an ordinary balanced diet would be. And yet people who are seriously involved in body-building apparently spend large amounts of money on regular purchases of these products. As part of this exposé, a reporter visited one of the companies that produces the supplements and confronted a company spokesperson with the charges against the product, as well as with one of the company's ads. The ad was a typical example of a cause-effect juxtaposition: on one hand, an image of the product; on the other, an image of a champion body-builder. Didn't the spokesperson think this ad was fraudulent? the reporter asked. Not at all, replied the spokesperson. Nowhere in the ad, he pointed out, was there any verbal claim that the product could bring about extraordinary muscle growth. As for the meaning of the pictures—that, he argued, was a completely subjective matter. The company could not be held responsible for what individual viewers saw in those images.

The spokesperson's response expresses in a nutshell what the value of images can be in such a situation. Because there was, indeed, no verbal claim of superior effects in the ad's body copy, the spokesperson was able to avoid being held accountable for customers' assumptions about what the product could do. And yet the images encouraged those assumptions even more vividly, if less explicitly. Unethical? In my view, yes, because of the underlying fraudulence of the product. But, having said that, let me add a final word about a question that may have occurred to some readers at this point, if not earlier. What should be the legal consequences for the various types of visual deception that we have examined in this book? Because I am neither a lawyer nor a first-amendment scholar, I cannot comment on technical matters. However, I would like to make a broader point about the desirability of government regulation of advertising images. In my view, official intervention in this area runs the risk of weakening the public's own sense of responsibility for critical viewing. If people think that a government watchdog—or should one say Big Brother?—is there to shield them from visual deception, they may be less inclined to invest their own energies in becoming "visually literate." For those of us who believe in the value of a self-reliant, self-educating citizenry, this side effect of government intervention would be unfortunate indeed. So I am skeptical about the ramifications of investing government authorities with the responsibility to protect people from pictures, and I think it would be regrettable if anything I have said in this book were to be seen as supporting such an intervention.

REFERENCES

Achebe, C. (1988). *Hopes and impediments: Selected essays*. New York: Anchor.

Adatto, K. (1993). *Picture perfect*. New York: Basic Books.

Adbusters spoof ad contest. (1995, Winter). *Adbusters Quarterly: Journal of the Mental Environment*, pp. 55-58.

Ads mocking subliminal advertising may bring fear of fostering bad image for advertising. (1991, June 17). *Advertising Age*, p. 18.

Ailes, R., with Kraushar, J. (1988). *You are the message*. New York: Doubleday.

Andrews, J. C. (1989). The dimensionality of beliefs toward advertising in general. *Journal of Advertising, 18*(1), 26-35.

Antin, T. (1993). *Great print advertising: Creative approaches, strategies, and tactics*. New York: John Wiley.

Appelbaum, U., & Halliburton, C. (1993). How to develop international advertising campaigns that work: The example of the European food and beverage sector. *International Journal of Advertising, 12*, 223-233.

Appleton, J. (1990). *The symbolism of habitat: An interpretation of landscape in the arts*. Seattle: University of Washington Press.

Arnheim, R. (1954). *Art and visual perception: A psychology of the creative eye*. Berkeley: University of California Press.

Arnheim, R. (1969). *Visual thinking*. Berkeley: University of California Press.

Arnheim, R. (1988). *The power of the center: A study of composition in the visual arts*. Berkeley: University of California Press.

Babyak, R. J. (1995). Demystifying the Asian consumer. *Appliance Manufacturer, 43*(2), 25-27.

Baker, M. J., & Churchill, G. A., Jr. (1977). The impact of physically attractive models on advertising evaluations. *Journal of Marketing Research, 14*, 538-555.

Baker, S. (1961). *Visual persuasion: The effect of pictures on the subconscious*. New York: McGraw-Hill.

275

Ball-Rokeach, S. J., Grube, J. W., & Rokeach, M. (1981). "Roots: The next generation"—Who watched and with what effect? *Public Opinion Quarterly, 45,* 58-68.

Bang, M. (1991). *Picture this: Perception and composition.* Boston: Bulfinch Press.

Barnicoat, J. (1972). *Posters: A concise history.* New York: Thames and Hudson.

Barthel, D. (1988). *Putting on appearances: Gender and advertising.* Philadelphia: Temple University Press.

Bazin, A. (1967). *What is cinema?* (H. Gray, Trans.). Berkeley: University of California Press.

Berger, J. (1972). *Ways of seeing.* New York: Penguin.

Biswas, A., Olsen, J. E., & Carlet, V. (1992). A comparison of print advertisements from the United States and France. *Journal of Advertising, 21*(4), 73-81.

Block, M. P., & Vanden Bergh, B. G. (1985). Can you sell subliminal messages to consumers? *Journal of Advertising, 14*(3), 59-62.

Blodgett, P. J. (1993). Visiting "the realm of wonder": Yosemite and the business of tourism, 1855-1916. In R. J. Orsi, A. Runte, & M. Smith-Baranzini (Eds.), *Yosemite and Sequoia: A century of California national parks* (pp. 33-48). Berkeley: University of California Press.

Bordwell, D. (1993). *The cinema of Eisenstein.* Cambridge, MA: Harvard University Press.

Bossen, H. (1982). A tall tale retold: The influence of the photographs of William Henry Jackson on the passage of the Yellowstone Park Act of 1872. *Studies in Visual Communication, 8,* 98-109.

Bourdieu, P. (1984). *Distinction: A social critique of the judgment of taste.* Cambridge, MA: Harvard University Press.

Bourgery, M., & Guimaraes, G. (1993, May-June). Global ads: Say it with pictures. *Journal of European Business,* pp. 22-26.

Bouse, D. (1991). *The wilderness documentary: Film, video, and the visual rhetoric of American environmentalism.* Unpublished doctoral dissertation, University of Pennsylvania.

Bouse, D. (1995, June). *In its original condition: Restoring the photographed past.* Paper presented at the Ninth Annual Visual Communication Conference, Flagstaff, AZ.

Brand, S., Kelly, K., & Kinney, J. (1985, July). Digital retouching: The end of photography as evidence of anything. *Whole Earth Review,* pp. 42-49.

Braile, R. (1994, Summer). Is racism a factor in siting undesirable facilities? *Garbage,* pp. 13-15, 18.

Brower, D. R. (1991). *Work in progress.* Salt Lake City, UT: Gibbs Smith.

Brower, K. (1994, November). Devouring the earth. *Atlantic Monthly,* pp. 113-126.

Brown, L. R., Lenssen, N., & Kane, H. (1995). *Vital signs 1995: The trends that are shaping our future.* New York: Norton.

Bushman, R. L. (1992). *The refinement of America: Person, houses, cities.* New York: Vintage.

Buss, D. (1989). Sex differences in human mate preferences: Evolutionary hypotheses tested in 37 cultures. *Behavioral and Brain Sciences, 12,* 1-49.

Buy me that! A kid's survival guide to TV advertising. (1990). Chicago: Consumers Union/Films Incorporated Video.

Canter, N. J. (1990). *The use of landscape photography in the environmental movement: A triple case study.* M.A. thesis, Annenberg School for Communication, University of Pennsylvania.

Cantor, G. N. (1972). Effects of familiarization on children's ratings of pictures of whites and blacks. *Child Development, 43,* 1219-1229.

Cappella, J. N. (1993). The facial feedback hypothesis in human interaction: Review and speculation. *Journal of Language and Social Psychology, 12,* 13-29.

Caron, A. H. (1979). First-time exposure to television: Effects on Inuit children's cultural images. *Communication Research, 6,* 135-154.

Carroll, J. B., & Casagrande, J. B. (1958). The function of language classifications in behavior. In E. E. Maccoby, T. M. Newcomb, & E. L. Hartley (Eds.), *Readings in social psychology* (3rd ed., pp. 18-31). New York: Holt, Rinehart & Winston.

Carroll, N. (1993). Toward a theory of point-of-view editing: Communication, emotion, and the movies. *Poetics Today, 14,* 123-141.

Chaffee, S., Pan, Z., & Chu, G. (1995, May). *Western media in China: Audience and influence.* Paper presented to the International Communication Association, Albuquerque, NM.

Chapman, S. (1986). *Great expectorations: Advertising and the tobacco industry.* London: Comedia.

Cheeky ad pains peach farmers. (1994, July 1). *Asian Advertising and Marketing,* p. 22.

Clark, D. (1995). Commodity lesbianism. In G. Dines & J. M. Humez (Eds.), *Gender, race and class in media* (pp. 142-151). Thousand Oaks, CA: Sage.

Clifton, N. R. (1983). *The figure in film.* Newark: University of Delaware Press.

Clinton, C. (1995). Gone with the wind. In M. C. Carnes (Ed.), *Past imperfect: History according to the movies* (pp. 132-135). New York: Henry Holt.

Cook, W. A. (1993). Lurking behind the ice cubes. *Journal of Advertising Research, 33*(2), 7-8.

Cooper, A. (1995, September 11). Eminent domain. *Adweek,* pp. 26-29.

Cox, D. S., & Cox, A. D. (1988). What does familiarity breed? Complexity as a moderator of repetition effects in advertisement evaluation. *Journal of Consumer Research, 15,* 111-116.

Crames, A. (1990). *Surrealism and linguistic complexity in ad messages: Viewers' interpretations of and responses to "difficult ads."* M.A. thesis, Annenberg School for Communication, University of Pennsylvania.

Creighton, M. R. (1995). Imaging the other in Japanese advertising campaigns. In J. G. Carrier (Ed.), *Occidentalism: Images of the West* (pp. 135-160). New York: Oxford University Press.

Cripps, T. (1983). Racial ambiguities in American propaganda movies. In K. R. M. Short (Ed.), *Film and radio propaganda in World War II* (pp. 125-145). Knoxville: University of Tennessee Press.

Cripps, T. (1993). *Making movies black: The Hollywood message movie from World War II to the civil rights era.* New York: Oxford University Press.

Cuperfain, R., & Clarke, T. K. (1985). A new perspective of subliminal perception. *Journal of Advertising, 14*(1), 36-41.

Cutler, B. D., & Javalgi, R. G. (1992). A cross-cultural analysis of the visual components of print advertising: The United States and the European Community. *Journal of Advertising Research, 32*(1), 71-79.

Dahl, H. (1993). *The pragmatics of persuasion.* Copenhagen: Handelshoejskolen i Koebenhavn.

Dahl, H., & Buhl, C. (1993). *Marketing & semiotic.* Copenhagen: Akademisk Forlags Semiotikserie.

Damasio, A. R. (1994). *Descartes' error: Emotion, reason, and the human brain.* New York: Grosset/Putnam.

Dambekains, L. (1994). Challenging notions of curriculum development: Questions of multicultural context and content in how we encourage students. *Visual Arts Research, 28,* 84-90.

Danesi, M. (1994). Introduction: Thomas A. Sebeok and the science of signs. In T. A. Sebeok, *Signs: An introduction to semiotics* (pp. xi-xvii). Toronto: University of Toronto Press.

Davidson, D. K. (1995, March 27). Marketers respond to virtual reality. *Marketing News TM,* p. 10.

DeMott, B. (1995, September). Put on a happy face: Masking the differences between blacks and whites. *Harper's*, pp. 31-38.

Diamond, E., & Bates, S. (1984). *The spot: The rise of political advertising on television*. Cambridge: MIT Press.

Domzal, T. J., & Kernan, J. B. (1993). Mirror, mirror: Some postmodern reflections on global advertising. *Journal of Advertising, 22*(4), 1-20.

Donsbach, W., Brosius, H.-B., & Mattenklott, A. (1993, May). *The guided eye: Channel and presentation effects in personal and televised perceptions of an event.* Paper presented to the International Communication Association, Washington, DC.

Dressler, W. W., & Robbins, M. C. (1975). Art styles, social stratification, and cognition: An analysis of Greek vase painting. *American Ethnologist, 2*, 427-434.

DuBois, W. E. B. (1903). *The souls of black folk: Essays and sketches.* (2nd ed.). Chicago: A. C. McLurg.

Dumas, A. A. (1988). *Cross-cultural analysis of people's interpretation of advertising visual cliches.* M.A. thesis, Annenberg School for Communication, University of Pennsylvania.

Dunn, S. W. (1966). The case study approach in cross-cultural research. *Journal of Marketing Research, 3*, 26-31.

Dyer, G. (1982). *Advertising as communication.* New York: Routledge.

Ebong, E. T. (1989). *Visual images in political advertisements: An analysis of their informational content and their demographic appeal.* M.A. thesis, Annenberg School for Communication, University of Pennsylvania.

Eco, U. (1975). *A theory of semiotics.* Bloomington: Indiana University Press.

Eisenstein, S. M. (1988). *Selected works.* Vol. I. *Writings, 1922-34* (R. Taylor, Ed. & Trans.). London: BFI Publishing.

Eisenstein, S. M. (1991). *Selected works.* Vol. II. *Towards a theory of montage* (M. Glenny & R. Taylor, Eds.; M. Glenny, Trans.). London: BFI Publishing.

Elinder, E. (1965). How international can European advertising be? *Journal of Marketing, 29*, 7-11.

Ellis, B. J., & Symons, D. (1990). Sex differences in sexual fantasy: An evolutionary psychological approach. *Journal of Sex Research, 27*, 527-555.

Espe, H. (1981). Differences in the perception of National Socialist and classicist architecture. *Journal of Environmental Psychology, 1*, 33-42.

Ewen, S. (1988). *All consuming images: The politics of style in contemporary culture.* New York: Basic Books.

Ewen, S. (1991). Desublimated advertising. *Artforum, 29*(5), 27-28.

Ewen, S., & Ewen, E. (1982). *Channels of desire: Mass images and the shaping of American consciousness.* New York: McGraw-Hill.

Farhi, P. (1990, December 11). Ad makers enter "hall of shame." *Washington Post*, p. C1.

Farley, J. U. (1986). Are there truly international products—and prime prospects for them? *Journal of Advertising Research, 26*(5), 17-20.

Fatt, A. C. (1967). The danger of "local" international advertising. *Journal of Marketing, 31*, 60-62.

Fincher, J. (1995). By convention, the enemy never did without. *Smithsonian, 26*(3), 126-143.

Finley, M. I. (1980). *Ancient slavery and modern ideology.* New York: Pelican.

Fiske, J. (1987). *Television culture.* London: Methuen.

Forbes, N. E., & Lonner, W. J. (1980). *Sociocultural and cognitive effects of commercial television on previously television-naive rural Alaskan children.* Final report to the National Science Foundation. Grant No. BNS-78-25678.

Fredrickson, G. M. (1988). *The arrogance of race: Historical perspectives on slavery, racism, and social inequality.* Middletown, CT: Wesleyan University Press.

Fridlund, A. J. (1994). *Human facial expression: An evolutionary view.* San Diego, CA: Academic Press.

Friedlaender, W. F. (1952). *David to Delacroix* (R. Goldwater, Trans.). Cambridge, MA: Harvard University Press.

Friedman, L. (Ed.). (1991). *Unspeakable images: Ethnicity and the American cinema.* Urbana: University of Illinois Press.

Gable, G. C. (1983). *Point of view in television advertising.* M.A. thesis, Annenberg School for Communication, University of Pennsylvania.

Gable, M., Wilkens, H. T., Harris, L., & Feinberg, R. (1987). An evaluation of subliminally embedded sexual stimuli in graphics. *Journal of Advertising, 16*(1), 26-31.

Galan, L. S. (1986). *The use of subjective point of view in persuasive communication.* M.A. thesis, Annenberg School for Communication, University of Pennsylvania.

Garfield, B. (1994a, February 14). CAA casts perfect spell in latest Coca-Cola ads. *Advertising Age*, p. 40.

Garfield, B. (1994b, August 22). Del Monte approach is fresh, though not quite subliminal. *Advertising Age*, p. 3.

Geiger, S. F., & Reeves, B. (1991). The effects of visual structure and content emphasis on the evaluation and memory for political candidates. In F. Biocca (Ed.), *Television and political advertising. Volume 1: Psychological processes* (pp. 125-143). Hillsdale, NJ: Lawrence Erlbaum.

Goffman, E. (1976). Gender advertisements. *Studies in the Anthropology of Visual Communication, 3*, 69-154.

Goldberg, M., & Gorn, G. (1979). Television's impact on preferences for non-white playmates: Canadian "Sesame Street" inserts. *Journal of Broadcasting, 23*, 27-32.

Goldberg, V. (1991). *The power of photography: How photographs changed our lives.* New York: Abbeville Press.

Goldman, R. (1992). *Reading ads socially.* New York: Routledge.

Gombrich, E. H. (1972). The visual image. *Scientific American, 227*(3), 82-96.

Goodman, N. (1976). *Languages of art: An approach to a theory of symbols.* Indianapolis, IN: Bobbs-Merrill.

Gordon, E. R. (1983). *Television's potential for reducing racial prejudice in children: A cognitive moral developmental approach.* Unpublished doctoral dissertation, Claremont Graduate School, Claremont, CA.

Gorn, G. J., Goldberg, M. E., & Kanungo, R. N. (1976). The role of educational television in changing the intergroup attitudes of children. *Child Development, 47*, 277-280.

Goshorn, K. (1995). *Persuasive evidence: Visual argumentation in land use conflicts.* Paper presented at the Ninth Annual Visual Communication Conference, Flagstaff, AZ.

Green, J. D. (1985). Picasso's visual metaphors. *Journal of Aesthetic Education, 19*(4), 61-76.

Griffin, M. (1992). Looking at TV news: Strategies for research. *Communication, 13*, 121-141.

Grinnell prof studies manipulative film techniques. (1987, August 21). United Press International.

Grodal, T. K. (1994). *Cognition, emotion and visual fiction.* Copenhagen: University of Copenhagen, Department of Film and Media Studies.

Gross, L. (1995). Out of the mainstream: Sexual minorities and the mass media. In G. Dines & J. M. Humez (Eds.), *Gender, race and class in media* (pp. 61-69). Thousand Oaks, CA: Sage.

Gross, R. (1993, June). *"Why is the gorilla flushing the toilet?" or Japanese advertising: Sights that tickle the eyes.* Paper presented at the Seventh Annual Visual Communication Conference, Jackson Hole, WY.

Haber, R. N. (1959). Public attitudes regarding subliminal advertising. *Public Opinion Quarterly, 23,* 291-293.

Haberstroh, J. (1984, September 17). Can't ignore subliminal ad charges. *Advertising Age,* pp. 3, 42, 44.

Halliburton, C., & Huenerberg, R. (1993). Pan-European marketing—myth or reality. *Journal of International Marketing, 1*(3), 77-92.

Han, S.-P. (1990). *Individualism and collectivism: Its implications for cross-cultural advertising.* Unpublished doctoral dissertation, University of Illinois at Urbana-Champaign.

Hasegawa, K. (1995, May). *Does the U.S. comparative advertising TV practice work abroad? The case of Japan and the United States.* Paper presented to the International Communication Association, Albuquerque, NM.

Hatcher, E. P. (1988). *Visual metaphors: A methodological study in visual communication.* Albuquerque: University of New Mexico Press.

Hausman, C. R. (1989). *Metaphor and art.* New York: Cambridge University Press.

Hayek, F. A. (1944). *The road to serfdom.* Chicago: University of Chicago Press.

Heerwagen, J. H., & Orians, G. H. (1993). Humans, habitats, and aesthetics. In S. R. Kellert & E. O. Wilson (Eds.), *The biophilia hypothesis* (pp. 138-172). Washington, DC: Island Press.

Hill, J. S., & Shao, A. T. (1994). Agency participants in multicountry advertising: A preliminary examination of affiliate characteristics and environments. *Journal of International Marketing, 2*(2), 29-48.

Hill, J. S., & Winski, J. M. (1987, November 16). Goodbye global ads: Global village is fantasy land for big marketers. *Advertising Age,* pp. 22, 36.

Hinsberg, P. (1991, June 10). Paseo ads run hot and cold—but that's the point. *Adweek,* p. 29.

Hitchon, J., Duckler, P., & Thorson, E. (1994). Effects of ambiguity and complexity on consumer response to music video commercials. *Journal of Broadcasting and Electronic Media, 38,* 289-306.

Hjarvard, S. (1994, July). *The global spread of a European model: The experiences of regional television news exchange networks using a public model of cooperation.* Paper presented to the International Association for Mass Communication Research, Seoul, Korea.

Homer, P. M., & Kahle, L. R. (1986). A social adaptation explanation of the effects of surrealism in advertising. *Journal of Advertising, 15*(2), 50-54, 60.

Homer, W. I. (1964). *Seurat and the science of painting.* Cambridge: MIT Press.

Horgan, J. (1995). The new social Darwinists. *Scientific American, 273*(4), 174-181.

Horovitz, B. (1990, November 14). Volvo agency steps down over ad flap. *Los Angeles Times,* p. D3.

Howard, J., Rothbart, G., & Sloan, L. (1978). The response to "Roots": A national survey. *Journal of Broadcasting, 22,* 279-320.

Huston, A., Greer, D., Wright, J. C., Welch, R., & Ross, R. (1984). Children's comprehension of televised formal features with masculine and feminine connotations. *Developmental Psychology, 20,* 707-716.

Ind, N. (1993). *Great advertising campaigns: Goals and accomplishments.* Lincolnwood, IL: NTC Business Books.

Jakle, J. A. (1987). *The visual elements of landscape.* Amherst: University of Massachusetts Press.

Jamieson, K. H. (1984). *Packaging the presidency: A history and criticism of presidential campaign advertising.* New York: Oxford University Press.

Jamieson, K. H. (1992). *Dirty politics: Deception, distraction, and democracy.* New York: Oxford University Press.

Jaubert, A. (1989). *Making people disappear: An amazing chronicle of photographic deception.* Washington, DC: Pergamon-Brassey's.

Javalgi, R., Cutler, B. D., & White, D. S. (1994). Print advertising in the Pacific basin: An empirical investigation. *International Marketing Review, 11*(6), 48-64.

Jensen, K. B. (1995). *The social semiotics of mass communication.* Thousand Oaks, CA: Sage.

Johansson, J. K. (1994). The sense of "nonsense": Japanese TV advertising. *Journal of Advertising, 23*(1), 17-26.

Johns, B. (1984). Visual metaphor: Lost and found. *Semiotica, 52,* 291-333.

Jowett, G., & O'Donnell, V. (1992). *Propaganda and persuasion* (2nd ed.). Thousand Oaks, CA: Sage.

Kahan, H., & Mulryan, D. (1995, May). Out of the closet. *American Demographics,* pp. 40-47.

Kaplan, S. J. (1990). Visual metaphors in the representation of communication technology. *Critical Studies in Mass Communication, 7,* 37-47.

Kaplan, S. J. (1992). A conceptual analysis of form and content in visual metaphors. *Communication, 13,* 197-209.

Katz, P. A., & Zalk, S. R. (1978). Modification of children's racial attitudes. *Developmental Psychology, 14,* 447-461.

Kelly, S. J. (1976). Subliminal embeds in print advertising: A challenge to advertising ethics. *Journal of Advertising, 8*(3), 20-24.

Kennedy, J. M. (1982). Metaphor in pictures. *Perception, 11,* 589-605.

Kennedy, J. M. (1990). Metaphor—its intellectual basis. *Journal of Metaphor and Symbolic Activity, 5,* 115-123.

Kennedy, J. M. (1993). *Drawing & the blind: Pictures to touch.* New Haven, CT: Yale University Press.

Kennedy, J. M., & Simpson, W. (1982). For each kind of figure of speech there is a pictorial metaphor: A figure of depiction. *Visual Arts Research, 16,* 1-11.

Kepplinger, H. M. (1987). *Darstellungseffekte: Experimentelle untersuchungen zur wirkung von pressefotos und fernsehfilmen.* Freiburg: Verlag Karl Alber.

Kepplinger, H. M. (1991). The impact of presentation techniques: Theoretical aspects and empirical findings. In F. Biocca (Ed.), *Television and political advertising. Volume 1: Psychological processes* (pp. 173-194). Hillsdale, NJ: Lawrence Erlbaum.

Kepplinger, H. M., & Donsbach, W. (1990). The impact of camera perspectives on the perception of a speaker. *Studies in Educational Evaluation, 16,* 133-156.

Kernan, J. K., & Domzal, T. J. (1993). International advertising: To globalize, visualize. *Journal of International Consumer Marketing, 5*(4), 51-71.

Key, W. B. (1973). *Subliminal seduction: Ad media's manipulation of a not so innocent America.* New York: Signet.

Key, W. B. (1976). *Media sexploitation.* New York: Signet.

Key, W. B. (1981). *The clam-plate orgy and other subliminal techniques for manipulating your behavior.* New York: Signet.

Key, W. B. (1989). *The age of manipulation: The con in confidence, the sin in sincere.* Lanham, MD: Madison Books.

Kilbourne, W. E., Painton, S., & Ridley, D. (1985). The effect of sexual embedding on responses to magazine advertisements. *Journal of Advertising, 14*(2), 48-56.

Kimle, P. A., & Fiore, A. M. (1992). Fashion advertisements: A comparison of viewers' perceptual and affective responses to illustrated and photographed stimuli. *Perceptual and Motor Skills, 75,* 1083-1091.

Kindem, G., & Teddlie, C. (1982). Film effects and ethnicity. In S. Thomas (Ed.), *Film/culture: Explorations of cinema in its social context* (pp. 195-208). Metuchen, NJ: Scarecrow Press.

Kobre, K. (1995). The long tradition of doctoring photos. *Visual Communication Quarterly, 2*(2), 14-15.

Kraemer, A. J., et al. (1975). *Vicarious attitude change and the design of "message" films: Application to race relations.* Alexandria, VA: Human Resources Research Organization.

Kraft, R. N. (1986). The role of cutting in the evaluation and retention of film. *Journal of Experimental Psychology: Learning, Memory and Cognition, 12,* 155-163.

Kraft, R. N. (1987). The influence of camera angle on comprehension and retention of pictorial events. *Memory and Cognition, 15,* 291-307.

Krieger, M. (1984). The ambiguities of representation and illusion: An E. H. Gombrich retrospective. *Critical Inquiry, 11,* 181-194.

Landau, T. (1989). *About faces: The evolution of the human face.* New York: Anchor.

Landler, M. (1994, November 18). Think globally, program locally. *Business Week,* pp. 186-189.

Lang, A. (1991). Emotion, formal features, and memory for televised political advertisements. In F. Biocca (Ed.), *Television and political advertising. Volume 1: Psychological processes* (pp. 221-243). Hillsdale, NJ: Lawrence Erlbaum.

Lang, K., & Lang, G. E. (1952). The unique perspective of television and its effect: A pilot study. In W. Schramm & D. F. Roberts (Eds.), *The process and effects of mass communication* (Rev. ed., pp. 169-188). Urbana: University of Illinois Press.

Lankford, M. D. (1992). *Films for learning, thinking, and doing.* Englewood, CO: Libraries Unlimited.

Larrabee, M. H. (1994). *Orthography and affect: Roman text in Japanese magazine advertisements.* M.A. thesis, Annenberg School for Communication, University of Pennsylvania.

LaTour, M. S. (1990). Female nudity in print advertising: An analysis of gender differences in arousal and ad response. *Psychology and Marketing, 7,* 65-81.

Lee, M. A., & Solomon, N. (1990). *Unreliable sources: A guide to detecting bias in news media.* Secaucus, NJ: Carol Publishing Group.

Leiss, W., Kline, S., & Jhally, S. (1990). *Social communication in advertising: Persons, products and images of well-being* (2nd ed.). New York: Routledge.

Lester, P. M. (1995). *Visual communication: Images with messages.* Belmont, CA: Wadsworth.

Levine, J. (1991, September 2). Subliminal advertising theoretician Wilson Bryan Key survives ridicule. *Forbes,* pp. 134-135.

Levitt, T. (1983, May-June). The globalization of markets. *Harvard Business Review,* pp. 92-102.

Lippert, B. (1995a, July 31). Calvinist youth. *Adweek,* p. 34.

Lippert, B. (1995b, September 18). The naked untruth. *Adweek,* p. 26.

Lombard, M. (1995). Direct responses to people on the screen: Television and personal space. *Communication Research, 22,* 288-324.

Lonner, W. J., Thorndike, R. M., Forbes, N. E., & Ashworth, C. (1985). The influence of television on measured cognitive abilities: A study with Native Alaskan children. *Journal of Cross-Cultural Psychology, 16,* 355-380.

Lorenz, K. Z. (1970). *Studies on animal and human behavior.* Cambridge, MA: Harvard University Press.

Lorimer, E. S., & Dunn, S. W. (1967). Four measures of cross-cultural advertising effectiveness. *Journal of Advertising Research, 7*(4), 11-13.

Lovelace, V., Schneier, S., Dollberg, S., Segui, I., & Black, T. (1994). Making a neighborhood the *Sesame Street* way: Developing a methodology to evaluate children's understanding of race. *Journal of Educational Television, 20*(2), 69-77.

Lull, J. (1995). *Media, communication, culture: A global approach.* New York: Columbia University Press.

MacLachlan, J., & Logan, M. (1993). Camera shot length in commercials and their memorability and persuasiveness. *Journal of Advertising Research, 33*(2), 57-61.

Mandell, L. M., & Shaw, D. L. (1973). Judging people in the news—unconsciously: Effect of camera angle and bodily activity. *Journal of Broadcasting, 17,* 353-362.

Marchand, R. (1985). *Advertising the American dream: Making way for modernity, 1920-1940.* Berkeley: University of California Press.

Marling, K. A., & Wetenhall, J. (1991). *Iwo Jima: Monuments, memories, and the American hero.* Cambridge, MA: Harvard University Press.

Marr, D. (1982). *Vision: A computational investigation into the human representation and processing of visual information.* New York: Freeman.

Marra, J. L. (1990). *Advertising creativity: Techniques for generating ideas.* Englewood Cliffs, NJ: Prentice Hall.

Martin, E. (1991). On photographic manipulation. *Journal of Mass Media Ethics, 6,* 156-163.

Martinez, W. (1992). Who constructs anthropological knowledge? Toward a theory of ethnographic film spectatorship. In P. I. Crawford & D. Turton (Eds.), *Film as ethnography.* Manchester, UK: Manchester University Press.

Mayne, J. (1993). *Cinema and spectatorship.* New York: Routledge.

Mays, L., et al. (1975). *On meeting real people: An evaluation report on "Vegetable Soup": The effects of a multi-ethnic children's television series on intergroup attitudes of children.* Albany: New York State Education Department.

McCain, T. A., Chilberg, J., & Wakshlag, J. (1977). The effect of camera angle on source credibility and attraction. *Journal of Broadcasting, 21,* 35-46.

McGinnis, J. (1969). *The selling of the president.* New York: Penguin.

McLuhan, M. (1964). *Understanding media: The extensions of man.* New York: McGraw-Hill.

Messaris, P. (1981). The film audience's awareness of the production process. *Journal of the University Film Association, 33*(4), 53-56.

Messaris, P. (1990). Ethics in visual communication. Broadcast Education Association *Feedback, 31*(4), 2-5, 22-24.

Messaris, P. (1992). Visual "manipulation": Visual means of affecting responses to images. *Communication, 13,* 181-195.

Messaris, P. (1994). *Visual "literacy": Image, mind, and reality.* Boulder, CO: Westview.

Messaris, P., & Nielsen, K. (1989, August). *Viewers' interpretations of associational montage: The influence of visual "literacy" and educational background.* Paper presented to the Association for Journalism and Mass Communication, Washington, DC.

Messaris, P., & Woo, J. (1991). Image vs. reality in Korean-Americans' responses to mass-mediated depictions of the United States. *Critical Studies in Mass Communication, 8,* 74-90.

Meyers, A. (1984). *Perception of formal elements in photographs: Differences between trained and untrained viewers.* M.A. thesis, Annenberg School for Communication, University of Pennsylvania.

Meyers, G. (1994). *Words in ads.* London: Edward Arnold.

284 ◄◦► VISUAL PERSUASION

Meyers-Levy, J., & Peracchio, L. A. (1992). Getting an angle in advertising: The effect of camera angle on product evaluations. *Journal of Marketing Research, 29*, 454-461.

Meyrowitz, J. (1986). Television and interpersonal behavior: Codes of perception and response. In G. Gumpert & R. Cathcart (Eds.), *Inter/media: Interpersonal communication in a media world* (3rd ed., pp. 253-272). New York: Oxford University Press.

Miller, M. C. (1990, April). Hollywood: The ad. *Atlantic Monthly*, pp. 41-54.

Mitchell, A. A., & Olson, J. C. (1981). Are product attribute beliefs the only mediator of advertising effects on brand attitude? *Journal of Marketing Research, 18*, 318-332.

Mitchell, G. (1992). *The campaign of the century: Upton Sinclair's race for governor of California and the birth of media politics*. New York: Random House.

Mitchell, W. J. (1992). *The reconfigured eye: Visual truth in the post-photographic era*. Cambridge: MIT Press.

Moog, C. (1990). *"Are they selling her lips?" Advertising and identity*. New York: Morrow.

Moore, T. E. (1982). Subliminal advertising: What you see is what you get. *Journal of Marketing, 46*(2), 38-47.

Moriarty, S. E. (1987). A content analysis of visuals used in print media advertising. *Journalism Quarterly, 64*, 550-554.

Moriarty, S. E. (1994, June). *A semiotic approach to visual communication*. Paper presented at the Eighth Annual Visual Communication Conference, Feather River, CA.

Morreale, J. (1991). *A new beginning: A textual frame analysis of the political campaign film*. Albany: State University of New York Press.

Mueller, B. (1987). Reflections of culture: An analysis of Japanese and American advertising appeals. *Journal of Advertising Research, 27*(3), 51-59.

Mueller, B. (1992). Standardization vs. specialization: An examination of Westernization in Japanese advertising. *Journal of Advertising Research, 32*(1), 15-24.

Nasar, J. L. (Ed.). (1988). *Environmental aesthetics: Theory, research, and applications*. Cambridge, UK: Cambridge University Press.

Nebenzahl, I. D., & Secunda, E. (1993). Consumers' attitudes toward product placement in movies. *International Journal of Advertising, 12*(1), 1-11.

Nevett, T. (1992). Differences between American and British television advertising: Explanations and implications. *Journal of Advertising, 21*(4), 61-71.

Ogilvy, D. (1983). *Ogilvy on advertising*. New York: Vintage.

Onkvisit, S., & Shaw, J. J. (1990). Global advertising: Revolution or myopia? *Journal of International Consumer Marketing, 2*(3), 97-112.

Orton, P., Reeves, B., Leshner, G., & Nass, C. (1995, May). *Effects of subjective camera angle (POV) and negatively-valenced footage*. Paper presented to the International Communication Association, Albuquerque, NM.

Oyeleye, A. A. (1990). *Advertising and commodity fetishism: Praxis in a peripheral theatre of consumption. A study of advertising in Nigeria*. Unpublished doctoral dissertation, University of Leicester.

Pals, T. (1995). *The effects of video editing speed on viewer comprehension and evaluation of public service announcements*. M.A. thesis, Annenberg School for Communication, University of Pennsylvania.

Panofsky, E. (1995). The ideological antecedents of the Rolls-Royce radiator. In I. Lavin (Ed.), *Three essays on style* (pp. 127-164). Cambridge: MIT Press.

Parameswaran, R., & Pisharodi, R. M. (1994). Facets of country of origin image: An empirical assessment. *Journal of Advertising, 23*(1), 43-56.

Paret, P., Lewis, B. E., & Paret, P. (1992). *Persuasive images: Posters of war and revolution*. Princeton, NJ: Princeton University Press.

Patterson, J., & Kim, P. (1991). *The day America told the truth.* New York: Plume.

Pechmann, C., & Stewart, D. (1988). Advertising repetition: A critical review of wearin and wearout. *Current Issues and Research in Advertising, 11*, 286-329.

Peebles, D. M. (1989). Don't write off global advertising: A commentary. *International Marketing Review, 6*(1), 73-78.

Peirce, C. S. (1991). In J. Hoopes (Ed.), *Peirce on signs: Writings on semiotic by Charles Sanders Peirce.* Chapel Hill: University of North Carolina Press.

Penn, R. (1971). Effects of motion and cutting rate in motion pictures. *AV Communication Review, 19*, 29-50.

Phelan, J. M. (1992). The pseudo context of the processed image. *Media Ethics Update, 4*(2), 9-10.

Poff, M. (1995, October 25). Critic pans advertising's cinema verité. *Roanoke Times & World News*, p. B8.

Pratkanis, A., & Aronson, E. (1992). *Age of propaganda: The everyday use and abuse of persuasion.* New York: Freeman.

Prince, S. (1990). Are there Bolsheviks in your breakfast cereal? In S. Thomas & W. A. Evans (Eds.), *Communication and culture: Language, performance, technology, and media* (pp. 180-184). Norwood, NJ: Ablex.

Prince, S. (in press). The digital threshold: Perceptual realism and unreal images. *Film Quarterly.*

Quelch, J. A., & Hoff, E. J. (1986, May-June). Customized global marketing. *Harvard Business Review*, pp. 59-68.

Reaves, S. (1991). Digital alteration of photographs in consumer magazines. *Journal of Mass Media Ethics, 6*, 175-181.

Reaves, S. (1995a). Magazines vs. newspapers: Editors have different ethical standards on the digital manipulation of photographs. *Visual Communication Quarterly, 2*(1), 4-7.

Reaves, S. (1995b). The unintended effects of new technology (and why we can expect more): A theory-driven framework for analyzing images of the O.J. Simpson story. *Visual Communication Quarterly, 2*(3), 11-15, 24.

Reeves, B., Detenber, B., & Steuer, J. (1993, May). *New televisions: The effects of big pictures and big sound on viewer responses to the screen.* Paper presented to the International Communication Association, Washington, DC.

Reeves, B., Lombard, M., & Melwani, G. (1992). *Faces on the screen: Pictures or natural experience?* Stanford, CA: Social Responses to Communication Technologies Paper #103.

Reichert, T., Morgan, S. E., Callister, M., & Harrison, T. (1995, June). *Men are taking it off! A visual analysis of male portrayal in magazine advertising.* Paper presented at the Ninth Annual Visual Communication Conference, Flagstaff, AZ.

Rex, J., & Mason, D. (Eds.). (1986). *Theories of race and ethnic relations.* New York: Cambridge University Press.

Rhodes, A. (1976). In V. Margolin (Ed.), *Propaganda, the art of persuasion: World War II.* Broomall, PA: Chelsea House.

Ricks, D. A. (1993). *Blunders in international business.* Cambridge, MA: Basil Blackwell.

Ricks, D. A., Arpan, J. S., & Fu, M. Y. (1974). Pitfalls in overseas advertising. *Journal of Advertising Research, 14*(6), 47-51.

Ridley, M. (1993). *The red queen: Sex and the evolution of human nature.* New York: Penguin.

Riis, J. A. (1890). *How the other half lives: Studies among the tenements of New York.* New York: Charles Scribners & Sons.

Ritchin, F. (1990). *In our own image: The coming revolution in photography.* New York: Aperture.

Rochelle, L. (1983). Now you see 'em—now you don't: Those sexy sublims. *Journal of Popular Culture, 17,* 161-166.

Rodriguez-Ema, V. (1994). *Can Michelangelo sell jeans? The use of art in advertising.* M.A. thesis, Annenberg School for Communication, University of Pennsylvania.

Rogers, M., & Seiler, C. A. (1994). The answer is no: A national survey of advertising industry practitioners and their clients about whether they use subliminal advertising. *Journal of Advertising Research, 34*(2), 36-45.

Rogers, M., & Smith, K. H. (1993). Public perceptions of subliminal advertising: Why practitioners shouldn't ignore this issue. *Journal of Advertising Research, 33*(2), 10-18.

Rogers, S. (1993). How a publicity blitz created the myth of subliminal advertising. *Public Relations Quarterly, 37*(4), 12-17.

Rosenberg, S. (1995). *Age-specific responses to cutting in advertising: Recognition, persuasion, liking, and comprehension.* Undergraduate honors thesis, University of Pennsylvania.

Rosenthal, W. (1994). Standardized international advertising: A view from the agency side. *Journal of International Consumer Marketing, 7*(1), 39-59.

Ross, B. D. (1985). *Iwo Jima: Legacy of valor.* New York: Vintage.

Rossiter, J., & Percy, L. (1983). Visual communication in advertising. In R. J. Harris (Ed.), *Information processing research in advertising* (pp. 83-125). Hillsdale, NJ: Lawrence Erlbaum.

Rothenberg, R. R. (1994). *Where the suckers moon: An advertising story.* New York: Knopf.

Saegert, J. (1979). Another look at subliminal advertising. *Journal of Advertising Research, 19*(1), 55-57.

Saltzman, J. (1989, November). TV news theater. *USA today: Magazine of the American scene,* p. 89.

Sandler, D. M., & Secunda, E. (1993). Blurred boundaries: Where does editorial end and advertising begin? *Journal of Advertising Research, 33,* 73-80.

Savan, L. (1994). *The sponsored life: Ads, TV, and American culture.* Philadelphia: Temple University Press.

Sayre, S. (1994). Images of freedom and equality: A value analysis of Hungarian political commercials. *Journal of Advertising, 23*(1), 97-106.

Scherer, K. R. (1971). Stereotype change following exposure to counter-stereotypical media heroes. *Journal of Broadcasting, 15,* 91-100.

Schudson, M. (1984). *Advertising, the uneasy persuasion: Its dubious impact on American society.* New York: Basic Books.

Scott, B. M., et al. (1992). Alcohol advertising in the African American community. *Journal of Drug Issues, 22,* 455-496.

Scott, L. (1990). *Toward visual rhetoric.* Paper presented at the American Academy of Advertising conference, Orlando, FL.

Sebeok, T. A. (1979). *The sign and its masters.* Austin: University of Texas Press.

Sebeok, T. A. (1991). *A sign is just a sign.* Bloomington: Indiana University Press.

Severn, J., Belch, G. E., & Belch, M. A. (1990). The effects of sexual and non-sexual advertising appeals and information level on cognitive processing and communication effectiveness. *Journal of Advertising, 19*(1), 14-22.

Shatzer, M. J., Korzenny, F., & Griffis-Korzenny, B. A. (1985). Adolescents viewing *Shogun:* Cognitive and attitudinal effects. *Journal of Broadcasting and Electronic Media, 29,* 341-346.

Shepard, R. N. (1990). *Mind sights: Original visual illusions, ambiguities, and other anomalies.* New York: Freeman.

Shom, B. (1994). *Documentary video and ethnic identity: Audience sensitivity to South Asian stereotypes*. M.A. thesis, Annenberg School for Communication, University of Pennsylvania.

Sifry, M. L., & Cerf, C. (Eds.). (1991). *The Gulf War reader: History, documents, opinions*. New York: Times Books.

Slattery, K., & Tiedge, J. T. (1992). The effect of labeling staged video on the credibility of TV news stories. *Journal of Broadcasting and Electronic Media, 36*, 279-286.

Smith, C. (1992). *Media and apocalypse: News coverage of the Yellowstone forest fires, Exxon Valdez oil spill, and Loma Prieta earthquake*. Westport, CT: Greenwood.

Snowden, F. M., Jr. (1983). *Before color prejudice: The ancient view of blacks*. Cambridge, MA: Harvard University Press.

Solomon, M. R., Ashmore, R. D., & Longo, L. C. (1992). The beauty match-up hypothesis: Congruence between types of beauty and product images in advertising. *Journal of Advertising, 21*(4), 23-34.

Solso, R. L. (1994). *Cognition and the visual arts*. Cambridge: MIT Press.

Somasundaram, T. N., & Light, C. D. (1994). Rethinking a global media strategy: A four country comparison of young adults' perceptions of media-specific advertising. *Journal of International Consumer Marketing, 7*(1), 23-38.

Stabiner, K. (1982, May 2). Tapping the homosexual market. *New York Times Magazine*, p. D11.

Stange, M. (1989). *Symbols of ideal life: Social documentary photography in America 1890-1950*. New York: Cambridge University Press.

Stout, R. G. (1984). Pavlov founded advertising because he showed that imagery could be transferred. *Television/Radio Age, 31*(14), 160.

Strumwasser, G., & Friedman, M. (1992). Mona Lisa meets Madison Avenue: Advertising spoofs of a cultural icon. In S. R. Danna (Ed.), *Advertising and popular culture: Studies in variety and versatility* (pp. 83-92). Bowling Green, OH: Bowling Green State University Popular Press.

Suzuki, N. (1980). The changing pattern of advertising strategy by Japanese business firms in the U.S. market: Content analysis. *Journal of International Business Studies, 11*(3), 63-72.

Synodinos, N. E. (1988). Subliminal stimulation: What does the public think about it? *Current Issues and Research in Advertising, 11*, 157-187.

Sypher, W. (1955). *Four stages in Renaissance style: Transformations in art and literature, 1400-1700*. Garden City, NY: Doubleday.

Tansey, R., Hyman, M. R., & Zinkhan, G. M. (1990). Cultural themes in Brazilian and U.S. auto ads: A cross-cultural comparison. *Journal of Advertising, 19*(2), 30-39.

Target market: Selling to all types. (1995, June 19). *Adweek*, p. 27.

Tatlow, R. E. (1992). *Media literacy vs. critical thinking: Which is a better predictor of critical viewing skills?* M.A. thesis, Annenberg School for Communication, University of Pennsylvania.

Teitelbaum, M. (Ed.). (1992). *Montage and modern life: 1919-1942*. Cambridge: MIT Press.

Theus, K. T. (1994). Subliminal advertising and the psychology of processing unconscious stimuli: A review of research. *Psychology and Marketing, 11*, 271-290.

Thorson, E., Reeves, B., & Schleuder, J. (1985). Message complexity and attention to television. *Communication Research, 12*, 427-454.

Tiemens, R. K. (1970). Some relationships of camera angle to communicator credibility. *Journal of Broadcasting, 14*, 483-490.

Turow, J. (in press). *Breaking up America: Advertisers and the new media world*. Chicago: University of Chicago Press.

Ulrich, R. S. (1993). Biophilia, biophobia, and natural landscapes. In S. R. Kellert & E. O. Wilson (Eds.), *The biophilia hypothesis* (pp. 73-137). Washington, DC: Island Press.

Veblen, T. (1953). *The theory of the leisure class: An economic study of institutions.* New York: Mentor.

Voight, J. (1995, May 15). A quaking bridge lifts BBDO. *Adweek,* p. 2.

Walker, J. A. (1983). *Art in the age of mass media.* London: Pluto.

Walker, P. (1992). The myth of surgical bombing in the Gulf War. In R. Clark et al., *War crimes* (pp. 83-89). Washington, DC: Maisonneuve Press.

Warlaumont, H. (1995). Blurring advertising and editorial photographic formats. *Visual Communication Quarterly, 2*(3), 4-7, 24.

Wasser, F. (1995). Is Hollywood America? The trans-nationalization of the American film industry. *Critical Studies in Mass Communication, 12,* 423-437.

Weiss, M. J. (1988). *The clustering of America.* New York: Harper & Row.

Welch, R. L., Huston-Stein, A., Wright, J. C., & Plehal, R. (1979). Subtle sex-role cues in children's commercials. *Journal of Communication, 29,* 202-209.

Wells, L. G. (1994). Western concepts, Russian perspectives: Meanings of advertising in the former Soviet Union. *Journal of Advertising, 23,* 83-95.

Wells, M. (1995, June 22). Luxury products push for mass appeal. *USA Today,* p. 4B.

Wernick, A. (1991). *Promotional culture: Advertising, ideology and symbolic expression.* Thousand Oaks, CA: Sage.

Weschler, L. (1989, November 13). A grand experiment. *New Yorker,* pp. 59-104.

Wheeler, R. (1980). *Iwo.* Annapolis, MD: Naval Institute Press.

Wheeler, T., & Gleason, T. (1995). Photography or photofiction: An ethical protocol for the digital age. *Visual Communication Quarterly, 2*(2), 8-12.

Whittock, T. (1990). *Metaphor and film.* New York: Cambridge University Press.

Williamson, J. (1978). *Decoding advertisements: Ideology and meaning in advertising.* London: Marion Boyars.

Wolf, H. (1988). *Visual thinking: Methods for making images memorable.* New York: Rizzoli.

Wolfflin, H. (n.d.). *Principles of art history: The problem of the development of style in later art.* New York: Dover.

Worth, S. (1982). Pictures can't say "ain't." In S. Thomas (Ed.), *Film/culture: Explorations of cinema in its social context* (pp. 97-109). Metuchen, NJ: Scarecrow Press.

Wright, R. (1994). *The moral animal: Evolutionary psychology and everyday life.* New York: Vintage.

Zanot, E. J. (1992). Subliminal seduction: Real or imagined? In S. R. Danna (Ed.), *Advertising and popular culture: Studies in variety and versatility* (pp. 56-62). Bowling Green, OH: Bowling Green State University Popular Press.

Zanot, E. J., Pincus, J. D., & Lamp, J. E. (1983). Public perceptions of subliminal advertising. *Journal of Advertising, 12*(1), 39-45.

Zettl, H. (1990). *Sight sound motion: Applied media aesthetics* (2nd ed.). Belmont, CA: Wadsworth.

Zuckerman, C. I. (1990). *Rugged cigarettes and sexy soap: Brand images and the acquisition of meaning through associational juxtaposition of visual imagery.* M.A. thesis, Annenberg School for Communication, University of Pennsylvania.

INDEX

Valentino (print ad), 48
Vanden Bergh, B.G., 71
Veblen, T., 231-232
Versace (print ad), 48
Viewers' perceptions of advertising:
    Awareness of computer manipulation,
    156-160
    Beliefs about subliminal advertising,
    70-71
    Interpretations of visual syntax, 203-218
Vignette ad, 198
Virtual reality, xv, 156
Voight, J., 166
Volvo (print ad), 143-144, (TV
    commercial), 271-272

Wakshlag, J., 35
Walker, J. A., 229
Walker, P., 148
War-mobilization posters, 36-38
Wasser, F., 93, 99
WDRE FM Radio (billboard), 243-246, 244
Weiss, M. J., 238
Welch, R.L., 79, 80, 82

Wells, L.G., 92
Wells, M., 231
Wernick, A., 62
Weschler, L., 99
Wetenhall, J., 93
Wheeler, R., 94
Wheeler, T., 153
White, D.S., 91
Whittock, T., 10, 175-176, 178
Wilkens, H.T., 69
Williamson, J., 224
Winski, J.M., 92
Wolf, H., 13
Wolfflin, H., 83
Woo, J., 115
Worth, S., xvi
Wright, J.C., 79, 80
Wright, R., 48

Zalk, S.R., 122
Zanot, E.J., 68, 70
Zettl, H., 32, 34
Zinkhan, G.M., 108
Zuckerman, C. I., 204-207

About the Author

Paul Messaris is an associate professor at the Annenberg School for Communication, University of Pennsylvania. His area of scholarship is visual communication, and his previous research has dealt with how people make sense of visual media. He is the author of *Visual "Literacy": Image, Mind, and Reality*, published in 1994 by Westview Press.